The Intervention

Patrick Gilbert-Roberts

Cover Design: Bespoke Book Cover Designs.

Copy Editing: Sally Odgers.

Formatting: Polgarus Studio.

Published by: Patrick Gilbert-Roberts.

ISBN: 978-0-6482375-1-8

Copyright: © Patrick Gilbert-Roberts 2017

This book is dedicated to my lovely, long suffering wife, Lyndy, who has a real job and would, I am sure, rather that I had one too, instead of disappearing into the spare bedroom all the time, writing silly stories.

Part 1

Chapter 1

It was back in 2029. I was sixty-eight, not in bad shape for a man of my age. I kept reasonably fit, nothing fanatical—I didn't run, or cycle, go to the gym or do yoga or anything. I walked a fair bit, swam in the sea—body surfing, that sort of thing. My diet was good, and I hadn't smoked since I was a teenager. Of course, I had my aches and pains, who doesn't at that age?

I think I was secretly rather proud of this, and tended to cultivate my swashbuckling appearance. I'd not lost any of the thick mane of hair on my head which I kept tied back in a ponytail and, although the blond was, by then, mainly grey, it still had a yellowish tinge. My beard was also mostly grey, and I kept it trimmed. I was deeply tanned and wore a silver earing in the pierced lobe of my left ear.

I had sailed yachts ever since I was a child and had owned several over the years. My wife and I had accumulated several thousand nautical miles of sea time, cruising mainly the east coast of Australia but with the odd trip to Vanuatu and New Caledonia and, once, even to Fiji.

Andrea (that's AnDRAYah she'd insist, not Andreeya! Not that it made any difference, everyone always called her Andie!) was only fifty-eight when she succumbed to breast cancer. I was sixty, and I was devastated. I had a moderately senior management position in the corporate sector. The company, with some reluctance I thought, gave me a couple of months' compassionate leave, during which, as some semblance of emotional stability began to return, I gave some serious thought to my future which led, ultimately, to me concluding I'd had enough of corporate life. The kids were grown up and had gone their separate ways. I no longer had need of so large a house. I reasoned I could sell it and, with the proceeds, buy a cottage in some quiet coastal town and take life at my own pace. My superannuation, I calculated, would be adequate to fund a modest lifestyle and, as I was qualified to marine Master 5, I could always augment that income with the odd yacht delivery.

In fact it was when I was on my way to Sydney to pick up a yacht when this strange tale really begins.

I love the sea and cannot live for long away from it, but I also love the vastness, the grandeur and the peace of outback Australia. I had been on a pilgrimage to Uluru, that spectacular, sacred lump of rock almost in the center of Australia that we once arrogantly renamed Ayers Rock. Now restored to its aboriginal name and jointly managed by the Anangu people (who seemed to manage it perfectly well all by themselves for 40,000 years before the white man arrived!) and Parks Australia, it drew, even back then, a quarter of a million visitors from around the globe each year.

My phone rang early one evening as I was washing down the dust of the day with a long cold beer, the setting sun casting fantastic shadows and improbable colors on the massive bulk of Uluru. Could I deliver a yacht from Pittwater, Sydney, to Auckland?

And so it was, late Sunday morning, the 25th of November, as I sped south on the Stuart Highway, Uluru 250 miles behind me with 1,500 still to go to Sydney, that I spotted her standing by the side of the road! Now let me put this into perspective: there is nothing, and I mean absolutely nothing, out there. It was 110 degrees! There are no towns, no filling stations, no turn-offs—what the hell was she doing here? She didn't need to wave a thumb at me. Out there, if you see someone, you stop, or, in all likelihood, the person dies! That is no exaggeration; maybe the aborigines can find water out there, but no one else could and, as far as I could see, the place wasn't exactly teeming with native Australians.

I brought the Land Rover to a halt beside her. She opened the door, handed in a small shoulder bag and climbed in behind it. It was a much more comfortable 75° inside the car. I handed her a water bottle and she drank gratefully. She wasn't sweating but then you don't in those conditions. It may be over 110 degrees but there is zero humidity.

"May I ask what the hell you are doing on the side of the road out *here?*"

She smiled somewhat ruefully. "My boyfriend has anger management problems."

The arch of my eyebrows and dip of my head demanded more information.

"We had a row, he pushed me out of the car and drove off." She paused. "He's done this sort of thing before… well, not out here… but he always comes back."

I suggested to her that she was better off without him.

"Anyone who would leave someone on her own out here deserves to be locked up!"

"I fully agree," she said, "I don't ever want to see him again."

I slipped the car into gear and we set off.

"So, you think he'll turn around and come back for you?"

"When he cools off, yes."

"And then he won't find you."

"No."

"And you don't care?"

"No."

"I agree with you. Let him sweat, let him wonder what may have become of you; maybe it'll teach him a lesson." It occurred to me that we may not be going the direction she wanted to go. "Were you headed south?"

"No, we were going to Uluru, but I don't care. I just want to be out of here. Where are you going?"

"Sydney."

"I would like to go to Sydney, if you don't mind."

"Mind? No, glad of the company."

Over the next few miles I had the chance to look at her properly—she was, at a guess no more than 30 years old, with very large almond-shaped blue eyes, shoulder length brown hair bleached yellow in places by the sun, deeply tanned, not unattractive. She told me her name was Lauren

Mitchell. She had a strange accent that I couldn't place. She said she was English but had travelled a lot and tended to pick up elements of other people's speech.

We drove into Coober Pedy around four o'clock. The sun was sinking in the western sky but there was no indication it was getting any cooler; according to the car's instruments it was still 105 degrees outside.

"Have you ever lived underground?" I enquired.

"Underground?"

"Yes, it's so damned hot here that the only respite they can find is to live underground."

"Seriously?"

"Seriously! People came here, still come here, to mine opal. They have probably the best quality opal in the world here. It's also *seriously* hot. So, people created dugouts to live in. They literally dig their homes out of the hillside and when it's as hot as it is today, and believe me it can get a lot hotter, the temperature in their underground home is going to be about 74 - 75 degrees." Lauren looked suitably impressed. "Anyway, we'll be sleeping in one tonight."

There's any amount of subterranean accommodation available in Coober Pedy and most of the tourists avoid the area at that time of the year so there was no problem finding a room.

Lauren, it transpired, had her wallet, passport and personal papers but all her clothing and toiletries were still in her erstwhile boyfriend's car. Once we had booked into our rooms at the *Underground Motel*, we drove down town to find her a toothbrush and a change of underwear. I advised her to wait until we got to Adelaide the following night before replenishing her wardrobe.

We had a pleasant enough evening at the motel. The food was surprisingly good considering the location. Lauren, I noticed, refused all alcohol and had a bottle of some kind of salt, or powder, that she sprinkled lavishly on her food. I eyed her quizzically and she mumbled something about a powder her doctor had prescribed for a blood deficiency disorder.

She seemed little inclined to talk about herself, glossing over her recent past with:

"Oh, I've travelled a lot," and something about her being part way through a geology degree but having parked it for a while so she could see more of the world. She was far more interested in hearing about me and, I must confess, what with having spent a few weeks on my own, two or three glasses of red wine and the apparently earnest attention of an attractive woman I did rather warble on!

Chapter 2

Somehow, we had managed to spend the past several hours in each other's company without my ever having mentioned my own name.

"Well, that's very rude of me, my name is Jeff Ridsdale."

"And you are Australian?"

"Yes, born in Melbourne."

"Is that where you live?"

"No, too damned cold!"

Lauren soon knew considerably more about me than I of her. She was an active listener and I a willing talker, especially after a glass or two of wine. She seemed particularly interested in my upcoming yacht delivery and was soon cajoling me to take her along.

"Do you know anything about sailing? Have you ever sailed?"

"No, but I'd really love to and I'm a quick learner." There was no disguising her enthusiasm, nor my lack. She was a pleasant enough companion but, as I explained to her, this was no afternoon sail on Sydney Harbor; we would be crossing the Tasman Sea—whatever the weather.

Joe and Kathy would be meeting me in Sydney. They had sailed with me on two or three deliveries already. They were sound. Joe had his Coxswain's ticket and I'm sure Kathy could sit hers tomorrow and sail through it, if you'll pardon the pun. But the Tasman Sea is no place for beginners, it has a reputation as an unpredictable and often treacherous stretch of water. Perhaps it was the red wine, perhaps her eager young eyes, probably a bit of both but, anyway, I promised to sleep on it.

Coober Pedy to Adelaide is about a ten-hour drive. We left at 7.00, having persuaded the motel to provide us with an early breakfast. I can be a little slow out of the blocks first thing in the morning and that morning I certainly wasn't as garrulous as I had been the night before. We drove in silence for a while. I could sense that Lauren was tense with expectation. I remembered that she was waiting on my verdict as to whether I would take her on the delivery. Sleeping on it hadn't achieved anything, other than the usual benefits of sleep.

I glanced at her. She seemed to be watching me from the corner of her eye. I slipped a CD into the player to alleviate the taut silence in the cabin and began to give some thought to the conundrum. Looking back on it now it is hard to see that there was anything to think about. She was a young woman I had picked up along the way (the circumstances that led to her being there for me to pick up were irrelevant to my considerations). She was, otherwise, inconsequential to my life. I had a job to do, she was unskilled in that area and could contribute nothing to my endeavors. I entertained no romantic or sexual aspirations toward her—she was less than half my age! Clearly the only reasonable response had to be: "no, sorry, I can drop you off in Adelaide or Sydney or anywhere in between but I can't take you on the boat."

So, of course, I said: "Yes, okay, you can come. I'm meeting up with two others—Kathy and Joe—who've helped me deliver boats before. Kathy's about your size and I'm fairly sure she'll have a spare set of foulies you can borrow."

"Foulies?"

"Protective clothing, for when the weather turns foul—foul weather gear."

"Ah."

"You'll have to keep out of the way, do as you're told and help out where you can. I assume you can cook?"

"Erm yes." She didn't sound convinced.

"If the weather stays fine it'll be a pleasant trip and, no doubt, we'll be able to give you some sailing lessons along the way. But the Tasman Sea is notoriously unpredictable and can throw up some nasty storms. If that happens I only want to talk to people who can contribute something useful to the situation, and that will not include you! Do you understand?"

"Yes, yes of course, and I'm very grateful. I'll do just what I'm told." She looked across at me rather anxiously and I, concerned I'd been overly stern, smiled reassuringly.

We booked into a little hotel I've used before, just off Hay Street in Adelaide. It was nothing fancy but provided a bed for the night at a reasonable price. I've never been one to splash out on hotels—can't see the value.

The following morning, I steered Lauren in the general direction of clothing stores and, with a cautionary word to her about time, I took up station in a coffee shop where I tucked into a plate of eggs benedict washed down with a cup of strong black coffee. I also took the opportunity to call Joe to discuss the job and confirm that everything was on track.

Hay in New South Wales is about half way between Adelaide and Sydney, so we made that our destination for the day, arriving in Sydney late in the afternoon of the following day. The trip was uneventful. We made small talk, often prompted by the things we saw through the windscreen, and we listened to music. I wouldn't have expected Lauren to share my musical tastes but, while she teased me about my use of old fashioned media (CDs), she seemed oblivious to the music itself.

It was about 5.30 when we arrived at the Royal Prince Alfred Yacht Club. I explained our business and had someone sign us in. My priority was a long cold beer, so we headed directly to the Halyards bar. The first one barely touched the sides. I bought a second and we found a table with a view out over the water. I phoned the owner to let him know I had arrived.

Chapter 3

Con Theodorakis was proof of my theory that you can't go wrong with a coffee shop (much less a chain of coffee shops)—even in New Zealand. He oozed success, from the Zegna sunglasses perched upon his receding hairline, through the gold chain necklace heavy enough to bow a lesser man, his Hugo Boss shirt, Rolex Yacht Master watch, to his hand-crafted Italian leather shoes.

"Jeff, nice to meet you." His handshake was firm without being brutal. I introduced Lauren as a member of the crew and left it at that.

He led us out along one of the fingers of the marina almost directly into the setting sun. About two thirds of the way along, we stopped.

"Well, here she is," he announced.

She was a Moody 42. Built in the UK in 2026; center cockpit, a gorgeous boat, built and set up for cruising. I'd read about them but never sailed one. My first impressions were very favorable: great lines, all the creature comforts, and then some, an excellent galley and heaps of stowage. Her name was *Perseverance.*

Con showed us over her. I checked out the navigation systems. It seemed to have everything it should have: radar, AIS, chart plotter, all the standard instruments, auto-pilot and wind vane steering.

"Do you have paper charts for the passage?"

"No, I thought the chart plotter…'

"Is fine as long as it works. If you lose power or get a glitch in the electronics… what then?"

We discussed it and Con said he thought he could lay his hands on the charts, either by going to the shop or borrowing a set from someone at the club.

The boat wasn't provisioned, as he pointed out, he didn't know what we may like to eat. He gave me $500 in cash which, I assured him, would adequately cover our needs.

By the time we had ironed out all the details it was nearly dark. We walked him back to the club and farewelled him at the car park. I unloaded the Land Rover, borrowed a wheelbarrow and trundled my gear out to the boat. We were just about to return to the club for some dinner when my phone rang. It was Joe.

"Problem?" Lauren enquired. I had put the phone back in my pocket and doubtless the consternation I felt was written on my face. Problem? There was a problem all right! Kathy's mother had been involved in a car accident and was now in a critical condition in hospital. Kathy and Joe, quite understandably, couldn't just up and leave her and go sailing away to New Zealand. I did know other people who could, conceivably, help me make a delivery but certainly not on such short notice. To make the Auckland deadline I'd agreed with Con, I really wanted to leave the following day. In ideal conditions, I might average six knots over the entire trip which would mean it would take the best part of ten days. I don't think I can remember a trip that had ideal conditions all the way. Leaving the next day would give me fourteen days and I was comfortable with that.

I explained the situation to Lauren. She looked suitably concerned but said nothing—there was, after all, nothing she could say or do that would change the situation. While I was waiting for my dinner to arrive I phoned a friend, Paul, who delivered yachts for a living. He was my last chance, really. At least he lived in Sydney. It turned out he was lying at anchor in the Great Sandy Strait. He was in the process of delivering a Leopard 40 catamaran from Cairns to Brisbane, so he was in no position to help me.

"Well, it's not the end of the world," I said finally. "People sail solo around the world all the time. It's not ideal but I think we can manage."

The following morning, we went shopping. We returned with our provisions at about 11.00 and were in the process of stowing everything when Con arrived with the charts. As we talked, I downloaded the GRIB files so I could check the wind conditions for the next few days. There was nothing untoward there. I put them on a clip on the chart table and we walked back to the club for the last decent cup of coffee I could expect for two weeks.

Chapter 4

It was mid-afternoon when the last smudge of land dipped below the horizon. We had about fifteen knots on the beam and were making a steady six to seven knots. *Perseverance* was a sea-kindly vessel and rode the gentle five foot swell very comfortably.

"Well, it's just us and the sea now," I said. Lauren's smile was, I thought, a little strained. Well, fair enough, if she'd not been to sea before. "What do you think of the sails?" She looked alarmed. "I mean the trim, we went through this earlier." Now she looked relieved—she knew what I was talking about. She gazed intently at the sails.

"I think the headsail should be eased a little." She looked up at the mainsail again. "And the mainsheet should come in a bit because there is too much… er… twist at the top of the sail."

"Yes, good, Lauren, very good. You obviously pick things up quickly." She smiled. "But, how else might you adjust the mainsail?"

I had taken her through the elements of sailing but had

not expected her to take much of it in first time around. It's not rocket surgery, as my daughter would say, but there's a lot to it and it takes a while to put all the elements together. Lauren was very quick. She seemed able to grasp the basic concept of how sails work, and readily understand and apply the various controls to tune the sails to the prevailing wind.

I checked the chart plotter and adjusted the wind vane steering to compensate for the East Australian Current, which seemed to be flowing even more strongly than I had anticipated. I involved Lauren in the consequent necessary adjustment to sail trim; I needed her at least vaguely competent as soon as possible.

Over the next hour or so I showed her how to use the chart plotter, the AIS and radar and how they could be overlaid on the chart plotter screen. I had her set some intermediate waypoints and we discussed what she would do if the actual course over ground was failing to take us to the waypoint. I showed her how to trim the wind vane steering.

Next, I set a waypoint more northerly than our intended course.

"Okay, I'm asleep, you're on watch. You look at the chart plotter. What do you see?"

She looked at the screen. "Our current heading is well to the south of the waypoint."

"Okay, so what do you do? Don't tell me, do it."

I have to say I was impressed. She calculated a course that attempted to take into account the strong southerly current. She then made the necessary adjustment to the wind vane steering. A brief look at me for approval was cancelled with a shake of her head and her eyes went to the sails. She brought the traveler up and cranked the headsail on a few turns and then checked the results. A few more cranks on the jib sheet and she was satisfied. I clapped her on the shoulder.

"Well done! You *are* learning fast."

I spent a bit of time on rules concerning the wearing of life jackets and tethering on to the jack lines. In particular I stressed that under no circumstances should she be in the cockpit or on deck after dark without her life jacket on and the harness connected to the jack lines.

The breeze that had remained steady at about fifteen knots from the north was forecast to ease through the night, backing and strengthening the following morning. Indeed, it had already dropped out and was probably no more than ten knots, still from the north. If in any doubt I will normally reduce sail at night. The Moody was nicely set up so that you can reef the mainsail and furl the genoa from the cockpit. I ran through the reefing procedure with Lauren. I showed her how to do it and how to shake out the reef when you no longer wanted it. Then I had her run through the whole procedure herself, twice, until I was satisfied she had the basics.

We discussed watches. Personally, I prefer four-hour watches if conditions permit. I find I can't get proper rest if I sleep for three hours or less. I impressed upon Lauren that if she was in any doubt about anything while on watch she was to wake me.

We threw together some spaghetti Bolognese and, as it

was a fine evening, we ate in the cockpit. Lauren ate sparingly, shaking her mysterious powder on the food. She glanced at the container and my impression was that she was running low.

"You don't have any more?" I asked.

"Er… no," she replied, a touch awkwardly, I thought. "but it's okay; I'll live." She laughed a little nervously.

I didn't pursue it.

Lauren didn't seem tired and I doubted she would sleep if I took the first watch so, just before 20:00, I ran through my list of instructions about what to do under various circumstances, renewed my admonishment to wake me if in any doubt at all then, after checking she was warmly dressed, had her life jacket and harness on and was securely tethered to the boat, I went below and took to my bunk.

A few minutes before midnight I awoke to the vibrating alarm in my mobile phone. I lay awake listening. Everything sounded as it should: the sea sloshing and gurgling along the hull, the occasional creak from the rigging, otherwise silence.

I went to the head, dragged on some clothes, made a pot of tea, buckled on my life jacket and took a cup up to Lauren.

"Everything okay?" I enquired.

"Ay Ay Cap'n, all ship shape and squared away."

"Have you been reading pirate books?" I checked our position on the chart plotter and transferred the data to the paper chart. Our speed had dropped off with the breeze, but we were still making reasonable progress. I made some notes in the log book.

"Seen much shipping?" I asked.

"There have been a couple, but heading north and a fair way behind us."

I checked the AIS and there was nothing in range.

"Well you'd better get off to bed. I'll see you at four."

The next four hours were entirely uneventful. It was a pleasant mild night, there was no moon, and the stars, so far away from the city lights, were almost dazzling. I do love to sail at night.

I had expected to have had to dig Lauren out of her bunk but, a little before four, I heard movement below and soon enough she poked her head out of the companionway.

"Sleep well?" I asked

"Mm yes," she said, and nodded.

I updated the chart and log making a note to myself that, since she seemed so apt a pupil, I might teach her a bit about navigation in the morning.

I had not been asleep long when something woke me. It doesn't take much these days. Once upon a time I could sleep through a hurricane, but then Andie gave birth to my first son! I lay there listening. Some sound had seeped into my slumbers and I knew it wasn't right. I lay there listening. There it was again. Lauren was up on the cabin roof! What on earth was she doing there? She had no need to leave the cockpit, unless to come below. I rose and made my way silently to the companionway. I stood on the second step and turned to face the bow. Lauren was standing at the mast, she wasn't attached to the jack lines and, most intriguingly, she was using what looked to be a mobile phone!

I stood watching her for a moment. She appeared to be pointing the phone towards the sky and it seemed to flash and make barely audible beeps. We were most definitely not in range of any mobile phone network and the device looked nothing like any satellite phone I had ever seen.

"What the hell are you doing?" I growled.

She started and almost dropped whatever it was she was holding. Regathering it she attempted to conceal it from me.

"Well, what are you doing? You're not clipped on and what's that you've got?"

"Oh… well, it's really calm I…'

"I don't care if it's a millpond, the rule is you are *never* on deck alone without being attached to the jack lines. And what is that thing you've got there?" If I sounded pissed off it was because I was pissed off.

"It's just my mobile phone."

"So, what are you doing with it? There's no network available out here."

"Um, I was just writing my diary." That didn't convince me. "Show me."

"No, it's not your business," she protested.

"Show me!" I demanded.

For just an instant I could have sworn that her eyes blazed at me even though It was a dark night and I could barely see her eyes. She muttered something which I took to be in a foreign language. I advanced towards her with my hand extended. "Give."

She had nowhere to go, and very reluctantly she placed it in my upturned hand.

I ordered her back to the cockpit and glanced at the device in my hand. It looked unlike any phone or radio I had ever seen. I gestured for her to sit and, when she did, I attached her tether to the jack line. Her hostility was palpable. I glanced at the chart plotter. We appeared to be on course and there was no traffic. I went below and sat at the chart table and, with the aid of the red night light, I examined the strange object.

I had never seen anything like it. It was black, about the size of a small mobile phone, but shaped more like a tablet of soap. There was the merest hint of a light behind what I took to be the screen, but the whole thing appeared completely seamless. I could see no evidence of buttons or switches of any sort and nothing that I could think to do elicited any response from it whatsoever.

I was in a quandary. I didn't know what to do; I didn't know what to think! Throw me a sailing or seamanship problem and I can think my way through it, but this…? I didn't know where to begin. I had noticed a few things I'd thought odd about Lauren, but nothing that individually, or even in aggregate, would particularly concern me. Suddenly I had someone behaving in a completely unexpected manner. She had some strange device, the like of which I have never seen. She was clearly lying to me and wouldn't talk to me about the device or what she was doing with it.

I slipped the thing into a small compartment I had noticed adjacent to the chart table and tried to assemble my thoughts. Certainly, finding a young woman alone on the side of a remote highway in the middle of Australia is highly unusual but her explanation seemed plausible at the time. There was something strange about the way she spoke but, again, her explanation was plausible: she travels a lot. Her decision to come with me all the way to Sydney was, perhaps, reasonable if she was backpacking in Australia and no longer had a partner but, upon reflection, her eagerness to sail with me to Auckland might have invited a little more interrogation.

I was angry with myself. Why had I allowed this situation to arise? What possible justification could I have for taking someone who I really knew nothing about, someone with no sailing experience, aboard a client's yacht? She was bright, there was no gainsaying that. Sailing isn't rocket science but not many pick up the essentials as quickly as she had. And then there was the… what was it, some kind of salt… that she put on her food? I should have been all over that like a rash. What sort of blood deficiency? What were the implications? And now she appeared to be running low on the stuff and we had the best part of two weeks before we were to arrive in Auckland where she might replenish her supply. What would happen when she ran out of it?

"Oh God!" I groaned, grinding the heels of my hands into my eyes. "Here's another fine mess you've got us into!"

Chapter 5

There was nothing for it but to have it out with her. I resolved to be calm and reasonable, to eschew the authoritarian approach I felt entitled to take, and not be angry with her. I made us a cup of tea and cut a couple of slices of dark fruit cake.

I found her sitting in the corner of the cockpit, her back to the cabin wall, out of the breeze, with her knees drawn up under her chin, and her arms wrapped around her shins. I sat on the seat beside her and handed her the cup of tea. She didn't respond so I placed it and the plate with the cake on it on the seat between us.

"Okay, I get it that you're not happy," I said as gently as I could, "but you're going to have to tell me what's going on." She didn't respond. I sighed and took a sip of tea. "I can't just ignore this. You've been brilliant, picking up all the sailing stuff, you haven't put a foot wrong. Now this… getting about the boat without tying on is certainly worthy of a reprimand. Hell, if anything happened and you went overboard, I wouldn't know about it until I came back on watch. The chances of backtracking and ever recovering someone in that situation is pretty much zero.

"But then I find you with some weird device that I… well, I've never seen anything like it before. What the hell is it?" I looked at her. She barely glanced up. Again, I thought I saw a glint in her eye. I glanced over my shoulder. The eastern sky was lightening, heralding the dawn, but there was certainly not enough light to reflect in her eyes.

I tried to encourage her to drink some, tea, have some cake—she hadn't had anything for hours. She refused or, rather, continued to ignore me. I ate a piece of cake and drank my tea. I looked at her huddled, closed-off form.

"Lauren, we have probably another twelve days together. We can't continue like this. At some point you're going to have to come out of your cone of silence and we're going to have to talk about this. So why not make it now and let's get it over and done with."

She shifted in her seat, fidgeted with her jacket. "It's no use. You wouldn't believe me anyway," she mumbled.

"Try me." She continued to sit in silence. I became a little exasperated and, rather than say anything that would worsen the situation, I took my cup below, washed it up and put it away.

The eastern sky was beginning to glow. I checked our position on the chart plotter and checked the batteries—they were holding up well. We weren't drawing much power and the wind generator was ticking over. I heard a sound and turned around to see Lauren coming down the companionway steps. She removed her life jacket and stowed it where I had shown her to. She slipped off her windcheater and sat down on the settee. She placed her hands on the table and appeared to be examining her fingernails.

"Like I said," she started, "you won't believe me."

I sat down on the opposite settee. "As I said, try me."

There was a long pause. Finally, she said, "I'm not really a human, I'm an alien."

I guffawed, of course!

"You see, you don't believe me."

"Well of course I don't believe you: an alien! For pity's sake!" But, beneath my incredulity, there was a growing sense of alarm. Was I stuck on a boat in the middle of the Tasman Sea with a lunatic?

"Have you ever seen anything like my syncom before?"

"What is it you call it?"

"Syncom—synaptic network computing system. You've never seen anything like it before and you cannot begin to imagine what it can do."

I stared at her, dumbfounded.

"Give it back to me and I'll show you."

I continued to stare at her, my mind racing. What if I did give it back to her? God knew what it was—some new whizz-bang electronic toy she'd picked up on her travels maybe; certainly, I wasn't one to keep abreast of the latest gadgetry but, in any case, I didn't imagine it could do any harm. So, I got up and retrieved it from its little locker. Again, I turned it over in my hands but could see no discernible features. I shrugged and handed it to her, returning to my seat as I did so.

She held it in her hand, pressed against her breast as though grateful to be reunited with it. She stared at me, apparently deep in thought. Then, as if coming to a decision, she rubbed the device, sat up and stared at it intently, made a few more swift passes over the surface with her fingertips and the most extraordinary thing happened. Lights appeared in mid-air, hovering over the table between us. I gaped uncomprehendingly. Gradually, the lights rearranged themselves until I realized I was looking at a hologram. It took me a moment to see what it was. Then I understood: it was a representation of the boat—*Perseverance*—on the ocean, its position relative to the New South Wales coast (you could see a graphic of Sydney at the extreme), and its position relative to the sea floor which appeared to be shown in some detail.

I stood up and walked around it. Suddenly, on what I took to be the sea surface, there appeared figures. I looked closely. They were the distance we had come since leaving Sydney, in nautical miles, the depth of the sea beneath us in feet, the distance to go to Auckland, our current speed, our estimated time of arrival based upon our average speed since departure—all data I could have taken directly from the chart plotter, but how in hell could Lauren have summoned up these data and how could this thing create a hologram of it all? As I stood speechless, gazing at the image, our precise position in latitude and longitude appeared. Then most of the statistics disappeared, apart from our position. In their place, the image of the sea was overlaid with a GRIB file which, I at first thought, was the file I had put on the clip on the chart table. But, as I looked more closely, I realized it was an updated version and, a little alarmingly, there was an indication of a serious disturbance to the south.

As I watched, the image changed. I realized it was progressing through time in four-hour jumps. The 'disturbance' (high wind) was moving northwards and would begin to affect us in about six hours. Now I was in a real spin! Not only did I have to try deal with this strange woman and try to get my head around this new, incomprehensible piece of technology that should have been impossible, but now there was the promise of some very nasty weather to contend with.

I sat down again, my mind racing.

Lauren stroked the syncom, and the hologram disappeared. She stroked it over my forearm and a hologram of my body appeared together with my height, weight, body mass index, blood pressure, heart rate and blood sugar levels.

"Your heart rate and blood pressure are elevated but that is consistent with your current situation and your psycho/emotional state. These will normalize soon. Your blood sugar reading suggests you need to eat. I will prepare breakfast if you like."

I realized my jaw was slack and consciously closed my mouth. I shook my head, but my reality didn't change. Could I be dreaming? I thought of pinching myself but that seemed too corny.

"Breakfast would be great," was all I could finally find to say.

Chapter 6

Lauren started clattering around in the galley and I returned to the cockpit. I made a firm decision to put the whole alien business out of my mind and to focus on the practicalities of the here and now.

As forecast, the breeze was backing to the north west and had picked up a little. I checked our position. We had clearly sailed past the influence of the East Australian Current. There are well known eddies that flow off the lower reaches of the current, but they are not always predictable. Judging from our present track it appeared we were now sailing in a northerly current every bit as strong as the southerly one for which our helm was set to compensate! So now we were heading wildly off course. I reset the wind vane to a guesstimated course and adjusted the sails. Satisfied with their set, I went below and calculated a proper heading then returned to the helm and readjusted everything.

Shortly after that was all done, Lauren called me to breakfast. She placed a platter of scrambled eggs on toast before me and poured me a mug of tea. She apparently was not eating. I tucked in with gusto. I hadn't realized how hungry I was.

"Not eating?" I asked between mouthfuls. "You'll need your energy. We've got some nasty weather on the way."

Her response was noncommittal.

By the time I washed up and put away the breakfast things the sun was well up and the boat was rising and falling on a long regular swell arriving on our starboard beam. Lauren had gone on deck and I followed her. I was gratified to see she was wearing her life jacket and was connected to a jack line. She was adjusting the sails to a breeze that had backed a little. I gave her a hand.

Not long after that the breeze dropped out and we were almost becalmed, the sails flapping and clattering as *Perseverance* rode the long swells. I started the engine and set her in motion again, adjusting the sails to get whatever drive we could from any breeze that happened to turn up.

"Tell me more," I said as I seated myself opposite her in the cockpit.

"About what in particular?"

"Hell, I don't know! I'm so utterly bewildered I wouldn't know where to start!" I shook my head, closed my eyes, opened them again. "Why don't you tell me what you were doing on deck last night when I found you?"

She seemed to gather her thoughts. "Perhaps it would be better to start at what I was doing when you found me near Uluru."

I frowned. "I thought I already knew that."

"No. You know what I told you, but I couldn't tell you

the truth. There was no boyfriend."

"What? So how did you come to be there?"

The story that unfolded was utterly fantastic. That is, fantastic as the dictionary defines it:

"conceived or appearing as if conceived by an unrestrained imagination; odd and remarkable; bizarre; grotesque."

Or

a : based on fantasy—not real;

b : conceived or seemingly conceived by unrestrained fancy;

c : so extreme as to challenge belief : unbelievable.

I should make it clear that I was never one to give credence to UFO sightings, alien abductions or any of that kind of thing. So what Lauren had to tell me was extremely hard to accept.

Lauren claimed she was a Hybrid; a cross between an alien species called the Kareet and an abducted human. Although she could get by on Earth, breathe our atmosphere (which was not so different from that of the Kareeti home planet of Kareedias) and drink our water, her digestive system lacked certain enzymes necessary to break down our main food types. Hence the powder she put on her food.

She had been on a geological expedition with three Kareet and another Hybrid like herself when a coachload of tourists suddenly turned up and was about to park on the side of the road. Lauren had strayed farthest from their 'vehicle' and, in imminent danger of discovery, it had taken off without her.

"So why didn't you just refuse my offer of a lift and wait

for your 'boyfriend' to return?" I asked skeptically.

"Would you have driven off and left me? I don't think so. You'd have insisted on either taking me or staying until he returned."

This was, of course, absolutely correct.

The reason she was so keen to come on the yacht to New Zealand was because it gave her a chance to get somewhere entirely remote where she could arrange a rendezvous, which is, of course, exactly what she was attempting to do a few hours before when I had caught her untethered on the foredeck.

While we talked, the breeze picked up a little and veered back to the west. It wasn't strong, so I continued to motor. At 07:00 I tuned the HF radio in for the weather broadcast. It was as I had suspected: an east coast low had formed in Bass Strait and was travelling in a northerly direction. East coast lows are not common in late November, but you can be unlucky. The low had formed from a cold front that had crossed Victoria and moved over Bass Strait. They can intensify because of the warm waters associated with the East Australian Current. I recalled that I had noticed the night before when checking the instruments that the sea water temperature was high: 75°. Hell, that was warm! It would normally be about 72° maximum at this time of year. I hadn't thought that much more about it then but now, with a low-pressure system heading this way…!

I checked the barometer. It had been steady at about 1014 but now it had begun to fall—as you'd expect!

I went back up on deck. "The weather forecast confirms there's a low forming."

"Is that bad?"

"Well it can be," I replied, "there was a monster a few years back, wreaked utter havoc with the Sydney to Hobart Yacht Race."

"Oh," she said pensively, "do you think this one will be bad?"

"I don't know. I don't like the sea temperature."

"The sea temperature?"

"Yes, it has the potential to intensify low pressure systems. Normally it would be no more than about 72 degrees but it was about 75 last night, which is surprisingly high."

"Surprising?" she asked as though herself surprised that I may have been.

"Well, I guess that's climate change."

"*Anthropogenic* climate change!" she parried, with some asperity.

"Yes, yes, I know it's down to us," I replied, mildly irritated by her confrontational approach.

"Yes, but you're not doing much about it."

"Fuck's sake Lauren, I'm a 68-year-old retiree who delivers the odd boat to augment his retirement income! What am *I* supposed to do about *global* warming?"

"I didn't mean you personally. I mean the human race."

"Well I can't speak for the human race but, if it's any comfort, I have been banging on about climate change for at least the last forty years. It's not made a damned bit of difference."

"Well the Kareet are going to make a difference!" she said

with the air of someone who has just used her trump card to win the decisive trick.

"What are you saying?" I asked, shocked. "Are you telling me that these aliens, which frankly I'm still struggling to believe actually exist, are planning an intervention?"

"That's right."

Chapter 7

The breeze was gradually intensifying. I turned off the engine, judging we could make as much speed under sail alone. Although we continued to sail under a cloudless blue sky, way off to the south-east mares' tails were beginning to appear in the sky. In view of the unusually warm sea temperature I wanted to adjust our course to the north-east to get us out of harm's way as quickly as possible. We were in the danger quadrant relative to the storm and that's certainly not the place to linger.

A course of approximately 60° would take us well out of our way but it would give us our best route to safer waters if the storm continued on what I had calculated to be its current course. Furthermore, it put us on a broad reach, which was a faster point of sail. I went below and dug out a set of storm sails and made sure the para anchor was readily accessible should the need arise.

Throughout the next few hours we continued to make good way. I maintained an eye on the position of the storm. In the southern hemisphere, if you stand with your back to the wind the center of the low pressure system is to your right.

The breeze was gradually intensifying, and, by the middle of the day, we had 25 knots with gusts over 30. I had reefed the sails and we were beginning to surf the steadily increasing waves.

In between keeping a weather eye on the developing situation and making sail and steering adjustments I grilled Lauren about the Kareet and their plans. I learned that she had little sympathy for the human side of her heritage and was clearly fully indoctrinated to the Kareeti view of the universe. She spoke scathingly of the arrant stupidity of the human race and was quite taken aback when I wholeheartedly agreed with her.

"Hell, most of the problems faced by the world today we've known about for decades. In most cases, if we'd acted straight away we could have averted the worst effects. I mean global warming was first postulated in 1896!"

"So why wasn't something done about it?"

"Greed, fear and stupidity. Some people became incredibly rich selling coal and oil. Incredibly rich people have a lot of power and influence and politicians both crave and fear power. Also, human beings are fat, apathetic and lazy. If you tell them you're going to close down their hospitals or double their taxes you might cause a bit of a furor, get them out on the streets protesting, but something as nebulous and seemingly remote as climate change or species extinction—can't be bothered!"

"Sounds as if you don't really care for your fellow humans."

"No, not much; they've been a bit of a disappointment, sorry excuse for a species really!"

"Well then, you won't be sorry to hear that the Kareet plan to get rid of them."

"What did you say?" I spluttered, aghast.

"The Kareet intend to save this planet."

"That's not what you said."

"The only threat to this planet, other than a random meteor strike, is human beings."

"Yeah, but you can't...' I searched but could find no words. "You surely don't mean to simply eradicate the entire species?" I finally settled upon, and actually laughed. The whole situation was far too phantasmagorical. I couldn't yet take it, or her seriously. On the one hand I had witnessed her use technology that I was quite sure, if humanity had actually developed it, would certainly not be in the hands of a backpacker but, on the other, how could I believe she was an alien and there was an extra-terrestrial plot to wipe out humanity? It was laughable.

"No, they don't intend eradication; just to balance the population. I am not privy to the fine details for I am not in the command chain."

"Holy shit!" My head was spinning. I became engaged dialectically with the proposition; the notion of vast numbers of people wiped out, "You couldn't do that! You'd cause catastrophic global chaos. You'd make matters worse!"

"As I said, I don't know the details," she said as though that were the end of it.

We didn't speak much for a while after that. The wind was

rising steadily, and the barometer was falling alarmingly. I was busy reefing sails and preparing the ship for the worst. I had Lauren stow away everything that was loose in the cabin. I ensured all cupboards were secured so no doors would fly open and spray the contents all around the cabin. I secured the cabin sole, having once before been belted in the back of the head by a loose floor in a knockdown. In the cockpit, I made sure everything was shipshape and secured. I found a couple of screws and some shock chord and fashioned a pair of cinches to hold the winch handles in their holsters.

The wind was at 30 knots, gusting to 38. It was very noticeably cooler. We were, by now, fully kitted out in our foul weather gear. I took the para anchor up on deck and secured the bag to the life lines. I put a 300 foot coil of single braid nylon rope in the anchor well and, disconnected the anchor chain, replacing it with the parachute rode.

It is a good idea, on a blue water sailer, to attach a second track on the mast parallel to the mainsail track. The second track is for the storm 'trysail. That way, when you decide to douse the mainsail you don't have to remove it from the track to get your 'trysail up. Unfortunately, *Perseverance* wasn't set up that way, which meant I was going to have an almighty struggle when the time came. I was torn. To avoid the difficulty and danger of working at the mast when conditions became extreme, I should probably drop the main now. On the other hand, we were trying to outrun the storm. We were running before the wind so the double reefed main was perfectly fine in the current conditions and allowing us to make good speed.

I tuned in for the weather report at noon. The system was intensifying, storm-force winds were forecast, heavy rain and seas to 20 feet. Lauren was in the cabin. She heard the report. She didn't say anything, but she took her syncom out of her pocket and… well, I don't know what she did to it, but suddenly a holographic wall sprang up, and depicted the Australian coastline, and our location overlaid with a current synoptic chart. You could clearly identify the storm center and, after she made a minor adjustment, the track of the storm. These things typically stay close to the coast and we were moving very deliberately away. This storm, however, was on a north easterly trajectory and seemed to be coming after us. What particularly alarmed me was the pressure at the center of the storm: 988 hPa! The storm that hit the 1998 Sydney to Hobart fleet had a central pressure of about 982. The only reason I could see for optimism was that we were heading away from the coast and these storms tended to lose their sting quite rapidly as they got farther out to sea.

I made some quick calculations. We were certainly not going to outrun it.

"We'll get the storm sails set now while it's still not too bad," I told Lauren.

We went on deck. Spatters of rain began to fall. I made sure we were tethered on and talked through the process with Lauren—she would manage the halyards. I was impressed at how calmly she was taking all of this; her first sail and with a major storm on our heels.

As I anticipated, it was a mongrel of a job trying to get the mainsail free of the track, so I could insert the storm trysail slugs but, after what seemed an eternity of being thrown about and having fully exhausted my extensive vocabulary of profanities and expletives, the job was finally done. Furling up the rest of the genoa and hanking on the little orange storm staysail to the inner forestay was easy enough.

"What's that bag over there?" asked Lauren as I flopped back into the cockpit.

"That's the parachute anchor," I replied. Clearly that meant little to her. "There will probably come a time," I continued, "when we will need to heave to…'

"Heave to?"

"Yeah, it's a maneuver used to stop the boat almost completely, with the sails still up. The theory is to use the mainsail and headsail to work against each other to balance the boat at an angle to the wind. The jib is back winded and attempts to turn the boat away from the wind, while the mainsail and rudder are trying to turn the boat into the wind. If you can get this all nicely balanced the boat will hold a steady position."

"Why would you want to do that?"

"Well, once she is 'hove to' the boat will ride the waves in a very much more comfortable way. It gives you the chance to rest, make a cup of tea and basically just sit the storm out."

"Oh, I see," she said thoughtfully.

"Yes, an interesting thing happens when a boat is hove to: a kind of 'slick' of calm water forms on the windward side of the boat and, if the waves are breaking at their crests the slick stops the waves from breaking over the boat. The problem is, when you are hove to, you do still tend to move forward, albeit very slowly, and what can happen is you sail out of your protective slick and waves start to break over your bow, and that's where the para anchor comes in. You attach it to the front of the boat and chuck it over the windward side. You let out about 250 - 300 feet of line, which is called a rode, and there's a bridle, or pennant line, that comes back to the winch in the cockpit, so you can control the set of the parachute. That stops you sailing forwards."

By now the wind was very strong. I glanced at the wind speed instrument during a gust and it was damned near 50 knots. The rain, which had begun as intermittent salvos, was now persistent and stinging to the face.

"In fact," I said, "now would probably be as good a time as any to put all of this into practice."

Once we were hove to, the difference was immediately evident. Whereas we had been bucking and diving, surfing down waves as we ran before the wind, now we surged gently up and down the swells as they passed beneath our hull.

"Right let's get this thing out there." The para anchor was my own—I always carried it with me on delivery jobs— part of the essential gear really.

It didn't take long to deploy. I let out about 250 feet of rode. I checked that the plastic hose I used for anti-chafing was in the right place, then I wound the pennant line around a winch and cranked it in to fine tune the set of the chute. Once I was satisfied with the set we went below to get out of the horrible weather.

As the wind howled through the rigging with increasing intensity I put a pot of soup on the stove and made some reassuring remarks to Lauren concerning our predicament. Although she had seemed reasonably sanguine before we set the storm sails, the seas had grown significantly since then and I had little doubt the waves were getting up over the 20 feet forecast. Just before we had come below I had seen her eyes, like saucers, taking in the mountains of water that roared towards us.

"Don't worry too much," I said, cocking my head toward the sea, "you'd be amazed at how well a small vessel like this can handle big seas. I've been in bigger storms in lesser boats than this and had no real problems. This boat's a beauty, well designed, very seaworthy."

"Will it get much worse?" she asked, a little apprehensively.

"No, it won't get much worse than this," I lied. No point in terrifying her. I handed her a mug of soup. "These east coast lows get pretty intense, but they tend to be short-lived. The farther they get from the mainland the more likely they are to run out of puff."

She asked me to hold her mug while she went to her bunk and rummaged around for her bottle of 'salts'.

"Anyway," I went on, "as you can see, it's not too bad down here now we're hove to."

She gave me a look that told me she wasn't convinced, took her mug and wedged herself into a corner.

I had missed out on my sleep during the dawn watch which was not, of itself, much of a problem but, what with the storm and all the extraordinary things I was hearing from

Lauren, I was becoming mentally exhausted. Nevertheless, as much to keep her mind off our predicament as anything else, I attempted to keep a conversation going. She seemed unwilling to talk about herself, the Kareet or anything to do with them so we ended up in a misanthropic rant on the myriad vile misdeeds of the human race.

It was becoming dark outside. I had switched on the navigation lights and the red cabin lights half an hour or so before. I thought it prudent to check the set of the chute while I still could see, and make sure there was no chafing at the attachment points of the lines. I pulled on my foulies, opened the washboards and reached for the tether, attached it to my harness and climbed into the cockpit. I replaced the lower washboard and looked about me. The wind was screaming, blowing the rain horizontally. The waves were, without doubt, as big as any I had experienced, many of them breaking at their crests. I think, at that moment, I was as apprehensive as ever I had been at sea. However, the slick appeared to be preventing the waves from breaking over us so, so far so good; the chute appeared to be doing its job.

I made my way cautiously forward to check the rode at the anchor cleat. The protective hose was still in place and showed no undue signs of wear. Keeping my knees bent, my center of gravity low and always keeping one hand on a lifeline, I worked my way back along the high, windward side of the deck. Although the waves were enormous the boat rode over them with a degree of predictability in her movement. I was just about in line with the mast when it happened. I don't know what caused it, perhaps a wave running at an angle to the prevailing set. In any case, we were just starting the ride down the back of a wave when the boat bucked like a bull at a rodeo. I was hurled forward. My head drove into the mast. There was an instant of brilliant light, intense pain, and then I felt myself falling into blackness.

Part 2

Chapter 8

The first thing I noticed was the pain. My head throbbed. My mouth was dry. I lay there, eyes closed, consciousness emerging slowly and warily from the blackness. I couldn't, at first, remember anything at all, but then, it was almost as though someone had thrown open the door and memory flooded in: the boat, the storm, the impact with the mast— where was I, why wasn't I being thrown around the deck? My eyes fluttered open.

Everything was still, quiet. I lay on my back on a comfortable surface in what appeared to be a hospital room. The subdued light, not much brighter than moonlight, came not from a point source but was, rather, a luminance that appeared to suffuse the space. I sat up abruptly and instantly wished I hadn't. A spasm of pain ran down from the crown of my head into the middle of my back and I felt giddy. I gripped the sides of the bed and sat there, clenching my teeth and screwing up my eyes, waiting for the pain to subside and the dizziness to go.

Where on Earth could I be? My mind raced. When I hit

my head, I was on a yacht, in a storm, about 180 nautical miles from the coast. How could I now be in a hospital on dry land? How long must I have been unconscious, if there had been time for Lauren to call for emergency services to fly out in a helicopter, find us in the dark, in all that wild weather, hoist us into the chopper and fly us back to Australia? I couldn't believe I had been unconscious that long. And, what was happening to *Perseverance*? God, that was a $200,000 boat and I was responsible for her!

At that moment I heard a whoosh. To my left, a sliding door had opened. In the opening, silhouetted against the brighter light beyond, stood a figure I didn't immediately recognize. The door whooshed shut. Lauren stepped towards me.

"Hello, are you feeling better?"

I attempted to reply but no words came. I signaled for water. She walked swiftly to an anteroom and returned with a metal flask. I drank greedily. The water felt wonderful in my mouth and tasted delicious. I emptied the flask and handed it back to her.

"More?" she asked.

I nodded. When she returned I asked, "Where are we? How long have I been unconscious?" She didn't reply immediately but watched me reflectively as I drank more water. "Well?" I persisted.

"Perhaps an hour," she replied.

"An hour? Don't be ridiculous! A helicopter couldn't even fly to where we were in an hour, let alone hoist us aboard, fly back and get me into a hospital."

"Well we're not in a hospital and there was no

helicopter." I gazed at her blankly. "We're in the Kareeti main vessel and it was they who rescued us," she said in a matter-of-fact tone. I continued to stare blankly, uncomprehendingly, at her. There was a moment or two of complete silence. I did notice she had changed her clothes and now wore a tunic over what appeared to be a body suit or perhaps leggings and form-fitting long-sleeved shirt. The outfit was made from olive green, metallic-looking fabric.

"So, how are you feeling?" she asked.

"Not very well," I grumbled.

"Someone is going to take a look at you."

I looked up at her from under my eyebrows, my mind racing. There was too much information to process and frankly, under the circumstances, I couldn't even see a place to begin. The door whooshed again, and I looked up.

If my head was in a spin before, it was at the point of imminent shut-down when I saw what entered the room next! I may have said before that I had never been a believer in UFOs, alien abductions and those funny little men with great big eyes, but that is exactly what walked into the room! It was maybe 160 cm tall with a disproportionately large head, the shape of an inverted teardrop, with a tiny nose and large, almond-shaped eyes. It was dressed in white but, otherwise, in the same style as Lauren,

"This is Zilzi," Lauren informed me. "She is… well, she is so much more than one of your doctors, but let's just say she is a doctor. Why don't you lie down?"

I don't have the words to describe my mental state at that time. Suffice to say that, in an almost trancelike state, I lowered myself , painfully, back down and lay facing the ceiling. Lauren and Zilzi started to talk. The language was like none I had ever heard before.

Zilzi produced a device that closely resembled Lauren's syncom and appeared to scan my body with it, although I saw no lights or holographic images. There was a short exchange between the two.

"Zilzi tells me you have fractured your skull and misaligned a vertebra low in your neck. Both these are easily fixed. I will give you something to drink and you will sleep. When you wake you will feel much better."

I wanted to remonstrate. I didn't know anything about this Zilzi, what her intentions might be or what was in this drink Lauren proposed to give me. But Lauren had never given me any reason to believe she would harm me and I was very, very, tired; I hadn't the energy to resist.

When I woke, the room was much brighter, perhaps to suggest daylight— morning. I felt remarkably well. I couldn't remember when I had last experienced such recuperative sleep. I ran my hand gingerly over my head, feeling for lumps, lacerations or tenderness. I found none! In fact, the only thing that detracted from my overall sense of wellbeing was a gnawing hunger in the pit of my stomach. I had no idea how long it had been since I last ate.

I propped myself up on an elbow expecting, at any moment, a jab of pain; none came. Beside the bed was the metal flask Lauren had brought me. I picked it up and found it to be nearly full. I drank deeply. As I set it back down, the door whooshed, and Lauren came in.

"How do you feel?" she asked breezily.

"Remarkably well, I must confess." I realized I had thought only of my physical sense of wellbeing. My bizarre circumstances came flooding back to me, doubtless casting a shadow on my countenance.

"Don't worry, Jeff. It'll be all right." She smiled reassuringly. "We have prepared quarters for you. I'm going to take you there now and I have arranged for food to be brought."

At the prospect of getting up I directed my attention for the first time to my state of dress. I was lying beneath a light coverlet. I flipped back a corner and realized I was dressed in a gown, beneath which I was naked. Clearly, I had been undressed while I was sleeping.

"My clothes?" I enquired.

"They're gone, I'm afraid. We don't have Kareeti dress in your size; we are none of us so big! You can keep the gown on, they are making you clothes and will soon be finished."

"So, what was wrong with the clothes I had on?"

"Are you serious? Do you think they would have allowed either of us on board with our Earth clothes on?" I suppose I must still have looked confused. "We have to guard against pathogens originating from Earth for which we may have no antigen."

"Ah," I said as the light slowly dawned. "So, you've sterilized me, have you?"

"Yes, in a manner of speaking. We were brought aboard straight into the quarantine hold. We were scanned for pathogens, bathed and irradiated."

"Irradiated?" I asked in alarm.

"Yes, but don't worry, we have the science perfected."

"And what other probes and examinations have I been put through without my knowledge or consent?"

"Why, none at all. The Kareet are very respectful of an individual's right to privacy."

"Oh really?" I replied. "You've removed all of my clothing without my knowledge or consent; I'd call that an invasion of my privacy. Wouldn't you?"

"You were unconscious!" she said, rolling her eyes. "You needed medical treatment. What were we to do? If you had been conscious your privacy would have been fully respected. You would have been given the gown to change into, in private, and then you would have been scanned for pathogens; simple." She sounded exasperated. Well, I was irritated too. I hadn't asked for any of this crap!

There was a moment of silence as the tension between us eased. She inclined her head to suggest we go. I hesitated a moment, then swung my legs over the side of the bed and carefully stood up. I need have had no concern; I felt remarkably well and not the least dizzy or unsteady.

"What about all of the bacteria that are part of my natural body's flora and fauna? Surely all of those are alien to the Kareet?"

"There are some commonalities, believe it or not, and many we have been able to assimilate and adapt to. Others we have developed antigens to. The Kareet have been interacting with humans for over forty years. We've had plenty of time to study and understand your microbiologicals. In fact, we're way in front. We have antigens for all the cold and flu viruses that still perplex your scientists; Ebola, Lyssavirus, Hendra virus, herpes, hepatitis—we can deal with all of them."

We left the room and entered an evenly lit corridor. We turned to our right. I followed half a step behind Lauren. At an intersection with another corridor I saw a small huddle of perhaps four Kareet engaged in conversation. They stopped abruptly as they saw us and stared as we walked past. I imagine they watched us with the same incredulity that I felt.

We stopped in front of a door in the wall. A moment passed and then the door slid open. It appeared to be an elevator. We stepped in. Lauren touched a glossy pad on the wall. There was a slight jolt and the lift began to rise. When it stopped, we turned to our left and followed a corridor, indistinguishable from the previous one, for about thirty yards. We stopped outside yet another door. Lauren placed her palm against another glossy pad. The door slid open to reveal a hexagonal vestibule accessing another five doors. We crossed to the door directly opposite, which slid open and we walked in.

The room we entered was not large. There was a bench along the wall to my left with a couple of stools beneath it. Along the wall opposite the bench, was a bunk which looked a little too short for comfort. There was a small sitting area with a comfortable-looking reclining chair. Behind that was a divider and, as I later discovered, behind that a bathroom enclosure. All very utilitarian but adequate and, I supposed, comfortable enough.

As we stood there taking it all in, a purple light beside the door flashed twice with a soft accompanying buzz.

"Ah, that will be your food," said Lauren, touching a panel on the wall. The door slid open. A small Kareet stood at the threshold bearing a metal tray. It was almost laughable! Here I was, suddenly and bewilderingly caught up in a sci-fi movie, and here was this little guy holding a tray with a dish covered by a silver cloche that could have come from an episode of *Upstairs Downstairs*!

I don't know what I expected to be under the cloche; bacon and eggs would have been nice, but whatever it was didn't look like any breakfast I had ever eaten, or would want to eat. A metal pan, perhaps four inches by six and perhaps an inch deep, contained a mossy green, apparently gelatinous substance that emitted an odorless steam. Beside the pan was a small tray containing two... tablets, for want of a better word. They looked, perhaps, like iced biscuits or more like oversized Chiclet's chewing gum pieces; one was white and one a light caramel color. I looked askance at Lauren.

"All right," she said, "you are going to have to get used to a very different kind of food from what you're used to. I had to get used to yours. Zilzi has profiled your gut flora and confirmed that you can digest this."

"Okay, fine, but what is it?"

"Would you be any the wiser if I told you?" Upon reflection, I thought probably not. "That," she indicated the green stuff, "will provide you with essential nutrients. It will satisfy your need for protein, amino acids and carbohydrates.

It doesn't have much flavor compared to your food on Earth. These," she pointed to the 'Chiclet's, "are the closest you are going to get to a dessert. They are not particularly sweet, but they do provide other nutrients including salts, sugars and enzymes your body needs. Please don't ask me to go into further detail because I don't have that level of knowledge."

She swung out one of the stools and I sat down and picked up an implement from the tray. It resembled a broad butter knife with the hint of a spoon-like depression. I poked suspiciously at the green stuff. At first it merely deflected to the pressure of the spoon. I poked a little harder. The surface yielded. I scooped up a small amount and eyed it suspiciously.

"Go on, it won't hurt you!" Lauren taunted.

Hell, I had eaten snails, Fugu, and even witchetty grubs! I put the spoon in my mouth.

"Well?" I looked up at her arched eyebrows with a degree of irritation.

"Offensive!" I spat. "Its very blandness gives offence to the epicurean tongue!" But, banter aside, I was damned hungry. I scooped up spoonful after spoonful until the pan was empty. It did not seem such a great quantity of food, and yet, I was surprisingly full as I swallowed the last morsel.

I turned my attention to the 'dessert'. I wasn't going to give Lauren the opportunity to get in another jibe. It appeared to be finger food. I picked up one of the white ones and bit into it. It was crunchy. To its credit, it did have a distinctive flavor, although of what I had no idea. I had never tasted anything like it before. But then that was not surprising. It was a little sweet and, perhaps, slightly tart, although not citric.

I finished the white one and then, more from curiosity than hunger, tried the caramel-colored one. Again, it was crunchy, with a different new flavor and, again, a little sweet. By the time I had finished I was surprisingly replete. I had been ravenous and deeply skeptical that the contents of the tray would do much more than whet my appetite.

I pushed the tray to one side. Lauren had, by now, pulled out the other stool and was sitting at the bench beside me.

"Well, what now?" I asked. "How do I get back to the yacht?" I had been thinking it through and had decided that *Perseverance* would have managed, hove to, without us on board just as well as with us.

"You won't be returning to the boat," she replied in a measured tone.

"But I have to go back," I remonstrated. "I'm responsible for that yacht. You've been able to get back to your... er... people, which is great and, of course I'm very grateful for all you've done to help me, for bringing me aboard and fixing me up, but now you've got to return me; I've got no role here."

"I need to explain some things to you." Lauren encouraged me to sit down in the recliner and try to relax. Once I was comfortable, she began. She must have spoken for ten minutes or more, virtually uninterrupted by me, as I listened, spellbound.

She told me about the Kareet, how they had, for several decades, monitored Earth, its biosphere and mankind's activities. The vessel upon which I now found myself was recently arrived in the solar system. It was a medium-sized interstellar vessel capable of housing and transporting a population of some 800. On this particular vessel, for this mission, there were fewer than 200 on board. The personnel could be broadly defined into four distinct groups. The crew, who ran the ship, were military personnel. They could be identified by their blue uniforms.

The medical staff wore white.

The senior military commander, the captain of the ship, was named Guurtsaad Duurn. He was widely regarded as a very capable, experienced but hard-nosed commander. I gathered that, in our idiom, he would be considered a 'hawk'.

I was told I may see some Kareet in a dark, olive green outfit, they were the scientific team.

"So that's your lot?"

"Yes, there are about fifty of us, from all kinds of different disciplines."

The other contingent, considerably smaller in number, was what we might describe as the diplomatic corps. Their role was to support the Head of Mission, ambassador for the Kareet, and upon whose shoulders responsibility for the mission rested. Head of Mission was Alassay Harraan, a very senior, highly skilled, diplomat. She was selected for this undertaking not only for her outstanding diplomatic abilities, but also because she had a reputation for incisive analytical thinking, cool-headedness, and innate wisdom.

Members of the diplomatic corps could be identified by

their silver uniforms, although the senior echelon of diplomats wore gold tunics over their silver leggings.

Apparently, there were signs of tension between Commander Duurn and Ambassador Harraan. Lauren's interpretation of the situation was that the Commander had his own views on what was the best way to conduct the mission and diplomacy didn't come into it.

"Just what exactly is this so-called mission?" I enquired.

"That, I am not at liberty to tell you," she replied, "I have been severely reprimanded for speaking with you as openly as I did. However, Alassay Harraan will no doubt tell you everything she considers you should know. You are soon to meet her."

"Does she speak English?"

"Yes, most of the senior ranking diplomats speak your language."

"I've been wondering about that," I said. "How did you learn to speak English so well?"

"Compared with humans, the Kareet have very highly evolved brains; their ability to process streams of complex information is matched with vast memory capacity. I personally speak twelve human languages as fluently as I do English. Being only a Hybrid, my brain is nowhere near as highly evolved as most Kareet."

While I was, with my merely human brain, trying to process this information, the little purple light flashed on and off a couple of times. Lauren opened the door. A Kareet in a blue uniform stood at the threshold. Across his (or her— I couldn't yet tell) upturned arms he held a folded fabric which I imagined was the clothing Lauren had told me was being made for me. They exchanged no more than a word or two. Lauren took the fabric and the Kareet departed.

"Here you are," she said turning to me, "your tunic is ready." She handed the bundle to me. I shook it out. There was a pair of leggings, a long-sleeved, form-fitting shirt and a tunic. It appeared to be the same outfit that every Kareet that I had yet seen wore, except mine was a deep claret color. There was also a pair of matching ankle-high booties. The sole appeared to be made from some sort of polymer while the uppers were of the same fabric as the leggings.

"They are making you more, but these will do for now. Why don't you get changed? I'll be back soon." With that, she turned and left.

Whoever 'they' were, they had evidently measured me up while I was unconscious because the outfit fitted perfectly. I was a little uncomfortable with the absence of underpants as the form fitting leggings left little to the imagination, but the tunic, once I had pulled it over my head, fell to mid-thigh and modesty was restored.

I discovered a mirror on the wall of the ensuite and decided that, all-in-all, I looked quite debonair in the outfit, except that my hair was bedraggled, and my beard could have used a trim. There were no toiletries to be found. It occurred to me that none of the Kareet that I had seen appeared to have hair, so combs and scissors and, presumably, razors would not be things they would have any call for.

I folded myself into the recliner and awaited Lauren's

return. While I waited I tried very hard to think through, calmly and rationally, all that had happened in these past however many hours. It proved impossible. I could not rid myself of the feeling that it was all some bizarre dream.

Lauren returned and, bless her, brought with her a comb. She, at least, had hair! The comb, however, was no match for my matted thatch. Lauren left again, returning a few moments later with shampoo and conditioner which she had brought with her from Earth. Half an hour later, while I was combing back my hair into a pigtail, Lauren reached inside her tunic and retrieved her syncom. "They're ready for us now," she said, in a matter-of-fact voice. "Are you ready?"

I didn't think I was, but nor did I suppose my degree of readiness would be of much concern to 'they' who were ready.

Chapter 9

We opened the door to my quarters to find two, apparently armed, military Kareet facing us. They grabbed me by my upper arms, one on each side of me, and proceeded to frog-march me toward the outer vestibule door. Lauren snapped something to them in their language. One of them turned his head and snarled something back at her, but they didn't release me.

I looked back over my shoulder in utter confusion just as the door whooshed open and I was propelled out into the corridor.

Lauren was barely a step behind. She positively barked at my captors and I thought I discerned the name Alassay Harraan. The soldiers paused, hesitated, and there was a terse interchange. Finally, they released my arms. One took up position in front of me and the other fell in behind. The one at the rear barked something and prodded me in the back. I gathered I was expected to march!

"Jeff, I'm very sorry." Lauren's voice was plaintive.

"What's with these two guys?" I asked, bemused.

"They have orders from their commander and it seems you are considered an unwelcome intruder. I have told them you are the guest of Alassay Harraan."

"That seemed to do the trick!" I tried but failed to keep the sarcastic edge from my voice. The Kareet behind me growled something. Lauren snapped something back. "What's going on?" I asked.

"He had the nerve to order us not to speak! I told him to get stuffed!"

"Atta girl!"

"Things were a little tense between Guurtsaad Duurn and Alassay Harraan before I was accidentally marooned on Earth. I fear the situation has deteriorated."

I was nudged into a vacant lift, my captors to either side. Lauren squeezed in; there wasn't much room. The lift ascended, I knew not how far. The door opened, Lauren slipped out and I was shoved out somewhat unceremoniously. I was becoming peeved, I must confess. These two thuglets— they barely reached my shoulder—were coming very close to getting a thick ear if, indeed they had ears!

I restrained myself however, and instead, focused on my current whereabouts. Looking up I found myself in a large, brightly lit room. Directly ahead of me, on a raised dais, several beings sat at a long table. In the center was an elderly Kareet whom I deduced was Alassay Harraan. She wore a gold tunic over her silver sleeves and a matching gold wimple. A purple sash around her neck fell straight from her shoulders.

On either side of her sat other Kareet dressed in the silver and gold that Lauren had told me indicated high status. Away to my left, separate from the long table, an imposing figure sat in a grand seat or throne. His metallic blue uniform confirmed he was military, although his was a darker blue and the material more lustrous than any I had seen to date. He wore a bright yellow sash diagonally from his left shoulder to the waist on his right side, and an ornate medallion suspended on a scarlet ribbon sat a little above where a human heart would be. Guurtsaad Duurn, I assumed. Behind him, and to either side, stood a coterie of whom I took to be senior Kareeti officers.

There had been a subdued hubbub of conversation when we first arrived, but this soon died as those gathered noted our arrival.

"Mr. Jeff Ridsdale, welcome." Her voice was mellifluous, her accent unlike any I had heard, but crisp and clear. "Please, come forward," she said, and beckoned. I was suddenly self-conscious and unsure of myself. "Mr. Ridsdale, my name is Alassay Harraan. I am the leader of this expeditionary mission. Those to my left and to my right are senior members of my cabinet. Over there," she indicated with a small flourish of her right hand, "is the captain of this vessel, Guurtsaad Duurn." I looked to where she had indicated. Guurtsaad Duurn's large eyes were fixed on me. If he wore an expression, it was not one I could read.

Alassay Harraan spoke again; this time in Kareeti. One of the silver-clad brought a chair and placed it perhaps five paces from the front of the long table. "Please," she said again indicating the chair with an eloquent gesture of her arm.

I shambled forward and, to my chagrin, found myself ducking my head in a small but undeniable act of obeisance, before sitting in the provided seat. As I sat, silently castigating myself for my deference, a harsh comment came from my left from the lips, I assumed, of Guurtsaad Duurn, followed by laughter from the group of officers at his shoulder.

Alassay Harraan looked in their direction with what I took to be a look of disapproval (I was still almost totally ignorant of Kareeti facial expressions, such as they were). She said something to them in a quiet voice.

At that point Lauren stepped forward and, with head lowered in respect, spoke with Alassay Harraan. There was a brief interchange and then Lauren smiled, bobbed her head and came to my side.

"I am to be your interpreter," she murmured in my ear. "I made the point that Guurtsaad Duurn does not speak English but has an interpreter, so he will know everything you say, but you would not know what was being said in Kareeti."

"Mr. Ridsdale, on behalf of our people I would like to welcome you aboard our vessel," Alassay Harraan began.

There was a comment from Guurtsaad Duurn.

"You don't speak for the captain or crew!" Lauren interpreted.

Again, there was the look of reproof from Alassay Harraan.

"Mr. Ridsdale, this must be a very confronting and confusing situation for you," Alassay Harraan continued with a note of forbearance in her voice directed, I presumed, at Guurtsaad Duurn, "so I would like to keep this meeting as short as possible. I gather that our young Hybrid here…' she looked meaningfully at Lauren, "has been talking to you of our purported mission." Her English really was exemplary, not just her vocabulary but also her use of intonation and nuance.

"Well I…'

"She had no authority to talk to you about any such matters and, in fact, has no diplomatic status whatsoever and is, therefore, not privy to our policies, plans or deliberations. You may be assured that she has been reprimanded appropriately and certain penalties have been imposed."

Guurtsaad Duurn growled something and Lauren began to interpret.

"He said…'

"Guurtsaad Duurn wants to know who else you have spoken to about what Lauren told you was our mission." Alassay Harraan overrode Lauren.

"Told…?" I began in confusion. "How could I have told anyone? Lauren only told me what she did after we had put to sea, I…'

"You had radio equipment on your vessel." Lauren interpreted a guttural riposte from Duurn.

I realized I was feeling very much on the back foot, out of my depth and defensive. I knew I had to pull myself together and get back on the front foot (to complete the metaphor). I took a deep breath and let it out slowly.

"I have told no one," I replied in a voice I hoped sounded calmly authoritative.

"He's insisting you respond to his question about the boat radio," Lauren informed me.

"I did not use the radio to tell anyone anything at all. If you pause for a moment and think about it," I said with a hint of dismissive disdain, "I had been confronted with what was surely the most improbable story I had heard in my entire life. Even as I began to conclude that there may be an element of truth to it, it is hardly likely that I would get on the emergency channel of the marine radio system and announce to the world that I had gone stark raving mad! For that is exactly what anyone hearing my transmission would have concluded."

A minor hubbub erupted between Guurtsaad Duurn and his officers that Lauren didn't bother to interpret for me.

"Mr. Ridsdale…' Alassay Harraan's voice was raised to reassert order. "Mr. Ridsdale, you were brought before this assembly at the request of Captain, Guurtsaad Duurn; the security of the vessel and, indeed, of the mission, is his responsibility. I am satisfied with your answers to his concerns…'

There was a retort from Guurtsaad Duurn followed by a brief but sharp exchange between the two protagonists. Lauren did not interpret.

"I do not believe it is necessary to subject you to this… court martial style of interview any longer. I would like, however, to speak with you at length, one on one, under more congenial circumstances. Do you think that might be arranged?"

This was clearly a rhetorical question but I, nonetheless, found myself nodding my assent. She smiled and lowered her head in a gesture I took to mean the interview was over.

I rose to my feet, as did Alassay Harraan and her entourage. She smiled briefly at me, turned and, with her coterie in tow, left the room by an entrance to the rear of the space. I looked around at Lauren who indicated we should leave. I glanced at Duurn. He appeared to be watching me with an expression I interpreted as malevolent. I didn't give him the satisfaction of a reaction, turned and headed for the door with Lauren.

Chapter 10

The door slid open and we stepped out straight into the waiting arms of the two thuglets. One of them stepped forward and grasped me by the upper arm. I had had quite enough of this by now. I pulled my arm from his grasp and pushed him away. As he fell back, the other surged forward and grabbed my tunic. My blood was up! I elbowed him in the gut and, as he doubled over, brought my knee up, catching his hip and sending him sprawling.

Well, that stirred the hornets' nest! The door behind me slid open, as did another a few feet down the corridor, and blue-clad Kareet swarmed out. In an instant, they had me pressed up against a wall, my arms immobilized. I heard Lauren shouting but to no avail. I was forcibly frog-marched away and thrown into a small holding cell, careering across the room and crashing headlong into the opposite wall. There was a sharp pain and I swore forcibly and volubly. Blood trickled down my forehead.

I sat on the floor, muttering pointless imprecations and planning lurid, if improbable, acts of revenge. Gradually I simmered down and began to consider my predicament. If this were not some prolonged, bizarre dream, I was locked up in a small, entirely unfurnished room (more a cupboard really) in an alien space ship surrounded by little green men (except they weren't green) and I had absolutely no control over my circumstances. If I could escape them where would I go, what would I do? I could hardly step out into space and make a quick getaway! I didn't like these military Kareet, or their malevolent master, and they were evidently the majority on this vessel. Alassay Harraan seemed all right, at least when compared to the military contingent. She seemed to have charm and style and, maybe, some concern for my wellbeing.

Clearly, I had to behave myself, not anger the crew any more than I already had, and try to nurture the relationship with Alassay Harraan. Meanwhile, I had a headache, I was becoming both hungry and thirsty and I was having difficulty subduing my irritation at being locked up. To divert my attention, I attempted to recall a poem I had long ago learned.

Take this kiss upon the brow!
And, in parting from you now,
Thus much let me avow-
You are not wrong, who deem
That my days have been a dream;
Yet if hope has flown away
In a night, or in a day,
In a vision, or in none,

Is it therefore the less gone?
All that we see or seem
Is but a dream within a dream.

I stand amid the roar
Of a surf-tormented shore,
And I hold within my hand
Grains of the golden sand-
How few! yet how they creep
Through my fingers to the deep,
While I weep- while I weep!
O God! can I not grasp
Them with a tighter clasp?
O God! can I not save
One from the pitiless wave?
Is all that we see or seem
But a dream within a dream?

It took me several attempts to get it right and I was quite amazed when I did. I was trying to draw parallels between the poem and my current situation when the door slid open. I looked up and saw what appeared to be a young man, as in a young *human* man! He leant, somewhat languorously, against the door frame.

"You must be Jeff Ridsdale."

I gathered my knees up and rested my arms upon them and eyed him speculatively. He had the same overly large eyes I had noticed in Lauren and appeared to be in his mid-twenties. Was he a Hybrid too? It made sense, I supposed.

He was dressed in the non-military silver garb although I saw a trio of blue uniforms behind him.

"My name is Carlos. I have come to get you out of here." He smiled. "Lauren," he added as though in response to my unspoken question, "has been assigned other duties." I clambered to my feet. "We'll take you back to your quarters, so you can freshen up and then Alassay Harraan is keen to talk with you again in private this time."

"Keep those idiots away from me!" I growled.

Carlos turned and spoke to the three foot soldiers, or whatever they were. He gestured for them to back away and they did.

Carlos led the way, I followed, and the three Kareet followed me at a respectable distance.

"I don't think they trust you," he said with a grin, having glanced back over his shoulder.

There was much I might have said but I let it pass. We came to my quarters. The door slid open and I went in. Carlos spoke to the boys in blue and they departed.

"I could use some food," I called out to Carlos from the ensuite. I dabbed cool water on the small wound to my brow, straightened out my tunic and poked a few stray hairs back into the band that held my ponytail. I heard him talking in Kareeti and walked out in time to see him replacing a hand set.

"That's how you would normally order your food," he said, and then as an afterthought, "Not that it would get you anywhere, there's no one at the other end that would understand you!" He chuckled.

We sat down. I stretched my legs out and crossed them at the ankles.

"So, Carlos, I take it you are a Hybrid too?"

"Yes, that's right."

"Are you related to Lauren?"

"No, no, not at all. What makes you think…?"

"Oh, I don't know, nothing really. I suppose there is a likeness. You could almost be her brother, perhaps it's the eyes. How does this whole Hybrid thing work anyway? I mean, I take it you are part human, part Kareet. Is your mother or your father human?"

"My father was."

"Was… so he's not still with you?"

"No. I've never met him. The Kareet gathered his semen."

"And then? I mean what happened to him?"

"I don't know. They don't tell you."

"So, they swoop down and scoop up some poor unsuspecting man or woman from… Earth… harvest sperm or eggs and then… and then what? We don't know. Maybe they're returned to Earth or maybe they're discarded?" My head was racing to keep up with this. "So why do they do it? What's the point?"

"Of making Hybrids? Well it gives them insight into the human species and it also allows them to infiltrate."

"You mean the Kareet send Hybrids such as yourself onto Earth to mix with humans and… and what… report back?"

"Yes, more or less."

"And Lauren?"

"Well, Lauren was part of a group undertaking some geological research when—'

"A tourist bus happened along. I got that from Lauren. Are there many Hybrids on board?"

"On this vessel, perhaps ten."

"Ten? Okay, and you said, '*this* vessel', how many are there?"

"Difficult to say, really. There's currently only one major vessel in the solar system—this one—but there may be anything up to ten or twelve scout vehicles whizzing around at any given time."

My eyes must have been like saucers. "How can you have all these vehicles in proximity to Earth and avoid detection?"

"I don't think we do, do we? Avoid detection I mean. Aren't there frequently reported sightings of unidentified flying objects?"

"Yes, but we don't take those seriously! They're just the ravings…' I stopped, speechless, as the import of my words sank in.

Carlos merely shrugged.

The little purple light flashed, announcing the arrival of my refreshments. Upon a small plate there lay what looked like a larger than normal pasta spiral, or rotini. It was the size of my index finger, and yellow, as you might expect pasta to be, only this was a little brighter and had a slightly glossy appearance. I knew better than to enquire. I picked it up, sniffed it, peered at it curiously, then bit off half of it. Upon contact with my saliva it erupted in a tingling effervescence reminiscent of sherbet, but savory, albeit a little tartly citric.

I swallowed and as it reached my stomach, it seemed to spread a warm glow. I popped the other half in my mouth. Within moments I felt fully sated, refreshed and energetic.

"Interesting stuff," I remarked.

Carlos smiled. He produced a syncom from his tunic and, with a hand gesture, drew an almost imperceptible glow. He spoke briefly and quietly in Kareeti. I heard a voice respond at the other end, then he replaced the device in his tunic.

"Alassay Harraan is ready for you now."

Chapter 11

Although austere in style Alassay Harraan's quarters were positively sumptuous in comparison to mine. Carlos had placed his hand on a panel beside a door, a small light flashed twice, he removed and then replaced his hand and the door slid open silently. He patted my shoulder, nodded his head in the direction of the apartment and strode off, leaving me at the threshold.

I stepped inside, a little tentatively, and glanced about me at the spacious suite. It took me a moment but eventually my eyes alighted upon her. She stood motionless, across the room, beside a large window, beyond which could be seen the star-studded blackness of space.

"Come in Mr. Ridsdale." She beckoned with a small gesture of her hand. I crossed the room and joined her at the window. "I gather you have not been getting on very well with our crew," she said in a neutral tone.

"They have not been easy to get on with," I responded dryly.

"Nevertheless, Mr. Ridsdale, I must discourage you from knocking them about!" She smiled.

"Perhaps you might discourage them from treating me like a common criminal. I certainly did nothing to invite their thuggish behaviour."

"No, I'm sure you're right, Mr. Ridsdale. I'm afraid the culture, as in all organizations, comes from the top." I refrained from comment. "Come, let us sit down. Let me pour you a drink. Over there, I think, beside the low table," she offered in response to my questioning look. "You won't be familiar with our food and drink, but I hope you will find this agreeable." She handed me what appeared to be a crystal goblet containing a pale amber liquid.

We sat down, across the table from each other in comfortable, low, semi-reclined chairs.

"I am quite sure that this must be altogether the most bewildering experience for you, Mr. Ridsdale. May I call you Jeff? I understand your people commonly resort to first names. Almost unheard of in Kareeti society but, nevertheless, you must feel free to call me Alassay." She raised her glass and took a sip. I followed suit. The liquid proved most agreeable. It was not entirely unlike a fortified wine. Perhaps a little more full-bodied, a little like a liqueur, although without the heat of a Drambuie or Benedictine.

"Mmm yes, very nice," I nodded my approval, "and yes you can certainly call me Jeff—everyone else does!"

"Thank you." She held her glass before her as though studying the contents for the first time. "It is not altogether unlike your earthly wines, from what I gather. It is fermented from Kareeti plant-like organisms so is probably, effectively a wine.

"I would like to be able to satisfy at least some of your curiosity as to what is happening, who we are and what our mission here is all about. It will not be possible to tell you everything but over the course of a few of these sessions I hope we may come to have a better understanding of each other."

"A few of these sessions?" I asked from under arched eyebrows. "Alassay, I have only one request of you and that is you return me immediately to my boat. I didn't ask to be brought aboard your vessel and I have a duty to deliver that very valuable yacht to its owner in New Zealand."

Alassay laughed. "Jeff, you were knocked unconscious in a terrible storm. You wouldn't have survived and I'm sure the boat will have sunk by now."

"On the contrary," I demurred, "I was attached by a tether to the boat. The boat was hove-to with a parachute anchor deployed. She was riding the sea with no major dramas. I would pretty much guarantee that she's still afloat now. If you'd taken Lauren and left me I would have recovered consciousness, ridden out the storm and continued the voyage when the seas abated."

"You had a fractured skull!"

"I didn't say I wouldn't have had a headache, but my injuries were not life threatening. I'm not ungrateful that your people have patched me up but, please, I need to get back now."

Alassay sighed, looked searchingly at me and shook her head. "Well I'm very sorry, Jeff, but there are many reasons why I cannot agree to your request."

I looked at her stonily.

"To begin with, I fear our young Hybrid, Lauren, has been somewhat indiscreet."

I can only imagine that, because of the phantasmagorical events of the past… however many hours—I had lost all concept of time—and the mind-boggling enormity of the things Lauren had told me the Kareet were contemplating, my mind had simply refused to entertain any further thought on the matter and had dismissed it.

As I now recalled the gist of what she had told me my expression must have darkened.

"I see that you do remember what she told you—stupid girl!"

I could think of nothing intelligent to say, so she continued.

"I had rather gathered from Lauren that you may not be entirely unsympathetic."

"Unsympathetic?" I spluttered. "What on Earth do you mean?"

"Well of course we're not *on* Earth!" she replied, dryly. "However, I understood you and Lauren had some quite lengthy discussions, during which you made it quite clear that you considered the human population was utterly out of balance and you are darkly pessimistic about the future of the planet."

"Well… I, er… I mean…' My mouth was suddenly dry and had apparently lost all connection with my brain. I reached for my goblet and downed its contents in two gulps. Alassay refilled the glass. I felt a warm glow from the liquor and began to detect a subtle calming of my agitated mind.

"You have to help me out here," I began in more measured tones. "Is it true, what Lauren said, that you intend to… *cull* the human race?"

"Yes, I suppose you could call it that," she replied watching me carefully.

I felt my senses reeling again. I took another swig of the wine. "Listen, there is a difference between holding a… philosophical… an *ideological* view on the world's population and actually colluding with someone to… to… to what… wipe out vast numbers of human beings." I shook my head, "The very thought is just too much to take in!"

"Well, collude may be a bit strong, at this stage."

"At this stage?" I asked incredulously. "What does that mean?"

"Oh, nothing really, a thought occurred to me, but it was just that: a thought, and doesn't bear discussion," she said with an air of finality.

I didn't want to even begin to imagine what she might have intended. Instead, I took another drink of the Kareeti wine. I was developing a taste for it and it really did seem to help to reduce my overall sense of agitation. I glanced at Alassay to see if anything in her demeanor suggested I was over-indulging; after all, I had no prior experience of this liquor and thus no idea of how strong it might be. If she were concerned she didn't show it.

"Jeff, the words you have used: philosophical, ideological, suggest to me that you are at least someone who has thought deeply about the problems facing the Earth."

"Well, yes, I have, for many, many years." And I had. I reflected for a moment. "When I was a mere child in primary school I remember my father talking to us around the dinner table one night. He told us that the world population was nearly 3.4 billion and it was predicted to double in fifty-seven years. That shocked the hell out of me! I could not believe that the entire population of the world could double in size in one human lifetime. It boggled my mind. I lay awake that night in bed thinking about it and I remember telling my friends at school the following day. Oddly they didn't seem all that impressed.

"In fact, it took just forty-three years to reach seven billion! It was around that same time, maybe a couple of years later, say 1968, that Paul Ehrlich published his now famous book *The Population Bomb*. I remember reading that when I was about fourteen. My parents were keen followers of an American: Ralph Nader. He brought the world's attention to the terrible effect human activities were having on the ecology; how our detergents were polluting the waterways, our industrial wastes were being dumped into rivers turning them into fire hazards! One river outside of Cleveland Ohio actually did catch fire!

"So yes, I think I first became horribly aware of the serious impact humans were having on the environment certainly by my early teens. It's never ceased to concern me," I replied reflectively, "and it is to my eternal discredit that I was so little involved in activism over the years."

"You think you should have been an activist, you think that would have made a difference?"

"It may have made a difference to me, to how I feel about myself. It would have made no difference to the current global situation, I'm sure."

"So, why did you not become an activist?"

"Oh, I don't know. There was always something else I needed to be doing—work, family, that sort of thing. I suppose I told myself that, realistically, my jumping up and down wouldn't change anything." I dried up, seeing my excuses for what they were. "Morally pusillanimous, if the truth be known! I'm sorry, I hope I'm not using… difficult vocabulary for you, am I? Only your English always seems so good, I forget it's not your first language."

Alassay chuckled. "The Kareeti brain is different to that of humans. Learning a language is very easy for us. I am as fluent in every major language on your planet as I am in English and I expect my English vocabulary is far more extensive than even your own. Certainly, I am aware that thousands of the words that I have learned are seldom if ever used in conversation and rarely even in texts."

"That's mindboggling!" I said with a shake of my head. "I never even managed to learn *one* other language."

"To return to our main theme," she continued after a brief smile of acknowledgement. "you are clearly very well aware of the predicament that faces your planet?"

"Yes."

"Mass species extinctions, gross pollution, climatic disruptions, depletion of the world's natural resources… I could go on, and on."

"Yes, yes, I know, I know, but you can't expect me to

turn around and say: 'quite right, well, off you go and wipe out half of the world's population, that should do the trick!'"

"But, by your own admission, Jeff, if half of the world's population were eliminated overnight, there would still be many more people on Earth tomorrow than there were when you were six!" She was, of course, perfectly correct. "If it took a mere forty-three years for a population of 3.4 billion people to double, it is surely reasonable to project that, notwithstanding improved education, health and living standards that mitigate against population growth, the population would be back to present levels well within a hundred years. So, halving the population would be a very temporary fix."

As the implications of what she was saying dawned on me I gaped at her in horror. What was she suggesting?

"But wait, what… what do you… how…?" I couldn't work out even where to begin! 'You can't just step in and take out the majority of human race!"

"Why?"

"Why? What do you mean why? Can't you see the enormity of what you're proposing? It's barbaric… it's…'

"Genocide?"

"Yes, yes, it is, it is genocide, the grossest genocide imaginable!"

"Not an activity entirely unknown to the human race. You're quite good at it by all accounts!"

I was speechless. Well, what can you say, what is there to say in that situation? Instead, I drank the rest of my wine and Alassay, obligingly, topped it up for me. I sat and tried to focus on my breathing. I felt my heart thumping in my chest.

"Genocide is not something that humanity condones," I said as evenly as I could. "We recognize it as both aberrant and abhorrent behaviour."

"But we can live with ecocide?" She didn't wait for me to try to formulate a response. "Jeff, I understand. I understand that you are a decent, concerned human being who, along with a vocal but essentially ineffectual minority, disagrees with much of what your species considers acceptable."

"You say ineffectual, but we are turning the tide. The world has agreed to limit climate changing emissions. We're...'

"Yes, yes, but all too slowly, it's all too little too late. If you could stop emitting greenhouse gases altogether this very day, harmful change would not be avoided. Species are going extinct on a daily basis. You're right at the point of catastrophically disrupting the food chain in your oceans. They will die, not just the coral reefs, everything!"

I sat looking at her, dumbstruck; not because anything she was saying was new to me but simply because—what could I say, what was there to say?

"We have been observing for a long time, waiting for the sort of response that could have been, should have been undertaken… at least forty years ago. Now it's too late; we have to act."

I simply had no answer. Thoughts were racing around in my head but there was nothing coherent that I could say. I couldn't escape the essential truth of what she was saying but nor could I accept the enormity of the solution she proposed.

"I think that is probably enough for one session, don't you?" she asked in a voice warm with compassion. I was struck by the irony of the situation. I took another drink. "You must be exhausted. We'll talk again when you are rested and have eaten." I finished my drink and stood up.

"There is a very noticeable tension between yourself and the captain of this vessel," I said as she too rose to her feet. "What's that all about?"

"Ah yes, Captain Duurn." She made the sound that I had come to interpret as a chuckle, and I held her gaze expectantly. She turned and, as we walked towards the door she continued, "Duurn is a man of action, a pragmatist. To him this is a straightforward mission; no need for diplomacy. The presence on board his vessel of the diplomatic corps is a source of considerable irritation to him. The fact that our Presidium has anointed me overall commander for the mission is a bitter pill for him to swallow." We had reached the door and, as we turned to each other, she smiled and said: "A word of warning Jeff: *do not* upset Captain Guurtsaad Duurn, *do not* rough up his minions. He has no compassion for you. To him you are simply vermin; without my intercession you would have been eradicated. If you anger him again, I doubt there is much I can do or say to save you."

Chapter 12

Carlos escorted me back to my quarters. We didn't speak much—I wasn't feeling particularly conversational. Back in my room I was restless; notwithstanding the calming effect of the Kareeti wine I was agitated. I paced back and forth in the limited space, my thoughts racing, and my pulse elevated.

Carlos watched me silently and speculatively. "I think," he said eventually, "you need to rest. But you can't do that in your present state. I will order you some food and some araanschoz. After that you will feel better and will sleep."

"What is araanschoz?"

"It's a drink."

"Is that the stuff Alassay Harraan gave me to drink?"

"No. That would have been some sort of liquor. Araanschoz is not intoxicating but it will relax you."

As I waited for my food to arrive, I tried to divert my attention away from the nightmare that possessed me by dreaming up the meal I'd really like to sit down to. I could almost smell the rare filet mignon, taste the herb roasted potatoes and see the Shiraz glowing in the candlelight. What eventually arrived bore no resemblance whatsoever to my mental images.

There was something that looked a bit like a thin piece of quiche, rather too green in color for my liking. It was warm, soft and tasted nothing like quiche. It didn't taste bad, just unlike anything really. I imagine it would fall into that category of tastes the Japanese call umami. There were another two of those Chiclet chewing gum-looking things that tasted nothing like their appearance suggested, and that was it. It appeared barely more than hors d'oeuvres, and yet I felt quite full once I'd eaten it all.

Carlos, who had been hanging around like a bad smell, removed my platter and, after wrestling with a small sealed flask, handed me a cloudy drink with the consistency of Yakult. His head gesture seemed to say, "knock it back' so I did. It didn't taste of anything very much at all. I put the cup back on the table and looked up at him with a 'well, what's next?' expression.

"I think you will start to feel better now, calmer. You should probably try to sleep." He smiled. I assumed it was intended as a gesture of reassurance.

"Yes, all right then, fuck off now, there's a good lad."

Once he was gone, and I was alone at last, I studied the switch panel beside the door and worked out how to dim the lights. Then I lowered myself into the recliner. I let out a great sigh and, with it, felt tension and stress flow from my body, and the maelstrom of thoughts in my head begin to slow. This Yakult stuff, what did they call it—araanschoz? – seemed to be the good gear.

I sat for a few moments savoring a gradually deepening sense of calm and relaxation. Then, aware I could soon fall fast asleep where I sat, I levered myself up and made ready for bed.

When next I woke (I have to guard against the tendency to say: 'the next day' or 'in the morning,' for I had no idea what time of day or night it was and, frankly, had no idea how much time had passed since I knocked myself out on the boat), when next I woke I felt better than I could remember feeling after a night's sleep for many a long while. I felt rested, relaxed and very comfortable. That in itself was unusual because normally, after a prolonged sleep, I would wake with pain in my lower back and twinges of arthritis in my knuckles.

The ensuite facilities included a cubicle which looked like a shower. It turned out not to be; well not as we might normally understand the concept. Once I had worked out how to make it work, a fine, warm spray—more a mist, really—filled the enclosure. The water was incredibly soft. I deduced it had a surfactant added to it. There was a square of some fabric which reminded me of the exfoliating gloves Andie used to have in the shower. I used that to scrub myself.

Shortly after I had finished my ablutions and dressed, the door buzzed softly, and a light flashed a couple of times. I stood not knowing what to do, and it buzzed again. A moment after that the door slid open. Carlos stood on the threshold, a smile on his face and a bundle in his arms.

"Delivery from Saville Row," he quipped.

"More like Carnaby Street!" I retorted. I took the bundle from him. "Come on in."

"Did you sleep well?" he enquired.

"Yes, very well, thank you. That drink you gave me—I'd like to take some of that home with me. Do you have a duty-free shop on board?"

He grinned. "I've ordered you breakfast."

"Ah, good. What's on the agenda for today, a trip to the movies, a football match?"

"I understand Alassay Harraan would like to see you again a little later. In the meantime, if you think you might be interested, we could spend a little time on the observation deck and, maybe, visit the Hybrid Club."

"Hybrid Club?"

"Yes, the Hybrids and the Kareet are not entirely comfortable in each other's company. Some of us probably wouldn't be entirely comfortable in human company either. I guess it's just in the nature of being a Hybrid. So, when we want to relax, let our hair down, so to speak, we prefer to be with other Hybrids."

"Well, as long as I won't make you all too uncomfortable, I'd very much like to come to your club. Tell me about the observation deck."

The observation deck was utterly fascinating. It reminded one of a futuristically styled nightclub, before the crowds arrived. The lighting was very low and bluish, the surfaces were metallic grey and a vast black oval window dominated the space. On the floor in the center of the window was a console that turned out to be a very highly sophisticated version of the sort of thing you see at scenic lookouts throughout the world—identifying the mountains and lakes and rivers visible from the lookout.

We walked up to the window. Our vista was that of the Milky Way. I have seen the Milky Way from a yacht hundreds of miles from land and any intrusive light source, I have seen it from Uluru and many remote locations across outback Australia and, believe me, it is an awe-inspiring sight. Nothing, however, could have prepared me for the spectacle that awaited me on the observation deck! Not only was there no light pollution, there was no atmosphere to add even the subtlest of filters to the view.

Carlos tapped a button and a stool swung out from the wall.

"Have a seat, Jeff."

I sat down and gawped, awestruck, at the splendor of our galaxy. After a few minutes Carlos chimed in again. "Get ready for this, I'll turn the ship around and show you something else that will impress you."

"Turn the ship around?" I asked, "How can you do that?"

"Our vessel is circular. It doesn't matter which way it's facing, except if you're on the observation deck and you want to see something, so we can turn the ship to face whichever way we want." He went to the console and appeared to be pressing buttons. "Brace yourself!" he said.

I suppose I was expecting a physical jolt from the change of orientation he was effecting. Instead, the jolt I received was entirely perceptual. All of a sudden, the Milky Way, spectacular as it was, was replaced by an almost dazzling wall of color.

"Whoa! My God! What the fuck is that?"

"Saturn," Carlos replied calmly.

"Holy shit!" I couldn't believe my eyes. The planet filled the huge glass portal. I pressed my nose to the glass and could just make out the rim.

"We are, let me see…' he peered at the console, 'Just under 30,000 miles above the planet."

"But, what about the rings?"

"We are above them. They extend much farther out." He attempted to maneuver the vessel so we could see the rings, but the light wasn't right.

From the observation deck of our speeding craft, Saturn began ever so slowly to diminish in size until it no longer completely filled the window. Briefly the rings did appear, and they were a spectacular sight. I was keen to see other planets, but Carlos explained there was no other planet any nearer to us than it would be to Earth, so I satisfied myself with watching in awe as Saturn gradually diminished.

"Had enough?" Carlos asked. "We could go to the Hybrid Club now, if you like."

I confess I was a bit like a kid in a candy store and I didn't really want to leave the observation deck at all, but I stood up anyway. "Okay, let's do it."

I suppose I had an image in my mind, although I cannot imagine why, of some version of a canteen with lots of stainless steel, bright fluorescent lights and refectory tables with a small crowd of Hybrids catching a bite to eat between assignments. The reality was, of course, entirely different. Carlos led me into a fairly small room, perhaps 16 feet by twelve, with subdued lighting and, most surprisingly of all, music. Not just any music but music I knew from Earth! I later learned that Lauren had brought it back with her after her unplanned, extended stay.

As my eyes adjusted to the low light I saw a comfortably appointed room with soft sofas, cushioned nooks and low tables. Four people lay around in varying degrees of repose.

"Jeff!" Lauren emerged from one of the nooks.

"Oh, hello Lauren; they haven't locked you up then?"

"Ha, ha, no, not yet; but I'm certainly not very popular in certain circles right now!"

Lauren introduced me to the other three. Miriam was the youngest; I guessed she was in her mid-twenties. Stephan was probably in his early forties and then there was Katarina who must have been at least my age. There was a similarity to their looks, perhaps because of the enlarged eyes, and yet all were distinctly different. Of course, they differed in both age and gender but, whereas Lauren, Carlos and Miriam would very easily pass as human, Stephan and, to a greater degree Katarina, had more Kareet in their appearance and would definitely have attracted attention were they to appear on a main street in Sydney.

With the introductions concluded, they made me comfortable on a sofa and Carlos went to a small cabinet and returned with a drink for me.

"Thank you. Is this the same stuff that Alassay gave me?"

There was an audible intake of breath from two or three of the Hybrids.

"*Alassay Harraan!*" Miriam corrected me primly.

I recalled Alassay mentioning that it was rare for the

Kareet to use first names only, but I saw no point in telling them she had told me I could call her Alassay.

"Alassay Harraan, of course, I'm sorry." I attempted to appear contrite.

Carlos chuckled. "No, I imagine she would have had something very much more refined in her cabinet," he said.

"Hiftervess, maybe," Stephan suggested.

"What was it like?" asked Katarina.

"It was a golden, amber color, quite full bodied, very smooth, warming; I liked it very much."

"Yes, sounds like hiftervess to me," Katarina said. "You are very lucky; not many have the honor."

"Sort of the equivalent of a rare fifteen-year-old single malt whisky," Lauren chipped in.

"I didn't know you were a connoisseur of malt whisky," I replied.

"I'm not; just a bit of trivia I picked up hanging around in bars with you!"

We made small talk for a little while, and I learned that Katarina and Stephan were part of the crew. Katarina was a systems engineer, part of the team that maintained the vessel's electronic and logic systems. Stephan was an engineer with defense systems. Miriam and Lauren were attached to the Science Team and had various research functions. Lauren was a physical scientist with specialties in geology, biology, environment and terraforming. Miriam, despite her apparent lack of years, specialized in demography and various sociological sub-fields. Carlos was a philosophy and ethics man, attached to Alassay Harraan's Diplomatic

Corp. He was on track to become Kareet's first Hybrid ambassador.

They were all clearly highly intelligent, very well educated and impressive people (If I can call them 'people'!).

I was keen to learn more about the Hybrids. "So, if you don't mind me asking, how did you get to be Hybrids… I mean… silly question really! Do you all have human fathers or do some of you have human mothers?" I really didn't know how to frame my questions.

Katarina came to my assistance. "We differ, some of us have human fathers, some mothers. I and two other Hybrids who are back on Kareet are the only survivors of the first cohort. It was not a particularly successful project. Several died early of genetic complications, and those of us who survived have never been particularly robust. Of the three of us, I am the one who has the most human appearance. As you can see, if the object was to create Hybrids who could infiltrate human society, I am hardly a success!"

I looked at Katarina. Certainly, she was no beauty and if she were to appear on Earth she would be considered strangely deformed, if not identified as an alien Hybrid. She had very large eyes—not as large as those Kareet that I had seen, but far larger than any human. Her head was almost hairless and had that distinctively alien shape although, again, not so much so as a Kareet.

"To give you some perspective, the first Hybrid program started about sixty of your Earth years ago. The Kareet had made their first reconnaissance of Earth and made several abductions. Eggs and sperm were harvested, and the abductees were returned to Earth. The vessel then returned to Kareedias where the Hybrid program was started.

"Considering the average life span of a Kareet is in the order of two hundred and fifty of your years, and Alassay Harraan, for example, is already quite a lot older than that, you can see that the Kareeti gene mingling has done little to improve my durability!"

I was amazed. I had thought Katarina was at least my own age but she was only sixty. Alassay Harraan, on the other hand, did not appear particularly aged and yet she was supposedly nearly three hundred years old!

"So, I presume they have done some fine-tuning to their program since then?" I asked.

"Oh yes, they learned quite quickly. Look at Stephan for example; he is a product of the next cycle. So he would be, what, fifty-eight, fifty-nine of your years?"

The difference was quite striking. I had thought Stephan to be in his mid-forties. He also had too alien a cast to his features for him to have blended into human society.

"Then, from the next cycle came Lauren and Carlos, making them about fifty-five." Now I was truly startled. I had taken them to have been no more than thirty. "And they will, in all probability, show few signs of ageing for the next fifty years."

"Wow! That's amazing!" I whistled.

"And Miriam, well, she is about forty-eight years old."

I was dumbfounded. I had thought her little more than twenty-four. Looking at her I could see they had ironed out the physical appearance issues to a very large extent. Had I seen Miriam on Earth I would only have looked twice at her because she was very attractive and had beautiful big eyes.

"And how do you all feel about Earth, humankind, the Kareet and what their stated mission is?" I asked as Carlos brought me a second drink.

The conversation that ensued was both interesting and enlightening. It was clear that their upbringing and education pre-disposed them to Kareeti values, principles and objectives and yet their part human ancestry apparently imparted a connection and sympathy with humanity. Stephan, in particular, and Katarina too, expressed grave misgivings about the Kareet interfering in Earth's affairs. Miriam and Carlos seemed more ambivalent, whereas Lauren gave us a glimpse of that asperity with which she had spoken on board *Perseverance* and railed against the ecological disaster that was the human race.

I was somewhat alarmed to find myself, although not expressing my opinions, siding more with Lauren than with Katarina and Stephan!

Chapter 13

Carlos received the summons on his syncom. I made my farewells to the Hybrids and followed Carlos through a maze of corridors, onto a lift, down more corridors and up a short flight of steps to Alassay Harraan's suite.

"Welcome back, Jeff. I trust you are well rested." The door closed behind us with a whoosh and we made our way back to the seats we had occupied before. "Your usual?" she asked archly.

"Hiftervess?"

"Oh, you have been doing your homework!"

We settled back into our respective seats. Alassay did not speak immediately, but seemed to be considering how to begin. I took a sip of my drink and savored the smooth, warm liquor.

"I have consulted at length with my senior aides," she began, "and I have decided that we will press you into service."

"Press me into service?" I repeated with a laugh, "That sounds very 18th century Royal Navy!" If she shared the humor of the moment it was not reflected in her expression.

"I need you to be my spokesman on Earth," she stated flatly. "Your people are too unpredictable; it would be far too risky for me to appear in person," she added. "It would also put our vessel at risk to attempt to establish communication between us and Earth."

I looked at her uncomprehendingly.

"We have technological capabilities far beyond any you have on Earth. We will implant a device that will enable me to speak through you."

"You'll what? What the hell are you talking about? You're not implanting anything in me. What right do you think—"

"Oh, do be quiet, Jeff! Do you really think you have any choice in the matter?" she interjected tersely. "We will do with you precisely as we see fit. It is only through my intercession that Guurtsaad Duurn hasn't already vaporized you!" The warm, friendly Alassay Harraan, in whose company I had come to feel moderately at ease, was showing a very different side to her personality! My heart raced and my stress levels were on the rise again. I took a gulp of hiftervess.

"Listen, Jeff," she continued in a more conciliatory tone of voice, "we have talked at length about the Kareeti mission. I know it is unpalatable to you but it's not negotiable. With your assistance we can facilitate a more favorable outcome for humankind. We can engage the world in the decisions to be made about which people are to be spared and certainly we can protect the people closest to you personally."

I drank the rest of my hiftervess and Alassay topped it up. The effect this stuff had on my cortisol levels was extraordinary. I drank a little more and tried to compose myself. I sat forward and gave her my full attention.

"Go on."

What Alassay Harraan and the Kareet had in store for me was truly mindboggling. Their medical team was preparing to implant a tiny device in the back of my neck adjacent to my cervical spine. Minute fibers would connect in to my nervous system. Once the surgery had healed, and I was advised that this would be a matter of hours not days or weeks, I would be effectively oblivious to the device's presence. Once activated, however, and when Alassay Harraan needed to communicate using the device, I would feel a tingle in my neck. Shortly thereafter she would actively control my vocal cords and receive visual and auditory input. She would be able to see and hear using my eyes and ears and the use of my voice to speak. I would have no control over my vocal cords while she was 'on-line' and no foreknowledge of what words may issue from my mouth!

I was dumbfounded.

"You can do this?" I asked. "You can just use me as a quiescent, uninvolved medium?"

"Yes."

"So, what, can you read my mind while you're in there?"

"No!" she said with a laugh. "No, we can't read your mind. We can tap into your visual cortex and see what you are seeing. We can utilize your auditory system to hear what you are hearing, and we can take control of your vocal cords to communicate to others. If we need to, we can block you from using your voice while we have control. If you are cooperative, we wouldn't exercise that option.

"It will take a little getting used to, I'm afraid." She smiled. "There is an upside, though. In order for this 'channel' to take… for your body to accept and not reject the device, we have to make some minor genetic modifications—nothing major—but while we're at it we'll be able to make some other minor changes which will get rid of your arthritis, restore your eyesight to how it was when you were young, make you feel younger and more vital and add a few years to your life expectancy."

I might have said any number of things at that stage, for plenty were whirling through my head. Instead, I sat there silently, shaking my head in disbelief at the enormity of it all.

"We will also provide you with a syncom, although you won't be able to use it properly. The Kareet have a small plate implanted in the palm of a hand during the first year of life. They need it to communicate with the syncom and they learn to do so over the course of a greater part of their childhood. We will teach you how to place the device in the correct proximity to the communication plate in your neck in order for you to alert me."

"What will I need to call you for?"

"I will need to know when you are in place, so to speak, when you are with the people I need to talk to."

"And then?"

"And then you should be sitting down in a position

where you can see as much of the room and the people in the room as possible. You will feel a tingle in your neck. A short time after that I will take over your voice."

"Who are the people you need to talk to?"

"Well, I imagine it will be the Security Council of the United Nations, don't you?"

"Oh yes, well they all know me well, so it should be no problem for me to pop in for a chat. They're probably missing me already!"

"Jeff, I don't expect you to be able to simply demand an audience with the Security Council, but I take you to be a resourceful man. It may be a many-stepped process, but find someone who has connections with people who have connections."

"And just how do you imagine that I am going to convince anyone in any place of influence that I haven't just simply lost my mind? I mean, even I have difficulty believing this isn't all just some wild figment of my imagination."

"We will also teach you how, with a gesture of the syncom, you can cause a holographic image of me to appear in the room in front of those to whom you are speaking… why do you smile?"

"I'm sorry." I shook my head. "In the face of all of this bewildering information my mind, for some strange reason, chose to remember an amusing story about Winston Churchill and ending sentences with prepositions." I was mildly gratified to see a mystified expression cross the face of this seemingly all-knowing being!

Chapter 14

There was nothing to the operation. I woke feeling rested and refreshed. I lay there appreciating the sense of wellbeing, not in any hurry to rise. After a few minutes I heard a door whoosh open. Someone came to my bedside. I reluctantly opened my eyes. I did not recognize the Kareet who stood over me. He or she wore a white tunic with blue epaulettes. A device resembling a syncom was held about an inch above me and was passed slowly over my body, it rested briefly upon my forehead before it was returned to a fold in the tunic. The Kareet turned and walked out.

I sat up and looked around me. There was little enough to see. It was a small room containing the bed upon which I sat and, against the wall, a small trolley with a jug and a cup upon it. I ran my hand over the back of my neck. It felt numb with a bit of a tingle as though a local anesthetic were wearing off. I stood up and went over to the trolley. The jug appeared to contain water, so I poured a drink and sipped tentatively. It was water, cool and fresh. I drank a cupful and replenished it.

The door opened, I looked over my shoulder. It was Carlos. He smiled.

"How are you feeling?"

"Well; very well in fact."

"Good; come on." He jerked his head towards the door. I shrugged, put down the cup and followed.

Of course, I hadn't the faintest notion where we were, but it took very little time to walk to my quarters. There was food waiting for me and as I sat down to eat Carlos fished a small, flat flask out of his tunic pocket.

"A small gift from Alassay Harraan," he said as he handed it to me. "Hiftervess, I believe."

I ate the food and took a sip of the hiftervess, planning to keep the rest for later.

"Well, if you're finished, Alassay Harraan is waiting for you."

We sat in our customary chairs. Alassay didn't offer me a drink on this occasion. She enquired as to my wellbeing and looked briefly at the back of my neck.

I put my hand to the site expecting to be able to feel the device under the skin, but I couldn't.

She produced a syncom from the folds of her tunic and placed it against the back of my neck. I felt a tremendous electrical jolt. I jerked and jolted almost out of my seat and onto the floor. I thought she had electrocuted me. As I gasped for breath, my heart pounding in my chest, she placed a hand on my shoulder.

"I'm sorry Jeff, I couldn't warn you. If I had you would have tensed for the shock and made it very much worse. You'll be pleased to know that will never happen again. The channel is now initialized."

I lay back in my chair, panting, blinking my eyes, waiting for my pulse to normalize, protestations of outrage forming in my mind.

"Well I have one piece of news that should please you: we are going to return you and Lauren to your precious boat."

"Straight up… seriously, I mean?"

"Yes, she is still afloat as you had surmised."

"And Lauren? I thought she was persona non grata these days."

"Ah well, she has been reprimanded and her place in the order of things re-explained to her. For you to more quickly establish contact with people useful to our cause it is important to tie you up in as little controversy as possible. We'll put you back on the boat. You can sail her into Auckland and tell them your radio and electronics were disrupted by the storm. If you were to turn up without Lauren, I imagine it could become a little complicated." That was an understatement. "Also, as I explained, you will have very limited ability to use the syncom. Having Lauren around may be useful."

The next thing on Alassay Harraan's agenda was some practice with the 'channel'. She gave me a syncom.

"This one is yours. As I've told you, you won't be able to do very much with it. Here," she placed it in my hand, "this way up, can you see?" I nodded. "Now, place it on the right-hand side of your neck, here," she took my hand and held it in the correct place. "With your middle finger, stroke it on the side." I tried.

"No, keep your index finger where I placed it." I tried to rearrange my fingers. She rearranged the placement of my index finger. "Along the center of the back with your finger tip pressed lightly against the edge. Now, stroke with your middle finger on the side." I tried again. I heard a buzz. Alassay beamed and produced her own syncom. It was glowing with a faint purple light and, clearly, was the source of the buzzing.

"On board this vessel you could now talk to me using the syncom, but when you are on Earth, that will not be possible because of our shields."

Next, she had me sit upright in my chair, feet flat on the floor, hands on the arms of the chair.

"You'll feel a tingle in your neck then, after about ten seconds, I will take control of the channel."

I sat there, feeling not a little apprehensive. The tingling came as promised. It was unmistakable without being unduly intrusive. I waited, counting down from ten. Suddenly I felt as though my head was held in a clamp. There was a sense of binding tightness between my temples. All of a sudden, I started talking! Not words that originated in my head. It was the most extraordinary thing—freaky! The voice was mine—it didn't sound any different to me than when I spoke normally, if that makes any sense (and of course it doesn't!)

"I can speak to you to give you advice or instructions," I said—no—she said—we said? "Or I can simply talk to others through you. If I ask you a question or would like to give you the opportunity to say something I can open the channel like this." Suddenly the vice that seemed to be clamping my brain released. I don't recall what I said. I doubt it was anything intelligent. I may have asked a question because the clamp came back on again and I heard my voice talking to me again!

She also showed me a gesture with the syncom that would, in effect, disallow her to open the channel. In the event that it was impractical for any reason for her to communicate then, by using the syncom I could let her know 'not now'.

We practiced for an hour or so and, by the end, it no longer felt so terrible. It still felt weird, totally weird, but I was beginning to be all right with it. I had mastered the skill of holding the syncom to call Alassay and my feelings of panic every time the clamp came on were definitely subsiding.

At long last she poured me a drink. I really felt I needed one by then. I was quite exhausted, and my heart was racing.

"I understand you are already familiar with araanschoz. I will ensure that you have a supply to take with you. You will find these sessions stressful and tiring, but you will find the araanschoz restorative.

"Now, pass me your syncom." I did so. "Hold it like this." She arranged it in my left hand. "It has to be your left hand for this. No, middle and index finger equally spaced, thumb there, no, pull it lower. Good. Now place it across your cervical spine like this." With the syncom held correctly she placed my hand on my neck. "With your little and ring fingers squeeze the syncom gently against the base of your thumb, yes, now apply a gentle pressure with the pad of your index finger." I felt a faint vibration in the syncom and then, falteringly at first but gradually intensifying, a hologram materialized about four feet in front of me. The hologram was of Alassay Harraan and she smiled at me. I looked across at the real Alassay and saw that she was smiling exactly as her hologram showed her to be.

After that she made me practice it time and again until I could call up the hologram with confidence and ease. Once she was satisfied that I was adept she poured me another hiftervess and then palmed her syncom and summoned Lauren.

We were briefed and drilled until Alassay Harraan was satisfied that we knew precisely what was expected of us and how we would deal with questions concerning our missing days. Alassay wanted to know how I planned to find my way to the Security Council.

"Well, it's no small task you've set me," I began, "I certainly don't move in those circles myself—very far from it. However, I did once deliver a yacht for a very powerful businessman who has some interesting connections. I think I would start with him."

Part 3

Chapter 15

We were transferred onto a small scout vessel with a crew of two and space for four passengers. Someone handed us each a package. I looked to Lauren for an explanation.

"Our clothes; what we were wearing when we were taken off the yacht."

"Ah, of course!"

I was given to understand that the main vessel was comparatively close to the Earth and, indeed, when the hatch opened, and we shot out into space, I was almost dazzled by the brilliance of Earth; it seemed to take up the whole of my field of vision. We were above the Pacific, the eastern third of which was covered in white cloud which accounted for the brilliance, the western Pacific was still in darkness.

We descended through the Earth's atmosphere and the experience seemed very much smoother and far less stressful than the images I had seen on television of vehicles re-entering the atmosphere. I assumed it was a function of the advanced technology available to the Kareet. As we swooped down over the dark sea, the eastern sky glowed with the promise of dawn. The pilot turned on a brilliant searchlight and swept the water. In a matter of moments, we spotted *Perseverance*; evidently the crew knew, to a high degree of accuracy, where she was to be found.

We flew around the abandoned yacht a couple of times and then hovered, stationary, above the cockpit. The pilot turned and nodded at us. I looked at Lauren. She slid out of her seat and beckoned me to follow. There was little enough room for her to maneuver her way into the small passageway, let alone a man of my size. I struggled, my feet getting impossibly caught up with no room to turn and my shoulders too broad to fit into the narrow walkway. Eventually, however, I worked my way to where Lauren crouched. I was on my knees! There was a fizzing sound and a hatch opened at her feet and a ramp extended like a telescope. I caught the wonderful smell of fresh sea air.

Lauren made her way down the ramp and I followed. It was an easy step onto the transom of the boat. Once we were both safely on board the ramp was retrieved, the hatch closed, and the scout departed at some impossible speed, almost without sound.

Finding myself back again on something as commonplace and familiar as a yacht, I half expected to wake up from this strange and elaborate dream but, of course, I didn't. I was still wearing the maroon tunic and leggings that had been made for me by the Kareet.

I went below into the cabin where everything seemed much as we had left it, however long ago it had been.

"Do you have any idea how long we were away?" I asked.

"Well, this is the morning of December the 4th," she replied. "We were rescued on the evening of November the 30th, so three and a half days, I suppose."

"Is that all? It seems like weeks to me!" I sat at the chart table to check our position. It was really only then that I began to appreciate the changes wrought in me by the Kareet. On the Kareeti vessel there was nothing for me to read and, of course, I didn't have my reading glasses with me. Sitting at the chart table I glanced at the chart while reaching to the rack where I kept my specs. As my eyes focused upon the chart I was startled to find that I could read it with absolute clarity! I had no need of my glasses.

I tried my eyes on the fine print. I could read chart data with no difficulty! Usually I had trouble seeing it clearly even with my glasses on. This was a bonus.

With the para-anchor set, and flying only a storm 'trysail and storm jib, the good ship *Perseverance* had made comparatively little progress. We appeared to be not much more than ten nautical miles from our approximate position when we abandoned her.

The south-westerly made dawn chilly at these latitudes, even if it was early summer. The Kareeti outfit was not warm enough.

I rummaged through my bag and found a pair of comfortable jeans, a tee shirt and a pullover. I kicked off the funny slippers they had given me and pulled on a pair of socks and some old sailing shoes. I dragged a beanie down over my ears and headed back on deck.

"Do you need a hand?" Lauren called, as I was climbing the companionway stairs.

"Yes, get some warmer clothes on and come up."

While I was waiting for Lauren I peeled the jib off the inner forestay and packed away the 'trysail.

~

The trip to Auckland was altogether uneventful. The weather remained fine, we had fair winds, mainly south westerlies and we made good progress. We sailed into Auckland harbor late in the afternoon of the 12th of December. I had contacted Con Theodorakis by satellite phone to let him know we were okay and that we had had a bit of a rough time in the storm losing our electronics, including the sat-phone, for a few days.

Con met us at Marsden Wharf where we were to clear in. As he had lodged all of the required paperwork and paid the import duty several days before, clearing in was a formality which took little time. New Zealand is a very yacht-friendly nation and they like to make life as easy as possible for sailors.

Once we were all done, Con came aboard, and we motored around to the Orakei Marina where *Perseverance* was going to live. Con was a member of the Royal Arakana Yacht Club and, once we were all packed and the boat was ship shape, that is where he took us for dinner. I don't think I have ever enjoyed steak and shiraz as much in my life as I did that night!

It transpired that when nothing was heard from us after

the storm an alert to shipping was broadcast but there had been no sightings. As there had been no Mayday call and we were not actually overdue no search had been instigated, which was fortunate. We had delivered the vessel undamaged and on time, so: another satisfied customer!

We booked into a small hotel for the night. I invited Lauren to come and sit with me in the quiet hotel bar while I partook of a much-needed nightcap.

"So, what happens with you now?" I enquired. "Now we've been seen to have delivered the yacht with the same crew that left Sydney."

"Alassay Harraan has asked me to stay with you for a time. She believes I may be able to assist you when it comes time to communicate with your people."

"Ah."

"It is most important that nobody suspects that I am anything other than human."

"Yes, I see," I said, although I was not entirely sure that I did. Rather than pursue it at that time when, frankly all I wanted to do was down a couple of large glasses of Dimple Haig and go to bed, I rather lamely asked whether she had brought adequate supplies of her special food additive. She smiled and assured me she had.

The following day we bought tickets on an 18:30 Qantas flight to Sydney and spent the rest of the day sight-seeing around the beautiful city of Auckland.

Chapter 16

Martin Barstock was not only a very wealthy man; he was also extremely well connected. As a young management accountant, he and a colleague, friends since their time together at Sydney University, saw an opportunity to seize control of a failing specialty retailer that was on the verge of going into receivership. He had done the analysis; the problem was not the business but the manner in which it was being managed.

They turned that business around and sold it on for a very handsome profit, which they utilized to buy another failing business. Again, they turned it around and, again, they sold it for a motza!

Martin established his own highly successful management consultancy agency and he and his friend continued to keep an eye open for profitable take-over targets. He was also on the boards of several very high-profile companies including one of the 'big four' banks. He was well known to politicians from both sides of the political divide and counted the then current prime minister as a personal friend. His commentary was frequently sought by the media and he was commonly invited to provide expert opinion to Senate Committees.

I had been introduced to Barstock by a man whose yacht I had delivered. Martin, who I guessed to be about fifteen years my junior, was in the process of buying a 'Bluewater Cruising Yacht'; one of the few world-class cruising yachts to be designed and manufactured in Australia. They are a brilliant ocean-going vessel and they come with everything you need to safely cross any sea, including a lifetime structural warranty! I'd have one if I could afford it. I can't. Martin could. He named it *Courtesan*. I gather his wife, Tanya, enjoyed the deft allusion to his other love.

Barstock was looking for someone who had genuine ocean sailing experience who could take him out into the Pacific and give him some intensive training so that one day he could confidently and competently sail the boat himself anywhere in the world. He asked for it; I delivered. We sailed south from Sydney to Hobart and then into the Southern Ocean across to the southernmost tip of New Zealand, rounding Stewart Island. We cleared into Dunedin and visited Wellington and Napier before heading out again into the deep blue yonder to Norfolk Island, then Lord Howe Island and back to Sydney.

By the time we finally tied up at the Royal Sydney Yacht Squadron, Martin Barstock was a very competent ocean skipper and I would happily sail anywhere with him. He, in turn, came to know me very well and, I hope, to hold me in high regard. When you've been through a Southern Ocean blow together you tend to get the measure of a man. I think we had mutual respect for one another.

~

"Bloody hell, here's a blast from the past!" was his reaction to my phone call. "What are you up to?"

"Oh, you know, a bit of this, a bit of that and not so much of the other!" He laughed. "I rather need to see you, if you can find the time."

"Sure. Where are you?"

"I'm back in Sydney—just finished a delivery to Auckland."

"I've got nothing on this evening; Tanya and the boys are in Brisbane for a few days. Do you want to come to my place or do you want to eat out somewhere?"

"Your place would be fine. Is it okay if I bring someone with me?"

"You dirty dog! Have you finally hitched up with someone?"

"No!" I laughed. "It's nothing like that, but it is a woman—my latest crew member."

"Yeah, of course, bring her around."

"What time?"

"Eight?"

"Fine by me."

~

"Jeff! Great to see you, come in. You're looking particularly well. Sailing obviously agrees with you."

"Good to see you too, Martin. This is Lauren." We made our way into Barstock's beautiful home in Cremorne. It wasn't a mansion or anything flashy, that wasn't the man's style. But style he had. The house was solid, spacious and beautifully appointed. The furniture in his living room would pay for my small cottage and I dare say I could have bought myself a Bluewater Cruising Yacht for the cost of one of the paintings on the walls.

We went up the stairs and the old traditional brick house was suddenly transformed into a modern wonder of glass and stainless steel and water feature. The glass folding doors were fully open and the room flowed out onto a deck from which there was a spectacular view of the city. Martin attended to drinks, and we sat out on the deck enjoying the view and the balmy conditions. We made small talk. I told Martin a little of how Lauren and I had met and a little about the delivery, but I had yet to find the courage to tell him of the real purpose of our visit.

"Martin," I finally said with what I hoped was appropriate gravity. He had just returned from the bar with another round of drinks. He sat and settled and glanced enquiringly at me. "Martin, I would like to think you know me pretty well." That didn't really warrant a response. I fought down the urge to abandon the plan altogether and continued, "We've sailed together… we've been through a bit… I'd like to think you'd take me for a pretty level-headed sort of a bloke." I looked at Martin. Puzzlement was writ large on his face. I made myself go on. "I need to tell you about something which you are not going to believe. You'll think I've lost my marbles." I looked at him. I think he was weighing up whether or not to say something flippant. I suspect my demeanor dissuaded him.

"Where do you stand on the whole issue of aliens, UFOs and the like?" God, I was making a hash of this!

He scrunched up his eyes and shook his head. "Are you serious? Of course I don't believe in that stuff."

"Yes, yes me too. That was, me too, didn't believe a word of it." I paused, not for effect but to find the courage to say the next words. "But now I've changed my mind. I've had my mind changed for me!" I looked at him.

He looked back at me, eyes wide. He glanced at Lauren perhaps to see if she was in on the joke. He got nothing from her and looked back at me.

"What on Earth are you talking about?" was all he said.

"I have been the victim of an alien abduction," I stated. What was going on in his head at that moment I can only guess but I'm sure it wasn't, 'well, I'm blowed! I was wrong all this time, there really are spacemen!'

I hurried on before he could dismiss me as barking mad. As succinctly as I could, I gave him the briefest outline of what had happened. I left out any information about Lauren being a Hybrid, because she had insisted that I didn't expose her, and I certainly said nothing of the intended Kareeti mission.

"They operated on me and installed a thing they call a channel along my cervical spine which they will use to communicate through me." Martin was looking at me like a stunned mullet. "They have given me a device… here," I said, pulling it out of my trouser pocket and handing it to him. "Have you ever seen anything like that?" He examined it. "No," I said, "you've never seen anything like that because it doesn't come from this world."

"Jeff, Jeff, stop. Is this some kind of elaborate joke?"

"No, no Martin, you have to trust me. You have no idea what I've been through. I thought I was losing my mind. I thought I was dreaming. Look, give me that syncom back." I held out my hand, and he gave it back. "I'm going to send a signal and shortly one of the Kareet, called Alassay Harraan, will communicate through me."

Barstock burst out laughing. "Fuck, Ridsdale you're good!"

I could think of nothing to say. How might I have expected him to react? I arranged my fingers correctly on the syncom, placed it against my neck and sat back in my seat. Martin's face was a picture of confusion. It was true, he did know me very well. He had never known me pull a humorous stunt like this and he'd never had reason to think me a space cadet, and yet here I was.

I felt a tingle in my neck. I rearranged my grip on the syncom and braced myself. A few seconds ticked by in silence, Barstock watching me warily. I felt the 'clamp' come on my brain.

"Good evening," Alassay Harraan said, although of course Martin thought it was me. I placed the syncom across my neck and caressed the syncom in the prescribed manner and, almost immediately, the air between Martin and me began to shimmer. Gradually the waves coalesced into an image of Alassay Harraan.

Martin gasped and fell back in his seat.

"Please don't be alarmed… Jeff, what is his name?" I felt the vice grip slacken.

"This is Mr. Martin Barstock."

"Mr. Barstock." The clamp came on a little firmer. "My name is Alassay Harraan. I am a senior diplomat and emissary of the Kareet. We are a civilization somewhat more advanced than your own and we have been observing you for many of your Earth years. I understand that all of this is extremely difficult for you to come to terms with, but it is very important that you do. I need you to assist Jeff because it is through him that I intend to communicate with your world leaders."

Martin sat in his chair, eyes wide, his mouth opening and closing a little like a goldfish. He was certainly not capable of speech.

"May I rely upon you to help him?"

After the two or three seconds it took him to comprehend, Martin nodded dumbly.

"Good. Thank you very much. Then I'll not keep you any longer and I'll say goodnight."

I felt the constriction in my head ease and the hologram faded away. I sat and watched Martin. He was breathing deeply, clearly still trying to process what he had just witnessed.

An hour or so later and with very much less left of the bottle of Talisker, Martin was a little more his old self. I had determined to tell him nothing of the Kareet's intentions. Lauren, I told him, was abducted alongside me. She had undergone a very similar experience, but had not received the channel implant.

We discussed how he might get me access to the Prime Minister for, clearly, this was not merely a local matter. He didn't think there would be any problem getting me in to see him, but he didn't envy me trying to tell him my story.

"Why don't the Kareet... is that what you call them?... why don't they just come to Earth, come and visit us? It would have to be easier than this!"

"I think they've studied the human race long enough and decided we are altogether too unpredictable. Or, more likely, all too damned predictable! Shoot first, ask questions after."

Chapter 17

Martin called me the very next day. Parliament wasn't sitting so the PM had a little more time than he might otherwise have had.

"If you would like to come around to my place at about 6.00, I'll take you over to Kirribilli House and introduce you."

Lauren was happy enough to stay at the small hotel we had booked into at The Rocks.

"I might take the opportunity to go for a stroll and do some sight-seeing," she said. It was an easy walk around Circular Quay to the Opera House from the hotel and there was much to see around The Rocks, which has a written history dating back to 1788.

Rather than battle the traffic, I caught a ferry from Circular Quay to Cremorne Point. From there it was an easy stroll to the Barstock residence.

~

'Honored to meet you, sir," I said shaking the proffered hand.

"No, no, call me Andrew," he said.

I have always tended to be a little overly respectful of 'powerful' people. I must have been some lord's vassal in an earlier life!

"Martin is being very secretive; he will not tell me what this is all about, but I'm sure you will shed some light on the mystery for me."

"I can well understand Martin not wanting to be drawn on this," I replied, "it does tend to strain one's credulity."

"Really, I am intrigued. Come, let's go and sit on the veranda. It's a beautiful evening." He led the way and soon we were seated around a teak outdoor table, beside a lawn that fell away to the water's edge, beyond which lay the Opera House and the Sydney CBD in all its glory.

"Well now…?" The PM smiled at me.

"Well… er… Andrew," I was having a little difficulty getting myself to use his name so informally, "I needed Martin to vouch for me because, well, obviously I suppose, you wouldn't have seen me otherwise." Oh God, I was babbling. I took a deep breath. "Martin couldn't tell you what this is all about because… well, frankly, you wouldn't have believed him." By now the PM was, quite justifiably, looking between the two of us, mystified. Barstock came to the rescue.

"What Jeff is trying to prepare himself to tell you is that we have been contacted by aliens and he is the communication channel." There was about three seconds of complete silence and then the PM burst into gales of laughter. While he was laughing I gripped the syncom in my pocket and arranged my fingers such as to notify Alassay Harraan.

"Excellent Martin! Where do you get this stuff from?" Andrew Baumann used the knuckle of his index finger to wipe the tears from his eyes.

"The alien race is called the Kareet and they have implanted a device in Jeff's neck which enables them to use his voice to communicate with others." The PM was taken aback. Of course, he had thought Martin was having a joke but Barstock had continued without a hint of humor. I felt the tingle in my neck.

"In a few seconds I will be able to introduce you to Alassay Harraan of the Kareet and she will appear before you as a hologram," I said. I was concerned that Baumann might swallow Alassay, his mouth was wide enough open! I placed the syncom across my neck. The air above the lawn in front of us appeared to shimmer. Within seconds Alassay Harraan's hologram materialized. Alassay was sitting in her favorite chair in her quarters. Beside her in the chair that I had customarily occupied when with her, sat another Kareet. I could tell from the outfit that he (I thought it was a male— the headwear seemed to suggest it) was one of the senior diplomats, one of Alassay's chief advisors, I assumed.

I felt the 'clamp' come on and glanced at the PM, half fearing he may be having a heart attack.

"Good evening Prime Minister," I (Alassay) said, "My name is Alassay Harraan. I am a senior diplomat, emissary for the Kareet and commander of our current mission to visit your planet." There was a pause. I don't know if Alassay was expecting a response, but Baumann was incapable of words. "Beside me here is Ilvik Runaal. He is one of my senior advisers." No doubt the PM's mind was racing. Improbable as this scenario undoubtedly was, he had to believe his eyes and his ears, and he certainly couldn't come up with any other rational explanation.

"I… er… I'm…' his voice was little more than a croak, "On behalf of Australia, I… er… I welcome you to earth." I could only feel sorry for the man; what, after all do you say in circumstances such as these? Alassay Harraan smiled, whether from warmth or amusement I couldn't tell.

"I thank you Prime Minister. We will not take up much of your time this evening. I am fully conscious of the deep sense of shock that you, Mr. Barstock and, before him, Mr. Ridsdale have all experienced as a result of our arrival. We think it essential that you keep our presence entirely secret. It would not be at all wise to announce our presence to the people of the world." Ilvik Runaal shook his head in steadfast agreement with his leader. "It is purely by chance that we have made initial contact with the people of Earth through an Australian connection. We cannot, of course, act in any way that may seem to prefer you over other world leaders.

"We have studied your world and its ways and its institutions for many years now. We believe that the most sensible forum for us to announce ourselves to your world would be the Security Council of the United Nations. Do you concur?"

"Why yes, yes, that would seem to be most appropriate." Baumann seemed to be pulling himself together. "Will you come to the United Nations to address the Council?"

"No, we have discussed the matter at some length and we

have concluded that it is in our best interests to communicate with your leaders in the manner I am communicating with you now."

"I see," Baumann replied neutrally, "A couple of points I might make, however: there are fifteen members of the Security Council but only 5 permanent members. If you want to maintain a high level of secrecy I recommend that only the five Permanent Members are invited. Also, although Australia is not one of the five I suggest that we attend anyway since we are now already aware of your presence."

"Your proposals seem appropriate. When you have arranged the meeting Mr. Ridsdale will alert me. Very well then, I shall not keep you. We wish you a good night."

"Oh, er yes, good night to you also." The two Kareet inclined their heads in a token of respect and, almost immediately the hologram began to dissolve, and the clamp was released from my brain.

Not much was said over the next couple of minutes. Certainly, our Prime Minister had much to think about. Finally, he shook himself out of his reverie. He looked at Barstock and then at me.

"That really happened, didn't it?" It was a rhetorical question really and elicited no more than a facial expression from Martin. "This is unbelievable! This is colossal! Holy fuck!" He got up from the table and started pacing. "The implications…," he trailed off. "Obviously no one can know about this. If either of you so much as breathe a word…' his eyes were flicking from side to side as he chased one thought after another across the screen of his mind. "I'll phone the President. Martin, not a word, mate, not a fucking word!" Barstock raised both hands in mock surrender.

"My lips are sealed."

"Mr. Ridsdale, Jeff, I need you to stand by. I need to be able to contact you and to have you available to come to me any time day or night."

"Yes, I understand."

"Now please tell me absolutely no one else has even the faintest notion that this is happening."

"Well, as a matter of fact there is one other. She was abducted along with me. Her name is Lauren Mitchell". I then had to relate, as briefly as possible, all that had transpired since that fateful November morning on the Stuart Highway.

Of course, I modified the story to protect Lauren's real identity; I stuck with her story of the boyfriend with anger management problems.

I also omitted to tell him of the impending cull. I was, of course, under strict instructions from Alassay Harraan to remain silent on this score. I felt under no obligation to do her bidding in this regard but, quite frankly, I was still unable to fully comprehend, let alone deal with the enormity of what the Kareet had in store for humanity. I had no doubt that Alassay Harraan would announce the visitor's intentions to the Security Council, better she tell the world leaders and let them deal with the information.

Chapter 18

By the time the meeting with the PM wrapped up Andrew Baumann was, outwardly at least, calm and collected. He took my contact details and assured me that someone would contact me the following day. That person would bring with him a special, dedicated mobile phone which I was to carry with me at all times but only use for the purposes of contacting, or being contacted by, the Prime Minister.

All costs associated with our stay in Sydney and any subsequent travel and expenses relating to 'this business' would be covered by the government; along with the mobile phone the contact would bring a credit card to cover all reasonable expenses. It is probably an insight into my dissolute nature that my mind went instantly to recalling the names of the better-known Sydney restaurants the like of which would, ordinarily, be well beyond my means!

Martin and I left with a firm handshake from the PM. We drove in his car back to The Rocks. We had neither of us eaten so we popped into The Lord Nelson. Reputed to be Australia's longest running pub/brewery. It brews its own very fine ales and has good food.

Martin was burning to ask me all about the Kareet, my experiences on the Kareeti vessel and indeed everything that had anything to do with the whole affair. I had answered a few of his questions in the car but I really didn't want to talk about it, not then.

"No more questions about this business tonight," I said as we walked into the Lord Nelson. He looked pained. "We're in a pub, Martin! This is supposed to be top secret." He nodded his head grudgingly.

Given that it was a Friday night we were quite surprised to get a table. Once settled with a couple of pints of their famous 'Three Sheets' and, with dinner ordered, I tried to steer the conversation to safer waters. I asked him about his family, but he answered briefly and seemed disinclined to elaborate.

"But what about you?" he said, "I can't believe how good you are looking!" I paused and thought about what he had said. It was true, I had been feeling pretty good. It's interesting; when something hurts or isn't working properly you tend to be very conscious of it and yet, when the pain disappears, you don't really notice that you are feeling so much better.

"Yes, come to think of it I am feeling pretty good."

"Which is interesting, given all you've been through of late."

"Yes," I lowered my voice and chose my words carefully, "when they did this…' I indicated the back of my neck with a vague swirling of my fingers, "they said they might be able to fix up a couple of things." I didn't think that, even were someone to be eavesdropping our conversation, which was highly unlikely, what I had just said could give them any inkling of what I meant or what had happened to me. "I've been so caught up in everything that I've not given it a moment's thought but, now you come to mention it, yes I do feel well."

~

When I got back to the hotel I noticed a light under Lauren's door, so I tapped on it. She opened it. I could hear the sounds of the television in the background.

"Not disturbing you, I hope?"

"No, of course not; come in." She switched off the television and indicated a chair. "What happened?" I recounted the meeting with the Prime Minister.

"You should have seen his face when the hologram of Alassay Harraan appeared in front of him! I thought he was going to have a heart attack!" Lauren looked alarmed. "No, no, don't worry; it's just a figure of speech," She looked relieved. "We also got to meet a man... er... er a male Kareet," I corrected myself—are male and female Kareet men and women? I really didn't know. Lauren didn't react one way or the other. "His name was Ilvik Runaal."

"Ah yes, Ilvik Runaal; he is a very highly respected, wise counsellor. Of all the Kareet on this mission it is he who Alassay Harraan trusts and venerates the most."

"Well, anyway, she has asked our Prime Minister to arrange a meeting of the permanent members of the Security Council of the United Nations."

Chapter 19

I once overheard my wife, Andie, say of me: 'Oh, Jeff, he's *pathologically* honest!" and, I suppose it's true. I guess it was the way I was brought up. My father was an honest hard-working man, my mother volunteered for several community based care organizations and both were concerned with justice and the rights of others. They were atheists and yet they were the personification of Christian morality and ethics, far more so than any self-professed Christian I have ever met.

So, it was something of a challenge I set myself when I invited my son Charlie and his wife Jessica out to dinner the night after meeting with the PM. Here I was burdened with the most appalling information concerning the future of life as we knew it, yet I could absolutely not speak of it, in any way, to my own flesh and blood.

I managed instead to regale them with tales of the sea and the nasty storm that caught up with us on the way to Auckland. I perpetuated the fabrication that the radio and electrics were taken out by the storm and then steered the conversation around to them: what were they up to, how was my darling grand-daughter, Millie?

Given the execrable position I found myself in without my ever having invited it, I had little difficulty overcoming my conscience when the eye watering bill for our mouth-watering meal arrived. I flipped the government credit card onto the bill folder and made sure the waiter got a decent tip!

"Dad, Christmas; you are coming?"

"Yes of course Charlie, if it's not too much trouble."

"Don't be an idiot! How can it be too much trouble? Midge's coming down from Brisbane, I don't think Asif can make it."

"Asif?"

"He's Midge's latest paramour!"

"Ah," I said. I had difficulty keeping up with my daughter's love life!

We had arrived at their car. There were hugs all round then I waved them away and walked back to the hotel wondering whether there really was any chance I'd be able to spend Christmas with them.

My wondering was interrupted by an unfamiliar ring tone. I stopped, confused, and then realized it was the phone the PM had given me. I flapped at my pockets until I found it.

"Ridsdale."

"Ah Jeff, hope I haven't disturbed you," Baumann's voice was unmistakable, after all he was on radio and television pretty much every day.

"No, no, of course not, no I was just returning to the hotel having had dinner with my son."

"Ah good. How soon can you and your companion be ready to leave?"

"Leave? I suppose about half an hour."

"Excellent. It is now, let me see, 9.40. There will be a car outside your hotel at 10.30."

"Yes, okay, we'll be ready."

I picked up my pace and strode down George Street with renewed vigor.

It was a white BMW Seven Series. Nice car; not every day I get to travel in one of these. Not that we travelled very far when we did get in. The driver tossed our carryalls into the boot. We slipped into the back seat and he sped off arriving five minutes later at the Opera House.

The driver handed us our luggage and with a curt 'Goodnight sir' he took off, leaving Lauren and I looking at one another in confusion. Standing nearby were a couple of blokes I took to be backpackers. They were casually dressed in shorts, sandals and lightweight jackets. They each had a backpack at their feet. One of them drifted over towards us. I didn't pay any particular attention.

"Jeff." I looked up startled. It was the Prime Minister!

"I… I didn't recognize you!"

"Excellent! That's the plan."

"Er, Andrew, this is Lauren. Lauren this is the Prime Minister of Australia Mr. Andrew Baumann." They shook hands, and each said something appropriate. I didn't actually hear what they said because of the noise of a helicopter.

Following years of inter-governmental bickering they had finally built a floating helipad, accessible from the walkway at the end of Macquarie Street. This is where the helicopter was making for. As the noise settled down Baumann beckoned us to accompany him. We walked towards the other backpacker.

"This is Kevin Barker, he is my personal assistant." We shook hands. "Well let's go," he picked up his backpack and made for the helipad. We followed.

Once we were buckled in, and before the noise of the engine made conversation too difficult, Baumann explained that he wanted his departure to go unnoticed. The press always kept an eye on his movements and "God alone knows what they'd make of me making an unscheduled flight to the US, just before Christmas!"

Eighty minutes later we disembarked at Canberra Airport close to an RAAF Boeing 737 -700 series which was making noises that suggested it was preparing to go somewhere. We were ushered on board.

The PM seemed at home. Well, he would, this was his plane after all, or the one he travelled on whenever he went overseas anyway. Normally there would be a huge entourage on board an official flight, including the PM's chief of staff, press secretary, personal assistants and members of the press. Baumann was keeping this trip very hush-hush. There was the four of us and an RAAF stewardess.

We dropped our bags on seats that would normally be

occupied by journalists and followed the PM to the front where there were comfortable seats facing across a table. A mini cabinet room if you will. No sooner had we buckled in when the plane began to move. Soon we were in the air, banking left, the twinkling lights of the Australian Capital filling the small windows.

"Kevin, why don't you take Lauren and show her round the plane?" Baumann suggested once we had levelled off. It was his way of saying he wanted to talk to me in private. When they had disappeared into the gloom of the rear of the plane he summonsed the stewardess and a bottle of scotch, a bucket of ice and two glasses were placed before us. "You do drink whisky?" I nodded 'would you like a mixer?' I shook my head. I spooned some ice cubes into the glasses, he added the scotch. He raised his glass to me and I reciprocated.

"I don't know if you have any idea of the time I've had." He said in a low voice. "You can probably imagine the reaction of POTUS when I told her we've had contact!" There had been, by Baumann's account, a few moments when the President had wondered whether the leader of one of America's staunchest allies had 'a few 'roos loose in the top paddock'!

"Do you have any idea as to their intentions?" he asked. I had to lie.

"No, I'm afraid I don't. They were not unkind to me and Alassay Harraan was even hospitable, entertaining me in her quarters and lavishing a very pleasant special Kareeti wine on me." I only mentioned the hiftervess to give myself some thinking time. "No, she told me that the Kareet were keen to make contact. She wondered who best to announce themselves to—I suggested the U.N." Once you start lying where do you stop? 'Then they implanted the channel into my neck and trained me in the use of it and the syncom."

"I don't know why she thinks she can't speak to the Council in person."

"They don't trust us not to do something silly," I replied

"But surely, she...'

"Have you taken a moment to consider mankind's track record?" I interrupted.

"Well anyway, Mrs. de Villiers has taken it upon herself to arrange the meeting with the other leaders."

Evidently the President wanted to keep all of this out of the public eye. Our flight was routed via Luke Air Force Base in Arizona, a little over 20 miles out of Phoenix. We were due at Luke at about 08:40 pm on the night we departed. In other words, we would fly for fifteen hours and then land three hours before we left! (Little wonder I prefer sailing!) We were to refuel at Luke and then fly direct to Andrews Field, Maryland. A helicopter would then transfer us the eighty miles or so to Camp David.

"Camp David? I thought we were going to the United Nations in New York."

"You can't fly the leaders of the world's preeminent nations into JFK, transport them to Turtle Bay and expect to keep that out of the news."

"Turtle Bay?"

"Manhattan."

As it turned out you couldn't even get the Australian PM into Camp David without it getting into the news. We had arrived on schedule at Luke Air Force Base. We had expected a wait of some two hours while they refueled and ran a maintenance inspection. That would have had us back in the air at about 23:00 and landing at Andrews four hours later at about 01:00, local time. Instead the maintenance crew found a faulty part which had to be replaced before we could take off again.

Our military hosts found us some accommodation and we finally departed at 07:30, which had us touching down at Andrews at 09:50. We didn't know it at the time, but it transpired that someone's curiosity was piqued by the non-scheduled arrival of an RAAF Airbus. That someone, presumably a civilian employee or a visitor to the base, recognized the Prime Minister and surreptitiously took a series of high resolution photographs of us disembarking and walking across the tarmac to the waiting helicopter.

The Washington Post published a couple of the photographs under the headline: 'Australian Prime Minister—We Weren't Expecting You!' on their website. The 'exclusive' that followed was a simple reporting of the unexpected arrival and mere speculation and conjecture as to the purpose of the visit and the apparent secrecy shrouding it. The journalist under whose by-line it appeared, had attempted to get information from the White house but had drawn a blank. He was of the opinion (given his relationship with his sources) that they genuinely had no foreknowledge of the visit. This in itself was strange indeed.

Katherine de Villiers had arrived before us at Camp David, with her Chief of Staff, and was impatiently awaiting our arrival. As soon as we arrived she hauled Baumann into her office and closed the door. After about half an hour I was called for. I was simply required to retell my story. As I did so I it occurred to me that her eyebrows began to mimic the 'Golden Arches' of the McDonalds logo! She looked repeatedly to Baumann for confirmation or reassurance that she was actually supposed to believe this, and it wasn't some crank story.

Finally, shaking her head in bewilderment, she told us that she had spoken to the leaders of the countries that comprise the other permanent members of the Security Council. She had advised them that we had received contact from the 'Aliens' and that they would be addressing us at our meeting. She had asked them to come to Camp David and, because it was paramount that this be kept secret until such time as we knew what the Aliens' intentions were, she had specifically requested that the leaders themselves, not their delegates, attend. She had asked them to bring no more than one personal assistant/advisor and urged them to refrain from telling their aides the purpose of the visit.

By the time we came out of her office there was a furor among the Presidents close personal staff. They had seen the Washington Post article. Katherine de Villiers was not happy She called the Whitehouse Press Secretary and told her to get her sweet fanny down to Camp David without delay!

I was exhausted. I had slept for several hours over the Pacific, but the jet-lag was playing havoc with my system. I retired to the room I had been assigned and fell into a deep sleep. I was shaken awake about three hours later by one of the staff. It would be better if I was able to sleep that night and begin to get my system back in tune with the circadian rhythm. It was after I had showered that I looked at myself in the mirror. What I saw shook me. My face looked younger! I stood there, naked, and examined my reflection. My flesh looked firmer. I may have said that I wasn't in bad nick for a sixty-eight-year-old but I was still, at the end of the day, sixty-eight. Skin loses its elastin, wrinkles form, hollows appear beneath the eyes. I looked more closely at myself. I was no spring chicken but the wrinkles were definitely no longer so deep and the hollows beneath my eyes were not as marked. I flexed my fingers and realized that I didn't have the familiar arthritic twinges in the knuckles. Alassay Harraan had clearly been true to her word!

Chapter 20

Jennifer Colebatch, as Whitehouse Press Secretary was quite used to spinning a good yarn to misinform the fourth estate but usually she knew the real story she was attempting to conceal. This time she did not. The President flatly refused to tell her what was going on.

"Jennifer, the press is onto it that the Australian Prime Minister is here. They have no idea why he's here, so speculation is rife. What they don't and, until this minute you didn't know, is that by this time tomorrow the presidents of Russia and France, the Chinese leader and the Prime Minister of Great Britain will also be here!" Colebatch gawped at her boss. "I *will not* tell you the reason I have invited them. You will have to concoct a story. Perhaps you can imply that we have received credible intelligence of a planned major, multi country, terrorist attack. You'll have to use your imagination."

"You're going to need the cooperation of the intelligence community and the Defense Department, at the very least."

"I'll contact Cliff Glasson. He'll arrange all of that."

National Security Advisor Cliff Glasson owed his current exalted position to Katherine de Villiers. She had selected him over several theoretically more senior contenders for the role. The newly elected president had not been impressed by the hawkish reputation of those presented to her as likely candidates. She chose, instead, the comparatively young but highly credentialed Glasson. De Villiers had heard him talk and had been impressed with his moderate views. He sought always to view any situation from the perspective of the other side and was always looking for ways to defuse tense situations rather than to confront them with force. Because of the faith shown in him by Katherine de Villiers he was intensely loyal to the President.

~

I don't think that, even in my wildest dreams, had I imagined myself having dinner with the President of the United States. Not that it has ever been, even vaguely, an ambition of mine but, nevertheless, here I was, and the crazy thing was, compared to my recent experiences, it seemed quite commonplace! Katherine de Villiers, I had decided, once the 'golden arches' returned to normal eyebrows, was an uncommonly attractive woman. Mind you, that is from the perspective of an old age pensioner! She was also charming company.

I had fallen prey to my instinctive deference to authority and had been minding my manners, "don't speak unless spoken to," I could almost hear my mother saying.

"So, Jeff, this whole thing has completely blown me away

I can't begin to imagine what it must have been like for you and Lauren." I glanced at Lauren, invisible Lauren! It was amazing how she could fade into the background and become almost indiscernible.

"Yes, it has been a bit of a wild journey!" I replied. I took a deep breath and attempted to gather myself. I had to get over this ridiculous obeisance; Christ I was Australian, wasn't I? Egalitarianism was supposed to be our paternoster.

"You were actually on board their… their… spaceship… er, craft?"

"That's right, as I think I mentioned this morning, I was effectively rescued from a yacht in a storm while I was unconscious. When I awoke I was in their vessel. As you can imagine that took a hell of a lot of processing!"

"And Lauren was on the boat with you. Why do you think, can you imagine, why they decided to rescue you?" The question was directed at Lauren. She put down her knife and fork and looked up at the President.

"I really have no idea," she replied, "Jeff was on deck and I was below. I heard a thump and called out to check if he was all right. He didn't respond so I went up to check on him. There was a bright light in the sky, very bright, I was dazzled. Shading my eyes, I could see Jeff slumped on the deck. I could only imagine that a ship had come across us and was shining a searchlight on us. Of course, it wasn't and, frankly, the next sequence of events is not at all clear in my mind."

"I just find it amazing, with all of the people in imminent danger at any given time around the world, that they should have suddenly decided to pull you out of the sea." I didn't like the way this conversation was going. We hadn't rehearsed for this. Clearly, we should have. It was, after all, a perfectly reasonable question.

"I think… er…'

"Katherine, you can call me Katherine."

"I think, Katherine, that when the very foundations of your belief system are turned upside down in so dramatic a fashion, you have more than enough to try to assimilate without asking 'why me?" But, I'm fascinated to know how the other world leaders received the news."

"Ah, ha ha," she laughed. "They were the most interesting telephone calls I have ever had to make!" It had worked; I had deflected her. "The French President was the funniest." She proceeded with a series of short, decorous, impeccably diplomatic vignettes of her conversations with the various leaders.

~

The first to arrive, late the following morning, was Laurence Winston the British Prime Minister. Even before his helicopter landed the Washington Post had the news on their website. Jennifer Colebatch swore under her breath.

"How the hell have they got hold of this information? This is supposed to be a clandestine operation!"

Other news platforms had picked up on the Post's announcement of the Australian PM's arrival and had sent teams to Andrews. By now speculation was rife. It was extraordinary enough that Baumann had flown in unannounced but now Britain was here. What in the world was going on?

Cliff Glasson arrived in a Robbins R44 which settled down beside the Sikorsky Gold Top that had brought Winston in. He and Colebatch were soon in a huddle.

De Villiers and Winston emerged from her office, an aide showed the PM to his room and the President motioned for Glasson and Colebatch to join her. The office door closed behind them. I was suffocating in all of this. Lauren was sitting calmly in a seat by the window looking out across the lawn.

"Fancy a walk?" I asked her.

"Sure."

I had surprised myself with my foresight—not always my strong suit—while in Sydney I had anticipated the cold weather in store for us and had taken Lauren out shopping for warm clothes. We had bought some nice gear and paid for it with the government credit card. I suggested we dig it out because it looked cold outside.

It was! There was an icy wind coming out of the north, the sky was grey and there was a hint of snow in the air.

"This is a bloody rip-off!" I growled, "This is my summer; I'd be strolling along the beach at home."

Lauren and I wandered around for a while appreciating the fresh air, even if it was a little fresher than we may have preferred. The big Sikorsky took off and, shortly after, another arrived. At least I assume it was another—they all looked the same to me.

"More dignitaries arriving, I imagine."

"I overheard one of the staff saying that they will all be here by this evening," said Lauren.

"Well I'm sure they'll all be impatient for a nice fireside chat with Alassay Harraan!" I said gloomily. How will she know when to call in?"

"I will send her a brief message."

"Oh, okay."

Chapter 21

We had dinner at Laurel Lodge at 7.00 that evening. I imagine the food must have been fairly special, given the guest list, but I don't recall. My stomach was churning with anxiety. The leaders of the world's greatest powers appeared to be regarding me with deep suspicion. I gather that Katherine de Villiers had briefed them on the story to date, so I wasn't given the third degree, but I still had difficulty dealing with the questions I did get asked.

As it became clear that we would shortly be rising from the table, Lauren (invisible Lauren!) excused herself demurely and left the room. A few minutes later we all assembled in the conference room. The leaders sat around one end of the long table, I along one side, toward the other end.

"Tell me, Mr. Ridsdale, how is this going to work?" Laurence Winston enquired.

"I have here," I held aloft the syncom, "a communication device given me by the Kareet. It is called a syncom. I should say that, as I understand it, syncom is an improvised translation. It is a contraction of synaptic network computing system. I have extremely limited facility with it. The Kareet have a chip implanted in their hand shortly after birth. They develop a relationship with their syncom from their earliest days. I have been taught skills sufficient only to facilitate this evening's proposed contact." I still needed to keep Lauren's true identity and level of involvement out of the spotlight, so I pretended to use the syncom to make contact. I just had to hope that Alassay was standing by ready to get this show on the road.

"How will this communication take place, Mr. Ridsdale?" The Chinese leader asked. I was about to respond when I felt the tingle in my neck. I raised my finger to ask his forbearance. I rearranged the syncom in my hand, carefully placing fingers in all the right place. I laid it across the back of my neck and waited.

Within a matter of seconds, the air above the conference table began to shimmer. Quite swiftly the strange optical aberration resolved itself into a perfectly clear image of Alassay Harraan. To her right, and to my dismay, sat Guurtsaad Duurn, to her left Ilvik Runaal. The five permanent members of the Security Council recoiled as one! There was an assortment of gasps and muttered expressions of disbelief. Even Andrew Baumann, who had already been subjected to a similar experience, seemed to be rocked by the appearance of the triumvirate.

I felt the clamp come on. I sat back and tried to relax while endeavoring to include all of the leaders in my field of vision.

"Good evening Madam President," Alassay Harraan began with appropriate solemnity and formality, "thank you for facilitating this meeting.

"My name is Alassay Harraan. I am an ambassador for my people, the Kareet. To my right sits the commander of the Kareeti fleet and captain of this vessel, Guurtsaad Duurn. My most senior advisor and our foremost scholar and expert on your world and its people, Ilvik Runaal, sits to my left." To say that the leaders looked startled is a gross understatement! The fact that Alassay spoke with my voice couldn't have helped. Katherine de Villiers gathered herself up to reply.

"I, would like, on behalf of the leaders gathered here and the peoples we represent, to welcome you, the Kareet, to our world. May I introduce…."

"There is no need for you to introduce these people Katherine de Villiers," Alassay cut across her, "we very well know all of those assembled. We thank you for your words of welcome however, although we wonder if you will still feel the same in a few moments when you have heard what we have to tell you." Her audience exchanged glances and a look of trepidation was on the face of the French President.

"We have observed your planet for many years now. We became interested when we first detected radio wave activity from this sun system. We were not previously aware of your planet. Yours is a very beautiful world, surpassing in beauty, resources and climate, any other planet that we are currently aware of in our galaxy. Regrettably this little gem of a world is under dire and imminent threat and will not survive very much longer." The leaders looked at one another in bewilderment.

"The fact that you appear surprised at this information is illustrative of the problem. You must, surely, be aware that the natural balance of the biosphere has been utterly disrupted by the gross over-population of your species?"

There seemed to be a collective sigh of relief at this, a sort of: 'Oh, is that all!' I had a sudden insight: this was the nub of the issue, people, including world leaders, simply did not see population as a problem.

"But the world population is stabilizing." Interjected Olivier Bouchard, the French President. In the hologram Guurtsaad Duurn seemed to react and lean across and speak animatedly to Alassay Harraan. I noticed what appeared to be a small earphone in his ear so, presumably there was an interpreter working in the background.

"Guurtsaad Duurn has noted that, like almost all of your species, you are blinded to the problem by your very membership of the species." Knowing something of Duurn's bluntness, I suspect that Alassay was exercising her highly lauded diplomatic skills. Ilvik Runaal took over the narrative:

"Monsieur Bouchard, the world population stands at a little under 8.5 billion. It is forecast to rise to 9.3 billion by 2050. Fifty years after that it is expected to reach 11.2 billion. Sixty years ago, one of your biologists, Mrs. de Villiers, raised the alarm in a book he called the Population Bomb; at that stage the population was only 3.5 billion."

"But he was proven wrong," the President replied. "He said that millions would starve and that we couldn't feed them, but we can, and we have. We have made enormous progress in our capacity to produce food."

"But at what cost?" Alassay Harraan interrupted.

"The cost to the planet is devastating," Ilvik Runaal continued. "In order to support humanity at current levels you are pumping water from global aquifers 3.5 times faster than rainfall can naturally recharge them; when they run dry hundreds of millions will suffer terrible water shortages. Your top soils are being lost at about 20 times the rate at which it can be replaced; you will not be able to sustain your current food production rates. Your oceans are being overfished jeopardizing the primary protein source of a third of your population. In addition to this your carbon emissions are being absorbed into the oceans causing acidification. As the oceans become more acidic, life forms that use calcium to form exoskeletons cannot do so. These life forms are a vital and fundamental part of the food chain in the oceans. As you require more food from the seas you are both over-fishing species into extinction and threatening the very viability of what life remains.

"The rate of species extinction and eco-system destruction is appalling. How long do you suppose your world can continue to support you under these conditions?" There was no immediate reply from the leaders. The Kareet remained silent, although I could see that Duurn was making remarks to Alassay.

"It may be that you are right in some of what you say," Liaoping Zhang ventured, "but this information is not unknown to us and we are always working towards solutions." There was a small pause during which, I assume, the translator was translating the Chinese Leader's words to Duurn. We could not, of course, hear what passed between the Kareet, only what Alassay Harraan said through me, however Guurtsaad Duurn's scorn was visible for all to see.

"I should like to know," ventured Prime Minister Winston, "why you have gathered us all together to tell us this and what you propose we do about it."

"That much at least is easy, Mr. Prime Minister," Alassay responded, "we no longer expect you to do anything about it. We have been waiting for you to address the problem for nearly fifty years. It has become abundantly clear that you have no plans to do anything at all. As you have not and, presumably, will not, we will come to your assistance and resolve the problem for you." There were gasps of alarm and the interchange of meaningful looks between the leaders.

"What precisely do you mean by 'resolve the problem,' may I ask?"

"Yes, MS de Villiers you may. The Kareet have deliberated over this for a considerable time. We have decided that in the interests of the planet and in the interests of all of the remaining species on the planet, including homo sapiens, the human population must be reduced to 1.5 billion."

"*One point five billion?!*" Olivia Bouchard almost exploded!

"That's outrageous, ridiculous!" huffed Winston. The Russian President, eyes wide, appeared to be groping for words as one in a dark room might for a light switch.

"Would it assist you, Mr. Sokolovski, if I were to speak in Russian?" enquired Alassay Harraan in a very calm voice.

"Ya tak zhe komfortno govorit' po-russki , kak ya govoryu po-angliyski."

"Er… no, no, I can manage in English, thank you. How, I would like to know, do you imagine we could reduce the world population so?"

"We neither imagine that you can nor ask that you do. We will do that."

Chapter 22

Having dropped that bombshell, it was not long before Alassay Harraan terminated the session with an agreement to reconvene in twenty-four hours. As the clamp came off my brain I slumped forward in my chair; I almost collapsed. I was utterly exhausted, my heart was racing, and my breath was coming in short, hoarse gasps. Baumann jumped to his feet and came to my side with a glass of water and a steadying arm. I croaked my thanks but pushed aside the water reaching, instead, into my inside jacket pocket where I had a flask of araanschoz ready for just this eventuality.

As soon as it was apparent that I was not in imminent danger of turning up my toes the leaders pretty well ignored me. It was not as though they were short of topics for conversation after all! I sat back in my chair with my eyes closed concentrating on my breathing. The araanschoz was quite remarkable stuff! It was only a matter of minutes before I felt calm, almost fully relaxed, and no longer so tired.

I listened to the leaders talking. I cannot remember the specifics of their conversation; it wasn't particularly coherent. I remember the Russian President talking in terms of locating the Kareeti vessel and launching an attack. Winston, the British PM, seemed unable to actually believe that he had seen and heard what he had, all too lamentably, actually seen and heard!

Olivier Bouchard groaned. "Quelle catastrophe, merde!" Pretty much sums it up, I thought.

"Gentlemen," Katherine de Villiers attempted to bring the house to order, "Gentlemen, we have to find a way to process this information and start to talk about it in an orderly and unemotional way." Of course they had! Thank God it wasn't my job to do so.

I didn't feel I had anything to contribute so I quietly rose and headed for the door. I glanced over my shoulder, Baumann was the only one who noticed my departure; I gave him a little three finger salute as I closed the door behind me. I caught the merest glimpse of a smile. A good man, I decided.

Lauren was in the outer room and saw me emerge. She rose immediately and came to my side.

"Are you okay?" she asked. "How did it go?" My only reply was a facial gesture. I had to keep in mind that no one else at Camp David knew what was going on and it was important that it remain that way.

There was a small group sitting on sofas around a coffee table. It comprised Jennifer Colebatch, Cliff Glasson, a young woman I had not yet met but who appeared to be an assistant to the Press Secretary, two or three people I didn't know who I assumed were aides to other leaders, and Tristan

Orford the Whitehouse Chief of Staff. It was Orford who called us over to join them.

"So, come on Mr. Ridsdale what's this all about eh? What's going on, what's the big secret?" Cliff Glasson was at me, even before we had sat down, trying to bluster me into talking. I couldn't blame him. He was the National Security adviser and he knew something big was happening and his President wouldn't confide in him.

"I am unable to…' I began.

"Now you listen here…'

"Cliff! Cliff, stop it, you know he can't." Orford intervened.

"I just don't get it!" Glasson fumed. "We're supposed to be the Presidents most trusted, something major is going down and she won't even talk to us."

"I'm beginning to think the tabloid press have got it right," Colebatch's off-sider chimed in. She had a laptop open in front of her on the coffee table which was throwing a bluish cast over her features. Several eyebrows were raised in silent anticipation. "They think its alien contact." Glasson and Orford scoffed dismissively but Colebatch's eyes swung immediately to my face to gauge my reaction. I don't know what she saw; I've never played poker, but I did try to make my face say: 'what'll these lunatics think up next?"

"Some guy has seen the photograph in the Washington Post of you and Lauren at Andrews. He's convinced Lauren's a Hybrid—half human half alien." To this day I cannot work out where the idea came from to do what I did, but I grabbed Lauren and hugged her to me so that my head concealed her face and, through my laughter, said: 'Ah that would explain a lot! I reckon she's a lot more alien than human though!" It was exactly the right thing to do though because my laughter was infectious, and it broke the tension at the same time as dismissing as ridiculous the notion that Lauren, or this situation, had anything to do with alien contact.

"I'm very sorry," I said after a moment, "I am under very strict instructions from your President and my Prime Minister that I cannot discuss this matter with you or anyone else. I would be surprised if, after tonight's meeting, they don't soon take you into their confidence. Now, I'm afraid that I'm still feeling somewhat jet-lagged…' I looked at Lauren and noticed that she was looking heavy lidded—I think she was actually trying to downplay the size of her eyes, "and I think Lauren is feeling pretty much the same so, if there is a driver handy, we would love to get back to our quarters."

"Hell, that was awkward!" I muttered to Lauren as we walked up the path to the door of Witch Hazel, the cabin that had been assigned to us. Keeping my voice barely above a whisper I said, "I don't think we should talk about this inside the cabin, I wouldn't put it past them to have the rooms bugged." I waved to the departing driver in response to his honk.

We went inside and sat at a small table. I poured myself a glass of hiftervess from Alassay's flask. Lauren settled for a glass of water. She produced her syncom and soon produced a holographic image of The Washington Post website. The headline story was 'Mystery Surrounds Secret Meeting of World Leaders." There were several opinion pieces, most accepting the major terrorist threat story released by Jennifer Colebatch, although clamoring for specific details of the threat. And then, under a heading: 'Close Encounter of the Third Kind?" was the story that Colebatch's assistant had found. The reporter referred to the story in the tabloid press and managed to effectively convey an appropriately tongue-in-cheek tone, however, she did describe in some detail the extraordinary claim by a man who swore that he had once been abducted by aliens and had met Hybrids and they looked just like the woman seen boarding a helicopter at Andrews Air Force Base.

We read through the article together. I wanted to talk to Lauren about it. I looked through the window; it had started to snow heavily so a late-night stroll was out of the question. Calling instead on my extensive knowledge of covert operations, gleaned almost entirely from Hollywood movies, I turned on the tap in the sink full bore and beckoned Laura over to stand beside me.

"If they've bugged the place they shouldn't be able to hear over the noise of that," I said just loudly enough for Laura herself to hear me. "Is that plausible?" I asked, "that man saying he had been abducted?"

"Yes," she replied simply, "There have been quite a few people abducted by the Kareet over the years. That is how they obtained the eggs and sperm to create the Hybrids in the first place."

"I'm surprised they were allowed to return to Earth. I mean weren't the Kareet worried that they would talk of their experiences?"

"Yes, I am told there was terrible trouble the first time a commander released a group of abductees. It was generally considered a monumental blunder, but the Kareet monitored the news and it soon became apparent that their story was treated with derision and was put down to hysteria. Clearly the people of Earth could not be persuaded to believe in Alien contact."

"Mm, people may be a little more inclined to believe soon," I speculated, "and there will be hysteria!"

"I've noticed your ability to fade into the background and I think you should keep that up, but I also wonder if it wouldn't be better if you kept a low profile, maybe stayed here in the cabin. I could tell people you're not feeling well and have someone bring your meals to you here. I can't imagine we'll be here much longer. It's almost Christmas."

~

The following day the leaders spent the whole day in conference. I was asked to come in at one stage, around about the middle of the morning. I was given the third degree. They wanted to know everything about my experiences from first awakening on the Kareeti vessel, the way I was treated, what I could tell them of their medical skills, the size of their vessel, what weapons they had, through to my meetings with Alassay Harraan and Guurtsaad Duurn.

I told them what little I actually knew about their medical science, I mentioned the insertion of the channel, I even told them how they had been able to ease my arthritis and make me look and feel younger.

"How old are you Mr. Ridsdale, may I ask?" Katherine de Villiers enquired.

"I'm sixty-eight," I replied. There was a general stir at my answer.

"You do surprise me," she responded, "I had taken you to be *fifty*-eight at most."

"Mm, well, I was perhaps a reasonably young-looking sixty-eight, but no one before would have thought me fifty-eight, so you can see that their technology is effective."

I told them that I had no real way to estimate the size of the Kareet vessel except that it was quite large enough for a complement of 800. That drew a low whistle! I told them I understood there was a fleet of some 10 or 12 scout vessels. These were very much smaller craft.

"I have only seen the one. It was the one they used to transport us back to the yacht in the Tasman Sea. It had a crew of two and seats for four passengers."

As to their weaponry, I had to tell them that I knew precisely nothing.

They grilled me on my assessment of the character and personality of Alassay Harraan and Guurtsaad Duurn. I told them that I was under no illusion that the Kareet were anything but deadly serious in their intentions. I offered the view that Alassay Harraan was sophisticated, cultured and highly trained in diplomacy.

"But at her core there is a steely determination and little sympathy for the human race," I told them. "Guurtsaad Duurn, on the other hand, is cold blooded and ruthless. He has no time for diplomacy and sees no benefit in its employment. He considers he has a job to do and would like simply to get on with it. He doesn't like Alassay Harraan and nor does she like him. There is a very real tension between the two."

"Perhaps we can use this knowledge to our benefit," mused Baumann.

"Perhaps," de Villiers said, "but let's park that for now and come back to it later."

"If they have every intention of carrying out this… this…," Winston couldn't bring himself to name it, "why are they bothering with diplomacy? Why haven't they just done it?"

"Can they do it? How do they plan to do this?" the Chinese Leader asked

"I have absolutely no idea how, but I have little doubt they can. Alassay Harraan would not discuss that side of it at all. I do know though that, if Duurn had his way, they would have 'just done it' and would be half way across the galaxy on their way home to Kareedias by now, leaving us to make of the chaos what we can," I replied. "Alassay, on the other hand, sees some benefit in discussing the matter with us. Perhaps she has in mind that we can select those who will be spared? I really don't know."

They released me shortly after that. There was an air of tension in the anteroom. Nobody liked being kept in the dark. There was, however, one positive thing that had come out of the morning conference: the leaders had agreed that it was pointless trying to keep the contact secret from their staff any longer.

"I think we will have to tell them that contact has been made, but certainly not the substance of the contact!" Katherine de Villiers concluded to general agreement.

It was almost lunch time. The conference door opened, and Andrew Baumann emerged. All eyes went to him. There was an expectant hush.

"Would you all like to come into the conference room?" he asked with a gracious smile.

"I'll round up the others," said Colebatch and scurried out to do so. I assumed that 'all' included me so I went in with the others. After a couple of minutes, the door opened again and Jennifer Colebatch, her assistant (whose name, I later learned, was Justine Morello) and two aides entered and closed the door behind them.

Most had found seats around the table, a couple remained standing, backs against the wall. MS de Villiers rose.

"I'd like to thank you all for your patience. I know this has been a trying situation for you all. Among those present in this room are the most trusted of my staff and, I am sure the most trusted advisors of the world leaders gathered here today. It is normal, when an event of major significance occurs, for us to immediately consult with you. On this occasion, it was determined that it was not appropriate for us to do so until we better understood the nature of this situation. We now do feel that we do, better understand it, and so we have resolved to share this information with you.

"Before I go on it is of paramount importance that you understand that what you are about to hear is of the very highest order of secrecy. Nothing that you hear in this room today is to go any further; you can tell no one, absolutely no one. Is that fully understood?" Her eyes scanned the room demanding signs of agreement from everyone present. Once she was satisfied she continued, "We have had contact from members of an alien race, extra-terrestrial life!" There was a collective gasp. I distinctly heard Morello say, "I *knew* it!"

"You will now appreciate the need for secrecy. This is a matter of supreme significance to the entire world. We cannot give anyone else access to this information before the leaders of the world's nations can gather at the United Nations to be informed and, subsequently, be addressed by representatives of this alien race. Is that fully and clearly understood?" She looked directly into the eyes of each and every person in the room.

"Last night the leaders gathered here were addressed by these extra-terrestrials. They are called the Kareet and they come from a planet within or own galaxy called Kareedias."

"May I ask, Madam President," Cliff Glasson interjected, what the role of Mr. Ridsdale here is?"

"Mr. Ridsdale and his companion were delivering a yacht from Sydney, Australia to Auckland, New Zealand when they were hit by a severe storm in the Tasman Sea. Mr. Ridsdale was knocked unconscious. When he awoke he was aboard the Kareeti vessel. They had patched him up. They have chosen to use Mr. Ridsdale as a conduit for their communications with us."

"Gee Ridsdale, where did you learn their lingo?" Orford chipped in sardonically.

"Actually, it appears that some of their people speak English fluently." The President replied with just enough edge to convey mild reproof.

"As a matter of fact," I ventured, "their head of mission speaks all of the major languages on earth, fluently." Incredulous muttering could be heard.

"What's their message? What did they have to say to you last night?" Glasson asked, clearly wanting to cut to the chase.

"Ah, well here's where I'm going to have to disappoint you Cliff; we have decided," and she gestured to indicate the Leaders, sitting to her left and to her right, "that this information will remain completely confidential, again until the other world leaders can be simultaneously appraised of it."

The President fielded a few more questions but made it clear she would divulge little more than she already had. Eventually she held up her hand.

"No more questions, please." She then solemnly and emphatically reiterated her expectation that not another living soul would hear one word of this information and again sought commitment from each and every one of us.

"Good," she said finally. "Jennifer, I want a briefing from you on what's happening in the media and, Cliff, I need you and Jennifer to concoct something rock solid around the terrorism story."

"Shouldn't be too hard," Colebatch replied, "it's almost Christmas, perfect timing for a Muslim extremist group to plan something dramatic."

Chapter 23

The staff had laid out a buffet lunch in the dining room. I spoke to someone in a white jacket about getting some lunch out to my 'ailing' companion at Witch Hazel and she was happy to assist. I took a plate of food and found myself a seat at a table away from everybody else. I had just started eating when Justine Morello slid into the chair beside my own.

"Do you mind If I join you, Mr. Ridsdale?" She sat down, "I just knew it!" she went on without waiting for a reply, "I just knew it had to be alien contact. It was the only thing that I could possibly imagine that could explain all of the extraordinary secrecy we've seen over the past two days.

"Isn't it exciting?" she bubbled on, "I always believed that there had to be extra-terrestrial intelligence out there somewhere, but I never imagined I would be here when they came! And you, how amazing for you, to have been on their ship! Wow, I can't imagine! And Lauren, what about Lauren, is she really a Hybrid like that man said?"

"MS Morello…'

"Call me Justine, call me Justine."

"Justine, I haven't known Lauren very long. I met her only recently. She kindly volunteered to assist me to deliver a yacht when my regular crew were unavoidably sidelined. Although I don't know her very well I have never doubted her terrestrial origins!"

"But that man...'

"There have always been cranks out there who report UFO's and who think they've been abducted by aliens. Usually the serious media don't give them much oxygen."

"But now we know there really are aliens, maybe...'

"Justine, I don't think Lauren is a Hybrid!"

She appeared to accept what I said but I felt she was reluctant to completely give up on the notion. We exchanged pleasantries after that and, as soon as I had finished my lunch I took my leave. I was keen to get back to the cabin and away from so many uncomfortable questions.

As I sank into the back seat of the car that drove me back to Witch Hazel I was pondering why it was that I was so willing to protect Lauren's identity. Why did it matter to me if they knew she was a Hybrid? I certainly owed no fealty to the Kareet, nor even to Lauren, although I quite liked her. I think I concluded that, in the overall scheme of things, Lauren was of no major importance; she was not a key player. It was not she who was threatening to wipe out eighty per cent of humanity. If these people came to know she was part alien they might... what, try to hold her for ransom, try to use her as a bargaining chip to try to force the Kareet to back off, soften their stance? That would never work. The Kareet couldn't care less about... well, that's not true; they probably would care, but they certainly wouldn't allow the wellbeing of one Hybrid to make one iota of difference to their mission.

If our people held her captive what might they do to her? What might they hope to learn from her physiology, her genetic make-up, the way her brain functioned? No, at the end of the day, there was no advantage to anyone in revealing her identity.

Lauren was poking at a log fire when I walked in the door. I think she was pleased to see me. There was a plate on the coffee table with a few scraps of food left.

"The food arrived okay then?"

"Oh, did you send it? Thank you." She threw another log on the fire. "Would you like to go for a walk?"

"It's cold outside."

"I'll get my coat."

I buttoned mine up to the neck and pulled my wool hat over my ears. The snow had stopped falling but it was quite deep. Someone had cleared the footpath that morning and the black top was visible beneath the car tracks, so we picked our way along the road.

"I have spoken to Alassay Harraan," she said once we were well clear of the house and any eavesdropping devices.

"Ah," I said.

"She is very concerned that that man identified me as a Hybrid. She wants me back as soon as possible."

"Oh," I said.

"Are they going to allow us to go back to Australia?"

"Well, I really don't know. I imagine they will. I haven't

talked to them about it yet. I mean, I can't see them keeping us here over Christmas." Lauren laughed out loud 'What?" I asked, puzzled.

"You humans, you're so funny!" I continued to look puzzled. "Here you are, visited by the extra-terrestrial intelligence you have been searching for these past forty or fifty years, threatened with the eradication of a large part of your people and you're worried about Christmas!" When she put it like that it did seem a little absurd.

"No, you don't understand," I tried to gather my thoughts. "The only people who know about the Kareet are the handful of people here in Camp David. Of those, only the Leaders of the nations that comprise the permanent members of the U.N. Security Council actually know about the…' I couldn't voice it. "No one else is to know until a meeting of the United Nations General Assembly can be called. With Christmas just days away there is no way a meeting could be called until afterwards. I'm sure that, when we meet with Alassay Harraan again this evening, this will all be discussed and I'm sure that she will accept that nothing can be done until early January at the soonest."

"Mm, well, if we get back to Australia I need you to drive me to somewhere remote where a scout craft can safely rendezvous." I was inexplicably irritated. It wasn't the prospect of driving her somewhere remote it was the notion that she thought me somehow complicit in all of this; as if I was a willing conspirator, part of the plot.

"Why the hell should I be helping you?" I growled. She looked surprised; confirming, in my mind at least, my supposition that she thought me in her camp. But I was on the wrong track. Her logic was impeccable.

"There is no benefit to anyone in you preventing me from returning to our vessel. All that would do would be to annoy Alassay Harraan and, probably, convince Guurtsaad Duurn that you are not to be trusted. Don't think that I do not appreciate the difficulty of your situation, but your cooperation is the only chance you'll have to influence the final outcome. Alassay Harraan, through you, is giving the world the opportunity to select the people that will remain to continue the human race into the future. Guurtsaad Duurn certainly wouldn't give you that chance." She was, of course, absolutely right

~

That night the meeting with the Kareet was brief and to the point. As I had predicted Alassay Harraan understood the difficulties associated with gathering the remaining world leaders at Christmas time. It was agreed that a General Assembly would be called at the earliest possible time after Christmas. I was to alert Alassay Harraan twenty-four hours before the scheduled convocation. She also instructed the leaders to nominate a highly competent, cool-headed and intelligent virologist or micro-biologist who could be relied upon to work with new and complex scientific material while maintaining unqualified secrecy. The inference was inescapable!

After the meeting, I found an opportunity to have a word with Andrew Baumann.

"So, when do we leave?" I asked him. He looked a little uncertain.

"I'm not sure they plan to let you out of their sight!"

"What, that's ridiculous! What do they think I'm going to do? Sell my story to the New York Times?"

"Well, that may be one of their concerns."

"You're not serious! Do you have any idea of the pressure I have been under from… well, everybody to tell them everything I know? Even you; you pressed me to tell you about the Kareet's motives and intentions. Did I tell you? Did I tell the President when she subjected me to the third degree? Have I blabbed about any aspect of this whole business to anyone at all? I think I have well and truly established my capacity to keep a secret, don't you? My family are expecting me for Christmas and I don't intend to disappoint them. And, I've no doubt, Lauren has plans too."

"Mm, well, I'll see what I can do."

"Please do." I said with some feeling.

An hour or so later Baumann found me with my nose in a snifter of particularly good cognac. I was, by now, feeling a little more congenial.

"All fixed, we leave in the morning."

"Excellent I said. Cognac?"

"Don't mind If I do."

"I don't mind if you do either—it's not my cognac!"

Chapter 24

We touched down in Canberra a few minutes before midnight on Saturday. It was the 22nd of December. There was a helicopter waiting to take us to Sydney. It was getting on for 2.00 in the morning when we reached Sydney. The PM's car met us and drove us to Kirribilli House. Andrew Baumann had phoned Martin Barstock from Canberra and asked him to meet us there. We were exhausted and thoroughly jet-lagged from the flight. After a hello and brief chat with Baumann, Martin put Lauren and me in his car and drove back to his house where my Land Rover was parked.

"You two look done in," he said, "best stay the night at my place." I was happy to accept his invitation. "So, tell me all about it," he asked enthusiastically.

"Martin, you know very well I can't tell you all about it."

"Well some at least?"

"I have been sworn to secrecy by no less a person than the President of the United States. Without which solemn pledge Lauren and I would be spending Christmas at Camp David!"

It was after 10:00 when I awoke on Sunday morning. I rose and showered and went to the car for a bag. I needed summer clothes. I fished out my mobile phone which had been switched off and left in my bag throughout the past five days. There was a string of missed calls from Charlie, half a dozen messages on Message Bank and a long text from my daughter Imogen. I rattled off a quick text message in reply to her, saying I'd been overseas and would see her on Tuesday. That was simple. Charlie, I predicted, would be more difficult. And so it turned out.

I called him. He was angry with me. He wanted explanations. I told him I'd been in the US. How could I just disappear overseas without even a word? We'd only had dinner the other night and suddenly, without warning I'd taken it into my head to fly to America! Was I crazy? Probably I was, I told him. I also told him that I was simply not at liberty to tell him anything further at that time. That, of course, gave rise to the third degree! I should have known better, but what could I have said? In the end, he had to settle for the story that I had seen something, while I was at sea, that I should not have. This had led to security concerns and hence my visit to the US. He attempted to get more out of me, but I told him I simply could not say any more, that I still had a couple of important things to get done and I'd see him on Monday night.

~

It was swelteringly hot that morning. We headed out along the M4, grateful for the Land Rover's air conditioning. It was a little after midday when we crossed the Nepean River. it hadn't really been necessary to leave as early as we did, but I wanted to get away from Barstock's questions; also, I thought the temperature would be more pleasant up in the Blue Mountains. It had been many years, I reflected, since last I'd been up this way.

We pulled into Wentworth Falls and stopped for lunch. I was right, it was a good ten degrees cooler.

"There's some great scenery around here," I said as I mopped up the last crumbs from my plate. "We've got a few hours to kill; I'll show you the sights."

We started at Rocket Point Lookout. Lauren was duly impressed but declined the steep steps down. We drove on to Valley of the Waters and took the walking track to Empress Falls. The cascades are almost other-worldly, they put me in mind of Lothlorien; one almost expected to see an ethereal Galadriel emerge from behind a dripping fern. There are just so many truly beautiful spots throughout this area and I silently castigated myself for not having spent a good deal more time there. Even the usually taciturn Lauren was effusive in her appreciation.

Overshadowing this otherwise perfect afternoon, of course, was the Damoclean prospect of the Kareet. My reason for being in the area was not, regrettably, to show off the beautiful landscape to Lauren, nor even to make a long overdue personal pilgrimage. Rather I had selected the Megalong Valley as a sufficiently secluded spot to have the Kareeti scout vessel pick up Lauren. To minimize the risk of the vessel being spotted it needed to be late in the afternoon, around about dusk.

We made our way down the Megalong Road, past the Megalong Valley Farm and drove some miles before I found a small paddock, surrounded by trees with no sign of human habitation in evidence. I pulled over to the side of the road and parked under a tree. We got out. It was surprisingly cool, having started the day in Sydney where it was 94 degrees with humidity in the 80% range!

"I think this should be okay, don't you?" Lauren, having returned to type, merely looked around and offered a grimace which I interpreted as saying: "It'll do." She palmed her syncom waved a hand over it and returned it to her pocket. I looked at her enquiringly.

"They're coming."

"How long?" She shrugged seeming neither to know nor care particularly. "Well," I ventured, just a little peeved at her off-hand manner, "I suppose this is goodbye." Another of her grimaces, open to interpretation. "I think I'd just like to say I've enjoyed meeting you. I'm not so happy about the circumstances, of course, but that's none of your doing." She smiled at me. "I'd like to take you sailing again—you showed signs of becoming a very good sailor."

"Well, I think I might like sailing again with you too. I don't think it will ever happen though, and we don't have sailing on Kareedias." Her eyes angled up to the sky. I followed the direction of her glance. At first, I saw nothing then, in the last rays of the setting sun, there was a flash. I lost sight of it again and then, taking my lead from the direction of Lauren's gaze, I picked up the scout coming in low over the trees. It was coming in startlingly fast and quite soundlessly. Defying everything I know about the laws of physics it came, suddenly, to an abrupt standstill, ten feet above the ground, just a few yards from where we stood. Lauren started towards it and I followed. By the time we had covered half of the distance a stepped gang plank or cat walk, for want of a better term, telescoped out from somewhere near the base of the vessel. The scout slowly lowered itself until the stair lightly touched the ground. A door opened, and a figure appeared. A familiar figure. It was Carlos!

I was distracted by the sight of Carlos so was taken quite by surprise when Lauren grasped me in a hug and planted a big kiss on my cheek! She continued to hold me for ten seconds or more and then, abruptly released me, said not a word, turned, picked up her bag and walked the remaining few yards to the scout. She and Carlos touched hands as they passed each other. Lauren climbed the steps. The door closed behind her. The cat walk was drawn back into the vessel. With almost no sound the scout shot vertically into the air, paused a second and then flashed across the darkening sky at incomprehensible speed.

"We meet again," said Carlos with contrived suavity.

"So it seems," I replied in a similar tone, "what brings you to these parts?"

"I'm to be your new Lauren, it seems."

"Ah, that promises to be fun! How, precisely am I to explain you away?"

"We hope you won't have to," he replied. "I'm really only here to help if you need me. I'll take a room in a hotel, buy a pre-paid mobile phone and then you can call me if you need me. If, in the highly unlikely event that someone sees me in your car driving into Sydney tonight, you can say I was a hitch hiker you picked up." I nodded my head, taking it all in.

"Money!" I said, I had been meaning to ask Lauren, "where do you… how do you get money?"

"Counterfeit."

"Counterfeit?" My eyebrows raised in skepticism.

"Very easy for us. Here," he pulled a small wad of cash from his shirt pocket and peeled off a twenty-dollar note, "this is your new format note—supposed to be more difficult to counterfeit." He handed it to me. I examined it carefully. I could detect no difference between it and any other twenty-dollar note in circulation. Of course, I was not an expert; but then nor was it likely that anyone to whom this money was passed would be either.

"That's a bit unethical, isn't it?" is all I could muster in response.

"Ethical?" Carlos laughed. "Ethics is a set of rules agreed upon by a group or culture that enable them to live and work together to prosper and succeed. The Kareet make no pretension to be part of your species."

"Except that you come among us, stay in our hotels and buy mobile phones."

"Purely pragmatic."

It was a strange drive back to Sydney. Carlos refused to be drawn on matters relating to the Kareet or their plans for the future of humankind but, instead, made various attempts at topics of conversation relating to current world and human affairs. These all seemed banal in the context of the Kareeti threat and I found it impossible to engage.

It was with some relief, then, that I dropped Carlos off outside a likely looking hotel, not too distant from the one I had been using in The Rocks. He took my mobile phone number, promising to call me as soon as he had a phone. I then booked back into 'my' hotel for the night. I was exhausted, no doubt still jet-lagged, and yet unable to sleep. I had some serious Christmas shopping to do the following day, and I had not given any thought whatsoever as to what I might buy for these people in my life!

Part 4

Chapter 25

It was early evening when I arrived at Charlie and Jessica's house in Turramurra. Imogen (Midge as we called her) had arrived that afternoon. Millie, at least, was glad to see me, running to meet me and jumping up into my arms. Charlie was distinctly pinch-nostrilled, and Jessica, no doubt influenced by Charlie's imprecations, was a little restrained. Midge was… well, Midge! Her usual insouciant self; too laid back to even come to the front door to greet me.

"Father dear!" was her laconic greeting when I walked into the living room where she lounged, glass of chardonnay in hand.

Mine was the guest bedroom, small but with an ensuite. I unpacked a few necessities and stowed the Christmas gifts in the wardrobe. It had been another hot muggy day in Sydney, and I'd spent most of it mooching around shopping centers and department stores. A shower would help me feel a little less shop-soiled. As I was tying up my hair, Charlie knocked on the door and walked in with a couple of Crown Lagers.

"Ah, are you not drinking?" I quipped. His face assumed his usual 'Dad joke' response expression.

"I must say you're looking very well," he said.

I glanced in the mirror.

"It's my life style: outdoors, stress free, doing what I love."

"Yeah, but you've been doing that for a while now and you didn't look this good. Have you been getting cosmetic surgery or something?"

"Cosmetic surgery!" I scoffed. But then I realized that the Kareeti treatment was going to be an ongoing source of comment, so perhaps I could use this idea. "No, not surgery, but I had a couple of injections to fill out the bags under my eyes. Not bad, eh?"

"Makes a difference!" He tried to look more closely at me. I held up the Crown Lager and clinked bottles with him.

"Happy Christmas!" I said.

"Yeah, happy Christmas. But why did you do it? Are you chasing the ladies or something?"

"Chasing the ladies! C'mon Charlie, I'm nearly seventy!"

"Yeah, but you're not in bad shape for an old guy. Seventy's the new fifty, they reckon."

"Yes, yes, but no, I'm not 'chasing the ladies'."

"What I really want to talk to you about is…'

"I know what you really want to talk to me about, Charlie, but I'm not going to talk to you about it."

"But why, what's going on?"

"I told you on the phone, I saw something at sea that I'm not supposed to have seen and now I'm sworn to secrecy."

"I don't see why that would entail a trip to the US. Were you part of that business where various world leaders all went secretly to meet with the American President?"

"Charlie, I don't mix in those sorts of circles! Who on Earth do you think I am?"

"I'm not sure I know anymore."

"Listen, I can't say any more at the moment. I think the whole thing may become public in the not too distant future but, just for now, it would make it a great deal easier for me if you'd just drop it, leave it alone, okay?" Very reluctantly he nodded. "Good; a couple more of these, I think," I said, holding aloft my nearly empty stubby.

~

Christmas was as Christmas is. On Boxing Day, we watched the start of the Sydney to Hobart Yacht Race on the television and then Midge and I made our farewells. I had promised to visit Andie's sister, Elizabeth, and her family at Port Stephens and to take Midge to see them. It worked well for me. I would stay overnight and set off in the morning and be home by mid-afternoon. Home! How long was it since I had been home?

It also gave me a chance to catch up with Imogen; get a feel for what was really happening in her life. She liked to project an image of herself which I knew to be untrue. She'd have you believe she was living the decadent life, partaking casually in drugs and sex, drifting from one music event to another, one party to the next and caring not a whit about the affairs of the world or even, for that matter, her own future. In reality, she was beavering away at a master's degree in linguistics at the University of Queensland, I had little doubt she dabbled in recreational drugs, but she was far too smart to get involved in anything that could do her any serious harm. As for men; she'd had a few but, as a young man I'd had quite a few young women, so who was I to judge?

"My supervisor wants me to convert it into a PhD."

"How do you feel about that?"

"I don't think so. I might do a doctorate but not on this subject; I'm reaching the extent of my interest in it."

"So, how far off is the Master's?"

"Effectively, I've finished. I've submitted it to Bill, my supervisor. If it's okay, it'll come back to me for a final edit and tidy up and that's it."

"Wonderful. Congratulations!" I was proud of her, very proud. "And Asif?"

"You know about Asif?" she asked incredulously.

"Well, only because Charlie mentioned him," I confessed.

"He's a very nice guy, very gentle, highly intelligent. He's from Pakistan. When I met him, he claimed to have no strong affiliation with Islam. He claims to be atheist, agnostic at the very least. As I got to know him better it became obvious that the Islamic faith still has a very strong influence on his values. I don't think I can see much of a future for a relationship with him."

"Ah, good, so then I won't have to travel to Karachi to see my grandchildren!"

Elizabeth and Tony are a great couple. I should make the effort to see them more often. Elizabeth is very different to Andrea, which is fortunate for, if she was more like her, I would be forever haunted by painful memories in her presence. Tony is a keen sailor too, which is why they chose to live in Port Stephens, but he's more into racing than cruising.

Tony tried to get me to go for a twilight sail, but I cried off. Frankly I hadn't the energy. Nevertheless, we spent a very pleasant evening on their deck overlooking Nelson Bay. We did the traditional Aussie BBQ, a few prawns, steak and snags, and drank a fair quantity of beer and, later, red wine.

The following morning, I was not as bright eyed and bushy tailed as I had intended to be. Nonetheless, I made my farewells over a light breakfast and a strong cup of coffee. Midge was still asleep, but she had planned to stay on with her aunt and uncle and catch a Greyhound back to Brisbane in her own time.

Chapter 26

It was late in the morning on Saturday. I was on my boat. An unfamiliar ringtone brought my head up out of the bilge. It took a moment but then I realized, of course; Andrew Baumann's phone! I scrabbled for my bag and managed to get the phone to my ear before it rang out.

"Good morning, Jeff. Hope I haven't caught you at a bad time."

"No, no, I was doing some work on my boat; took me a while to find the phone. How're you?"

"Jeff, you may recall that Al… ah, Alassay Harrim…'

"Alassay Harraan."

"That's it. You may remember she asked for a microbiologist. Anyway, it seems we've found one and she wants to meet up with you."

"Me? Why would she want to meet me?"

"I don't know, something about getting as much information on the Kareet as possible."

"So, where have I got to go?" I enquired with exaggerated resignation.

"Nowhere, it seems she wants to come to you."

"Really? Oh, okay."

"So where does she find you? As in, where are you?"

"Iluka, it's…'

"I know Iluka."

"Oh."

In the end, I offered to drive to Ballina airport to pick her up if she could get a flight. Baumann promised to text me her flight details.

"Oh, by the way, her name is Lena Sandmeier; Austrian I understand."

It was damned hot in the cabin and I figured the sun would be over the yardarm somewhere in the world, so I dug a can of beer from my Esky and went up and sat in the cockpit where a pleasantly cool sea breeze brought instant relief. I sat on the stern perch, drained about half of my can of beer in one go and shook my head in bemusement. This whole thing was just getting more and more bizarre!

~

I watched the seemingly endless line of people making their way from the plane, across the tarmac to the airport arrival lounge. I had Lena Sandmeier's mobile phone number from Andrew Baumann and, to save standing around like a hire car driver with her name written on a cardboard sign, I had sent her my photograph and she, in turn, had sent me hers, so I had some idea who I was looking for. As it happened she was almost upon me before I spotted her.

She walked straight up to me, extending her hand.

"Jeff Ridsdale?"

"Lena, hello!" I took her hand. She had a firm handshake.

"This is it," she said indicating the cabin bag she was wheeling behind her, "no luggage to wait for."

We made our way out to the car park.

"Ooh, it's very hot!" she said

"Middle of summer for us."

As we wound our way from the airport out to the Pacific Highway, I took the opportunity to look a little more closely at her. She was a strikingly handsome woman. I guessed her to be in her late forties. She was tall and fine boned with just a hint of the Helen Hunt about her. Her hair was tawny, shoulder length and, as we drove, she rummaged in her handbag, came up with an elastic band, scooped up her hair and tied it in a ponytail.

"That's a little cooler," she said with an engaging smile. Her English was perfect with only a hint of an accent. I smiled back at her. I suddenly realized I was attracted to her in a way that I had not been attracted to anyone since Andie died.

"The air conditioning will soon have you comfortable," was all I could find to say.

She turned half sideways in her seat to engage with me.

"You know, I am absolutely dying to ask you all about the Kareet. But also, I want to wait. I want to wait until we are able to sit down and relax and focus completely, without fear of interruption. Will that be possible?"

"Oh yes," I replied, "there's precious little to disturb you in Iluka!"

"Okay, good, so tell me about Iluka."

"You'll get to see it for yourself soon enough, but I can paint a few word pictures along the way if you like."

We put Lena's bag in the spare bedroom and I took her upstairs, through the kitchen, via the fridge where we collected a couple of beers (she had expressed a keen interest in trying our Australian beers), and out onto the deck.

"Oh my God!" she gasped. "This is incredible!"

My house overlooked Iluka Bay which, despite its name, is actually part of the Clarence River. In the late nineteenth and very early twentieth centuries a massive project to stabilize the course of the river during large floods had seen the construction of a long rock wall across the 'bay' in the river on which the small township of Iluka stood. This effectively created a very large, peaceful lagoon, free of current and ideal for mooring or anchoring boats.

The house was designed to take advantage of its position. The ground floor comprised double garage, laundry and two bedrooms with a shared bathroom. Upstairs, the kitchen, bathroom and study took up the back of the house while at the front, the living room and main bedroom opened onto a good-sized deck that ran the width of the house. From the deck, you look out over Iluka Bay and the Clarence River which together, at this point, are well over a mile wide, to Yamba on the south side of the river entrance.

A couple of dozen yachts at anchor in the bay were clearly visible, with probably another dozen or so tucked away in front of the fisherman's co-op away to our left. Three or four pelicans patrolled the calm waters, while many more watched on from where they sat upon the rock wall. The Yamba yacht club had a race on that afternoon, and the sea breeze was filling their sails and bearing them upstream on a beam reach. It was the epitome of peace and tranquility.

"This is absolutely beautiful."

"You can see why I was so keen to get home from Camp David."

We settled into comfortable recliners and made respectable inroads into our first beer before Lena gathered herself to sit more upright and turned toward me. "Now, tell me everything!"

By the time she had wrung me dry, after I had told her the story from the start and answered innumerable questions, many very insightful and penetrating, the westering sun was golden on the water. The yachts had finished racing and were laying off Dart Island packing away their sails, and an impressive number of empty beer bottles cluttered the low table between us. Lena Sandmeier could handle a beer!

"Are you hungry?" I asked.

"Yes, now you come to mention it, I am!"

"I've little to offer in the house, I'm afraid, but if you like fresh seafood, our local pub has a well-deserved reputation."

"Okay, sounds good to me."

"I didn't say what kind of reputation," I jibed. "Anyway, it'll give you a chance to see a real Aussie rural pub."

There is a concrete walkway along the river front and, from my garden, it is about 200 yards to Sedgers. Of course, we walked. It was a balmy evening and the setting sun was beginning to light the river with a blaze of red and gold. I don't quite know how it happened; was it the romantic setting, was it the beer, was it the rapport that had sprung up between us? In any case, as we walked along the foreshore, without premeditation, I took her hand in mine. It seemed so natural. She gave my hand a little squeeze.

I can barely begin to imagine how someone, particularly a well-educated and sophisticated someone, freshly arrived from Christmas in Europe, would react to Sedgers Reef Hotel!

It's ancient, well by Australian standards, completely un-renovated, dilapidated and, quite frankly, delightful. You'll find your local bloke dressed in singlet, shorts and rubber thongs, usually with a pair of sunglasses perched on his head, propping up the bar. The wives and girlfriends sit around the old timber tables. Some of the old geezers have their eyes permanently attached to the numerous screens with the sound turned down, showing racing, cricket or football (depending on the season) or some television soap opera.

Off to the right, as you come in the front door, is the bistro, with orderly rows of retro tables and chairs with a counter at the far end where you order your food. The menus are hand-written on whiteboards hanging on the walls.

Lena's eyes darted around the place, taking it all in.

"Bit of a culture shock?" I enquired.

She laughed and shook her head in wonderment. We went to the counter and, after I had given her the low-down on local fish, we ordered and paid, and carried the gizmo that would flash and buzz when our meals were ready, out to the front of the pub to one of the many tables facing the river. Once we were settled, I went to the bar and found a semi decent Pinot Grigio that would reasonably complement the seafood.

We had given the Kareet a fair hammering all afternoon, so we talked a little about ourselves.

"How did you get lumbered with this job?" I asked her.

"You obviously don't move in the world of the microbiologists," she replied with a smile. "If you did you would be familiar with my name. I seem to have managed to acquire a bit of a reputation!" She chuckled self-consciously. She began to give me a little of her scientific background which sounded quite amazing, but she soon stopped. "I can see your eyes are glazing over; I'll shut up!"

I tried to protest but she knew I was only being polite.

She asked me about my past and, as we worked our way through a large seafood basket and the bottle of wine, she came to hear about my former career in management consultancy and of Andie and Charlie and Midge. She asked if there had been anyone else since Andie died and I, a little sheepishly, confessed there had been no one.

I learned that Lena had been separated for two years and was currently negotiating a divorce. Evidently her husband, wearying of the long hours she put in at the lab and the frequent seminars and conferences she had to attend all over the world, found himself a young thing who stroked his ego, made him feel young again and was always there when he needed her.

As we talked, I gazed into Lena's eyes and felt a warmth and closeness that I hadn't experienced in years. She had a way of twisting a strand of her tawny hair around her finger as she talked and wrinkling her nose when she smiled which lit up my heart.

We strolled back along the foreshore to the house and went up to the front deck where I proposed a nightcap. It was a balmy 80^0, the stars blazed in the cloudless sky and the lights of Yamba mingled with the many navigation lights and twinkled on the water. Lena stood at the front rail, taking in the view. I came to her side with drinks in hand. She turned to me. I handed her a glass. We clinked. She took a sip then draped her right arm, holding the drink, over my shoulder. She gazed into my eyes and I could feel the pressure of her arm drawing me towards her. We kissed.

It was a soft lingering kiss, the first I'd had in over eight years, but it awoke something in me and I began to kiss her with more urgency. She responded, but then she pushed me gently away. I was scared that I had overstepped the mark but her smiling eyes told me otherwise. She drank from her glass, her eyes all the while on mine. I gulped at my own drink. She reached out with her left hand and took hold of the front of my shirt, just above my belt, turned and walked towards my bedroom, tugging me along behind her.

I awoke, as usual, at about 6:30. I looked to my left. Lena lay asleep, her back to me, not even a sheet covering her nakedness. I shook my head in silent amazement. Who could have foreseen this twenty-four hours ago? I slipped quietly from the bed and padded, barefoot and naked, to the bathroom and thence to the kitchen. I poured myself some juice and wandered out onto the deck. It was a beautiful morning. The sun, not long over the horizon, had yet to breathe its hot breath on the land. I watched a trawler glide up the river, back with the night's catch.

I heard a sound and turned to see Lena walking towards me. She was clutching a pillow to herself in a token, but utterly failed, gesture of modesty, while the back of her right wrist rubbed at an eye. She stopped in front of me and spread wide her arms to embrace me. She held the pillow against my back and I could feel all of her naked body against my own. I could also feel a predictable response in my groin! Lena felt it too. She stood back and looked down at it.

"Ooh, now it would be a shame to waste that!" she said. She picked up the remains of my orange juice from where I had sat it on the hand rail, downed it in one gulp, took me by the hand and led me back to bed.

My head, that morning, was seething with almost incoherent thought. I couldn't believe this had happened. Was I in love? I felt I was. Was this a betrayal of my love for Andie? What would the kids think? Where could this possibly lead? Lena would have to go back to Austria, ah no, I recall she told me she lived in Switzerland but, nevertheless…

I felt like I was teenager again. Yet I was sixty-eight years old. I certainly didn't feel that old; far from it. The Kareeti magic seemed to be working very well indeed! I had no aches and pains, I felt active and virile, and Lena seemed unconcerned about our age difference. In fact, at one stage during the morning, after struggling with the idea for quite some time, I brought it up.

"I'm, um," I started with some trepidation. "I, um, I wanted to say… er," She looked at me expectantly. "I guess I'm trying to say I'm really concerned at the big age gap between us and how you should probably be with a younger man," I finally managed to say. She looked at me incredulously.

"What on Earth are you talking about?"

"Well I'm just so much older than you, and I…'

"Wait a minute, just how old do you think I am?" she asked.

"Well, I… er…'

"I'm fifty-one!"

"Oh, I had thought maybe forty-seven."

"Good response! And you are… what? Fifty-six?"

"Fifty-six! Christ, I'm nearly sixty-nine!"

"Don't be ridiculous!" She snorted.

"No, it's true." She gazed at me as though trying to decide if I was pulling her leg. "I admit I'm not in bad shape for my age, but the real difference is something the Kareet did while I was on board their vessel."

Lena sat up and took notice. She was endlessly fascinated by our alien visitors. I told her all about the operation; I mean she knew about the operation to implant the channel, but not about the genetic tweaks.

"Wow!" was all she said. Then, after she had had some time to consider all I'd said, she grinned, "I suppose that makes me some weird gerontophile!"

I punched her on her arm and then we fell into a wrestling match and, next thing I knew we were making love again. I really was acting like a teenager.

~

"How do you feel about this whole Kareet thing?" Lena asked.

It was late afternoon. We had found a shady spot under the sand cliffs on Iluka back beach. We'd had a swim and were sitting back in a couple of beach chairs; I had just opened a couple of cans of ice cold beer from the Esky.

"Hell, what sort of a question is that? I mean 'the whole Kareet thing' is just so big that I don't know where to begin to think about it. It's like when people start talking about the distance between stars, the number of galaxies; I just don't have the mind power to process it."

"Yes, I know what you mean, but how about the idea that the human population is out of control and needs to be reduced?"

"No argument there."

"Nor from me."

"But what about some alien civilization coming here and literally wiping out most of our population?"

"Are they really, really planning that?"

"You'd better believe it!" I responded vehemently. "The only upside I can see so far is that if we cooperate with Alassay Harraan we'll be given the opportunity to select those we want to save. If Guurtsaad Duurn had his way, they would just cull the population to the size they thought appropriate and leave without another thought."

"But how will they do this?"

"Well, at this stage it is purely speculation, but the fact that they wanted a microbiologist involved makes me think they are going to release a virus, or microbe of some sort, and provide us with an adequate quantity of antidote to preserve those we wish to save."

"This is just appalling! Have they given any thought to how the remaining humans are going to cope with the completely overwhelming number of corpses that will result?"

"I don't know, but I doubt they much care. Their level of empathy for us is on a par with our own for an infestation of ants. I guess bodies decompose and, eventually, will be no longer a problem."

"But they are a very big problem while they are decomposing!"

~

That evening we took my inflatable and nipped across the river to Yamba. We had dinner at a steak house in Coldstream Street and I introduced Lena to a particularly fine Western Australian Shiraz. Damn the expense— it was all going on Andrew Baumann's card anyway!

"So, if I understand it, you can contact this Alassay woman any time?"

"Alassay Harraan, yes. I have a syncom, which is short for synaptic network computing system. The Kareet are paired with theirs from infancy and can do pretty amazing stuff with them. I've been taught a few elementary gestures sufficient to fulfil my role as the go-between."

"So, we could perhaps contact her tonight?"

"Why would you want to contact her?"

"I'd like to get some insight into what she's planning…'

"I really don't think that would be appropriate," I cut in. "Only the leaders of the countries of the Security Council are even aware of the presence of the Kareet. We are all sworn to secrecy, I very much doubt that Alassay Harraan would divulge anything to us at all."

Lena nodded her acceptance of my assessment. "Excellent wine," was all she said.

~

The next day was New Year's Eve. I took juice and a coffee to Lena, who adorned my bed like a pale Aphrodite. Unused as she was to the warm climate, she wore clothing only when she had to, which suited me just fine!

"It's New Year's Eve, do you need to be anywhere? Do you have to fly away somewhere?"

"Oh, I could fly back to Canberra and find some antiseptic hotel to languish in, if I'm cramping your style."

"Cramping my style? Don't be daft! God no, I was only asking because we haven't spoken at all about where you were staying or who you may know or want to spend time with in Australia."

"Jeff, I know a couple of scientists in Australia, but they don't even know I'm here and, even if they did, I certainly wouldn't be desperate to fly off and spend New Year's Eve with them! If I haven't outstayed my welcome…'

"I don't think you could ever do that! Of course you

must stay. We'll see in the new year together."

I'd no sooner said that than Lena's phone rang. It was Baumann. It could only have been Baumann because, other than I, there was no one who knew the number of the phone he had provided her.

"Yes, I'm fine thank you, Andrew… Yes, he's well too… No, Jeff has put me in his spare bedroom… Yes, very well, we're getting on just fine… well not everything I need to know but yes, as much as he can. The 3rd did you say? You'll book them? Okay… did you want to speak to Jeff? Okay, bye." She handed the phone to me.

"Hello Andrew."

"Jeff, I'm glad you are able to help Lena out with all she needs to know. I hope it's not too much of an imposition."

"No, no, no imposition. It's all good."

"We need you back on the 3rd. I'll book flights for you and send your tickets to your phones. I'll have someone meet you at the airport. The word is that they think they can pull off a General Assembly on the 7th. Katherine de Villiers would like you and Lena in Washington on the 5th'.

So, it was back on! Even though Lena and I had been talking, seemingly endlessly, about the Kareet, here in sleepy Iluka it seemed a mere abstraction. Now, with a call to Washington and then the prospect of a General Assembly, the whole reality of the situation came thudding back. It was only by dint of some serious effort on our part, and with the assistance of a couple of bottles of good French champagne (thanks again Andrew!), that we were able to derive any joy at all from that night's celebrations.

Chapter 27

I'm at a loss as to why Katherine de Villiers wanted Lena and me in Washington two days before the General Assembly. We were taken to the White House and she met us in the Oval Office. She looked drawn, as well she might, and seemed distracted as she spoke to us. Of all things, she wanted to know if we had a strategy in mind! I was so taken aback that my response may have lacked the courtesy one might normally adopt when addressing a person of such rank. I seem to recall I snorted derisively and said, "Strategy! What the hell kind of strategy do you cook up to deal with an alien force planning to wipe out the vast majority of humanity?"

She eyed me speculatively but, if I had offended her, she gave no sign. Instead, she got up from her chair and began to pace back and forth behind her desk, pausing once to gaze, unseeing, out of a window at the snow-covered Rose Garden below.

"We have to be able to do something." She said as though to herself, and then, more directly to me, "Did you see anything on board their vessel that might be a… a weakness? Something we might be able to exploit?" She looked searchingly at me.

"Madam President," I replied, minding my manners this time, "I'm afraid my head doesn't work that way. I'm not a military person. It wouldn't have occurred to me to look for holes in their defense systems and, even if it had, I'm not an engineer; I couldn't have recognized one if I'd seen it." I shrugged helplessly. "I was escorted to various rooms, my own cabin, that of Alassay Harraan, a large meeting room, a perfectly amazing observation deck and a small club room. At no stage did I see anything remotely resembling a flight deck or control room or anything at all technical."

"What about you MS Sandmeier?" The president turned her attention to Lena. "Have you any thoughts?"

Lena took a deep breath, her eyebrows arched, her eyes round. "The only thought I have had is that the Kareet must be planning to accomplish their ends using a virus, or something microbial. Why else would they want a microbiologist? I imagine they will have an antigen that they'll entrust to me to reproduce in adequate quantities to protect roughly the number of people they intend to survive."

"Why wouldn't you reproduce it in quantities to save everyone?"

"That would be a vast amount. They wouldn't give us enough time to immunize the whole population. Anyway, I don't know for sure, but I'm guessing the antigen will consist of genetic material that will have a limited reproduction cycle."

There really wasn't very much else to say. We shook hands at the door and were escorted to the main entrance where our driver awaited. Lena expressed an interest in doing some shopping. She had heard that Georgetown was the place to go. Shopping is not my thing; I would almost rather have dinner with Guurtsaad Duurn than go shopping! Of course, I feigned enthusiasm, but Lena saw through that in an instant.

"On second thoughts," she said, "perhaps now is not the best time."

We were booked into the Hyatt Place on K Street NW. We hadn't announced our 'engagement', so they had reserved two rooms.

"We'd better use them both, I suppose," I said.

"We'll make love in both beds and decide which one we prefer."

"You're a very naughty girl, but I like you!"

A little after we had returned to the hotel, Baumann rang me. He was keen to meet up. I think he wanted to know what the President had said to us. He was at the Hay Adams, only about 300 yards down the road, so we rugged up and walked.

The hotel had made a small meeting room available for the Prime Minister. A concierge showed us to the door. Andrew Baumann was his usual affable self. We took off our coats and sat in comfortable chairs around an ornate coffee table.

"So now," he said, becoming solemn, leaning forward, elbows on his knees, "how did the meeting with POTUS go?"

Lena and I exchanged glances.

"Oh well, you know, not much came out of it really," I said. "I think she's desperately looking for an angle… an edge really—some chink in their armor."

"Were you able to help?"

"Me?" I laughed. I gave an account of the exchange we'd had. "And then she asked Lena if she had any ideas."

Baumann now turned his attention to her. Lena explained what she imagined the Kareet had in mind and her theory about the likely limitations to the quantity of antigen, as she had to the President. As he shook his head he looked dejected, helpless.

"I don't know what we can do," he said resignedly. "I imagine the military will get all hairy chested and talk about blasting them out of existence but so far no one has even detected their presence in the solar system."

"Heaven knows I'm no military expert," I said, "but even if they could find them, I'm damned sure the Kareet will have defense systems that could easily handle anything we might throw at them."

"Didn't you tell me you were close to Saturn at some stage?"

"Yes, that's right."

"I seem to recall it took *Voyager* over three years to reach Saturn. I suspect the Kareet will have completed their mission and be long gone before we could send a weapon even a tenth of the way there."

The meeting broke up soon after that; what was there to talk about? It was just what I was saying about the trip to

DC in the first place. Lena and I walked back to the hotel, stopping off at a diner for a bite of lunch on the way. The somber mood of both the President and the Prime Minister had rubbed off on me. Lena sensed it. We didn't talk much.

~

New York, New York, so good they named it twice! Well it didn't seem so good that morning of the 7th of January. It was bitingly cold with a nasty wind coming off the East River. We were booked into the Grand Hyatt on East 42nd Street. It was too damned cold to go out, so we had lunch in the hotel.

In the early afternoon, the sun came out and New York looked a little more inviting. We put on coats and scarves and ventured out.

As we were wandering along East 42nd Street, Lena avidly window shopping, a street evangelist who was handing out what appeared to be small sheets of paper with scripture readings printed on them approached me. I don't do religion and I was about to brush him off when I saw, to my amazement, that it was Carlos! He gave no visible sign of recognition but, as he handed me the slip of paper he hissed, "Take it!" I did, and slipped it into my coat pocket. We wandered on. Lena had been oblivious to the event.

I had no idea how Carlos came to be in New York or how he had known where to find me but, while Lena slipped into a shoe shop to look at a pair of shoes that cost more than it would to anti-foul my boat, I slipped the piece of paper out of my pocket. In fine print, that would have truly challenged my eyes before the Kareeti rejuvenation process, were concise instructions on how to answer a call from Carlos on my syncom, with a proposed time of 16:00.

Lena reappeared from the shop with a bag containing a box and a happy smile on her face. As we wandered along I quietly told her of my recent encounter.

Just before four o clock, back in my room, I retrieved the syncom from my baggage and laid out the piece of paper on a small escritoire. Lena and I sat and waited. At precisely four o clock a small blue light flashed and the syncom vibrated quietly. I followed the instructions on the slip of paper. There was a shimmering effect over the bed which, quite quickly, resolved into a hologram of Carlos.

"Hi guys," he said cheesily. "You must be Ms. Sandmeier, the virologist."

Lena was, to her credit, quite calm in the face of this apparition; I suppose my tales must have at least partially prepared her. It was odd speaking with him like this. The voice came from the syncom rather like a normal cell phone on speaker, and seemed completely divorced from the holographic image.

"If you can speak using the syncom, how come I had to have this thing implanted in my neck?" I asked a little tetchily.

"The syncom is used for one-on-one conversations, Jeff. This is as loud as it gets. How many people do you think would hear this in a large meeting room?"

"Well, I could hold it up to a microphone."

"Hah, I don't think that would work very well and,

besides, my hologram can't see you. I can only see you through the lens of the syncom. Alassay Harraan needs to see and hear what's going on. The only practical way to do that is by using your eyes and ears and voice through the channel.

"Anyway, we have to ensure that everything runs smoothly for Alassay Harraan's address to the UN tonight."

He asked me how the arrangements were coming along and, of course, I had to tell him that I had absolutely no idea since I had nothing to do with the arrangements. I blithely suggested he contact the Secretary General of the United Nations as pulling together an extraordinary assembly of the 192 nations was a little above my pay scale!

"I have been advised that the Assembly will be called to order at 19:30 Eastern Standard Time," I told him, "beyond that I can tell you nothing."

He seemed to accept that; well, what else could he do? Carlos ran me through some syncom moves that would increase and decrease the size of the hologram. After several attempts, I seemed to get the hang of it. He made me practice it several more times.

"We have been studying the layout of the General Assembly Hall and we think you should be seated on the rostrum, at the green marble table at the Secretary General's seat. Alassay Harraan's hologram will appear behind you. You will need to enlarge it for such a large audience."

"What if I want to call you?" I asked.

"No point in confusing you with more stuff," he answered offhandedly.

"How do I contact you on the syncom, Carlos?" I
persisted.

"It shouldn't be necessary…'

"Carlos!" I said in a threatening manner.

"Oh well, if you really want to know." He had me
practice the moves several times.

Chapter 28

You cannot begin to imagine the terror that gripped my heart as we entered the United Nations Building that evening. In my professional life I had been a nervous and reluctant public speaker. Of course, it had been necessary, upon occasion, to rise to my feet in front of a room full of business people, but it was never something I was comfortable with and, since retiring, I had become even more, well, retiring! The fact that I didn't have to have a speech prepared and was to be merely the mouthpiece for Alassay Harraan did nothing to quell my fears.

One occasionally sees the General Assembly Hall on television, so one appreciates that it is a very large room. That does nothing to prepare you for walking into the space. The room is one hundred and sixty five feet long, one hundred and fifteen wide, and the ceiling is seventy five feet above your head!

We entered from a door adjacent to the podium, the Secretary General, Gustave Javier, on my right and Katherine de Villiers to my left. I felt like a man going to the gallows. The general hubbub subsided as people noticed that we had entered. No doubt I was a source of much curiosity.

The President of the General Assembly called the house to order and gradually people took their seats and the noise ceased. Once order had been restored, the Secretary General rose to his feet and addressed the Assembly. At this stage I was standing two or three yards behind him and a little to his left. He announced that the extraordinary session had been called in response to a momentous occasion—contact with extra-terrestrial intelligence. That announcement, needless to say, caused an uproar.

When, eventually the Secretary could again make himself heard he continued.

"Indeed, not only has contact been made but we are also to be addressed this evening by one of the leaders of our alien visitors."

There ensued yet another hubbub.

"However, I hasten to add," he continued, somewhat ironically, I thought (since two or three minutes of uproar had passed since his previous words!) 'that our visitor will not be here in person but will, rather, appear in the form of a hologram and will use Mr. Jeffrey Ridsdale," he waved a hand in my direction, "as a… well, as a sort of medium, if you will."

There was a speculative murmur from the assembled.

"They will, apparently, use his voice to convey their message. Mr. Ridsdale was sailing a yacht across the Tasman Sea. He was injured, knocked unconscious, in a storm; when he awoke he found himself aboard a spaceship!"

After a minute or two the ensuing noise subsided.

"I will ask Mr. Ridsdale to take my chair and…' he could not think of the words to finish the sentence. Instead he summoned me, and I shambled across the carpet and took the seat he indicated. He sat to my left in the seat normally occupied by the Deputy Secretary General. I looked out at the world's delegates and gulped. My hands were sweating, and my mouth was dry. As if in telepathic communication with me, an attendant appeared with a flask of water and a glass. I drank deeply and placed the syncom on the desk in front of me. I looked up at the domed ceiling high above and was struck by the uncanny resemblance the dome, with its ring of recessed lights, had to that of the classic image of a flying saucer as seen from below.

I tried to calm my shaking hands so I could perform the hand gestures to summon Alassay Harraan. I repeated them two or three times and then came a loud gasp from the audience. I glanced behind me and there, in crystal clear clarity, though rather small, sat Earth's nemesis. I reproduced the gestures Carlos had taught me that afternoon and watched as Alassay grew to three or four times her real size. I returned my gaze to the front. There was now complete silence. Every face I could see wore a similar expression of utter awe and disbelief.

"Er, ladies and gentlemen, this is Alassay Harraan, senior ambassador of the Kareet." I hadn't planned the introduction but somehow felt compelled to make it. "You may find her means of communication a little strange as she will be using my voice to convey her message to you. Please understand that although you will be hearing my voice none of the words you hear will be mine. Er, thank you." I positioned the microphone so I could sit back in the chair, and tried to relax (fat chance!) and then she began.

Lauren may have described Alassay Harraan as one of Kareedias's most highly respected diplomats and perhaps, like me, you may have formed the impression that diplomats choose their words with tact and delicacy. Not so Alassay Harraan; concise, economical yes, but about as delicate as a wrecking ball. I was reminded, starkly, of how she not only used my vocal chords to transmit her message but was also able to control the tone and intensity of my voice. The assembly was aghast! At times there were loud and emotional eruptions. Alassay paused for these to abate and then continued remorselessly.

She did not invite questions but answered some anyway. Many, she simply ignored, such as, "Even if we are overpopulated, what right do you have…," or, "Shouldn't we have the right to solve these problems ourselves?" She rounded contemptuously on one delegate who spoke of the devastation to the world economy.

"Your so-called economy is indicative of the stupidity of your species! It should be evident to any school student who has learned about compound interest that an economic model that relies upon perpetual annual growth is doomed to failure. As long as you persist with this folly you are forced to stimulate demand, consumption, and you perpetuate the devastation of your world's resources. There are many in your communities who know this, who bring it to the attention of those who purport to lead you, and yet they are ignored! Which arrogant buffoon named your species Homo Sapiens? Wise, you certainly are not!"

I formed the very distinct impression that Alassay Harraan was not in the best of moods! She was doing little for mine for that matter. I was feeling absolutely drained. Somehow, perhaps counter-intuitively, it is far more exhausting being the mouthpiece for someone else than it is to speak for oneself, even though that requires thought, concentration and the formulation of ideas and arguments. I reached into my jacket pocket and withdrew the flask of araanschoz. I had been taught a technique with the syncom to alert Alassay in the event that I needed time out, but I couldn't remember what it was. Instead I raised the flask in front of my eyes and waved it backwards and forwards for a second or two. Clearly, she got the message for there came a pause in whatever it was that she (I) was saying at the time. I took a grateful pull on the flask, swallowed two or three mouthfuls then screwed the cap back on and replaced it in my pocket.

The restorative effects of the fluid take a little while to kick in, but the fluid immediately refreshed my dry throat. Alassay seemed content to give me a short breather.

The President of the United States rose to her feet with a question. "May we know, Alassay Harraan, what time frame you have in mind for your program?"

An expectant hush fell over the hall. After perhaps five seconds during which, presumably, Alassay contemplated her response she said, "I will meet now, in private, in a conference room with the Secretary General and your micro-biologist. Following those discussions, I will advise the Secretary General who will no doubt pass the information on to you. That is all."

I heard myself murmur, "Reduce the hologram Mr. Ridsdale."

"Ah yes." I groped for the syncom where it lay on the desk in front of me and, holding it in my left hand, I closed my eyes and tried desperately to remember the gesture I needed. By now the araanschoz had taken effect and I realized I was actually quite calm. I took a deep breath, exhaled and then, with the appropriate pass of my right hand, reduced the hologram until Alassay was approximately half of her real size.

I looked up. The Secretary General was standing. I rose and followed him. I glanced across to the visitor seating area, to the right of the rostrum, where Lena had been sitting. She had risen to her feet and now walked, a little unsteadily, towards us. I looked at her closely. She looked ashen and drawn. Gustave Javier led the way, Lena fell in on my right. I was holding the syncom in my left hand and the hologram of Alassay Harraan drifted along with us at my left shoulder.

Once we were comfortably ensconced in a meeting room with the door closed behind us, I enlarged the hologram until she was approximately the same size as us. Perhaps Alassay doesn't like crowds but, in any case, away from the tumult of the General Assembly Hall her demeanor changed dramatically. Perhaps not sweetness and light but her manner reminded me very much of my first one-on-one, meeting with her in her quarters aboard the Kareeti ship. She was polite and spoke with apparent respect to the Secretary General; perhaps a shared diplomatic kinship? To Lena she showed warmth and, apparently, genuine interest.

Apparent warmth notwithstanding, by the end of half an hour there was not one of us who wasn't chilled to the very core of our being. The cold hard fact we faced was that, within a matter of no more than three months, we would witness… would be *party* to, the death of the vast majority of the world's human population. The Kareet already possessed the viral agent and the vaccine. They required Lena to manufacture the vaccine in the appropriate quantities and to distribute it to each of the UN delegates who would, in turn, allocate it to the chosen few in their own countries.

After Alassay Harraan had spoken with Lena and established a reasonable time frame for the manufacture of the vaccine, she told us, curtly, that she would speak with Lena and me, in private, the following day. She then took her leave of us.

The Secretary General did not seem overly impressed to be excluded from the planned meeting, but it was not of our doing and nor was there anything that could be done about it. Alassay Harraan, it seemed, was not in negotiation mode.

"I have trouble understanding," Javier murmured meditatively, "if we are to be given the vaccine, why would we not manufacture enough for everyone?"

"Well, to begin with," Lena responded, "there would not be anywhere near enough time to manufacture such quantities but, in any case, the molecule can be reproduced only a certain number of times. We will be given sufficient material to manufacture the specified quantity and no more."

"Ah, I see," was all he said.

When we returned to the assembly, the noise in the chamber was deafening. Everyone, it seemed, was clamoring to be heard. When the Secretary General returned to the rostrum, I stayed with Lena and returned with her to where she'd been seated—I'd had enough limelight for one lifetime! The noise in the chamber abated; more, I suspect from the delegates' need to know what had transpired than the frantic efforts of the President of the General Assembly to bring the rabble to order!

Javier took his place on the rostrum. He pulled his microphone to his mouth. An expectant hush fell upon the assembly. It was short lived. The Secretary General took no more than a minute to summarize what had transpired in the meeting room. The chamber erupted again.

I felt a tap on my shoulder. It was Martin Baumann. He said nothing, merely jerked his thumb over his shoulder. I've seldom been more pleased to see an Australian Prime Minister! Lena and I jumped to our feet and followed him out.

Chapter 29

Baumann had little to say. We stood in the main foyer close to the entry doors and he used his mobile phone to call the driver. He was tight-lipped and ashen-faced. He asked some perfunctory questions, seeming little inclined to hear the response. To his credit, he did seem genuinely concerned about our own personal wellbeing. After a couple of minutes of desultory conversation, the car pulled up outside. He placed a hand on each of our shoulders and mumbled something vaguely paternalistic, then he turned and walked back towards the main chamber.

Lena and I left the building to be greeted by an icy wind whipping in along the East River. We scurried across the footpath and clambered gratefully into the back of the waiting car. I had the driver stop at a liquor store along the way and used Bauman's credit card to buy a bottle of 18-year-old Glenlivet which was outrageously expensive but, what the hell, I'd paid my taxes and I figured I was worth it!

Back in my room at the hotel, I administered the Glenlivet to Lena as a doctor might have given medicine to a patient. She was badly in need of a tonic. I turned the lights down and found an on-line jazz radio station. Lena sat back in a comfortable chair and put her feet up on the coffee table.

"Tough night?"

"Oh, God, yes!" she groaned. "What a nightmare! But it must be terrible for you, so much worse, having to be the… what… the mouthpiece for her?"

I settled for a grimace and a shrug. I topped our glasses.

"There are some small compensations," I said, raising the bottle with a chuckle.

~

At some point during the night I rolled over, half awake, and Lena laid her hand on my arm.

"Are you awake?"

"Mmm."

"Can they eavesdrop on you?"

"Eh?"

"When you are talking to me, say, like right now."

"No, I don't think so. No, I'm sure they can't; why?"

"How do you know?"

"Well, I specifically asked about that when they implanted the channel. Alassay was quite adamant that they are incapable of reading my thoughts and I am physically very aware any time the channel is active, so she can't listen in on me using that."

"What about the syncom?"

"Well that seems to be inert most of the time."

"Is it in here, in the bedroom now?"

"No, I think it's in the other room in my shoulder bag. Why, what's this all about?"

"I want to talk to you about something."

Lena switched on the bedside light, sat up and pulled the bedclothes around her shoulders.

"Should I be getting us another drink?"

"Just water for me."

I poured us each a glass of water.

"Well?"

"Well, what if there was a virus, a highly contagious virus, that made people infertile?"

I looked suitably puzzled, because I was.

"If such a virus got loose it would put an end to human reproduction. That would reduce the population quite dramatically!"

"Yes," I said, uncertainly, where are you going with this?"

"Jeff, I've been worried, for years, well worried is not the word, I've been just appalled by the population problem. I simply couldn't see how the planet could survive unless something really dramatic happened to change the equation. So, some while back I got the idea... well, I'm a microbiologist... I...'

"You've created a virus!"

"Yes, it infects the ovaries, effectively preventing the production of eggs."

"Holy shit!"

"You see, this could achieve the Kareeti objective without killing anyone."

"But if it's highly contagious who's to say it won't make

everybody infertile and just put an end to the human race?"

"It would need a vaccine."

"Have you created one of those as well?"

"Not yet, but I thought the Kareet may be able to help me with that. They seem to be way ahead of us scientifically. If they could create a vaccine using the same principles of limited reproducibility then, instead of me manufacturing an antigen for a virus which will kill, I can be making one to allow some humans to continue to reproduce."

"And the world population will take care of itself through natural attrition."

"Exactly."

"Wow!"

"You don't think I'm awful?"

"Awful? No, certainly not. I think if I had been a microbiologist I might have done the self-same thing!"

We didn't sleep again that night. We discussed whether Alassay Harraan might be willing to consider Lena's idea. I rather thought she might because, when I had met her face to face, she had shown a decent humane side to herself.

Lena had weathered the General Assembly onslaught and had only been partially mollified by the milder approach she had taken with us in the meeting room. She was not at all confident that Alassay would accept a compromise.

We also talked about how best to broach the subject with her.

"Alassay is supposed to be contacting us today; we could talk to her about it then," I suggested.

"I think I'd like to gauge her mood before showing our

hand. I don't think we'll get more than one shot at this, so we need to get her in the right frame of mind," Lena said.

"What if she won't go for it?" I asked.

"We will have to find a bargaining chip."

She was right, of course, but what, what could we possibly use that would give us leverage? We couldn't think of anything on the spur of the moment.

The sky showed signs of lightening. I proposed Lena go and roll around in her bed for a few moments while I made us a cup of coffee. I didn't see any point in telling the world we were an item at this stage.

I had a quick shower and pulled on some clothes. The coffee machine was one of the nearly ubiquitous capsule kind. I've never much liked the coffee they make but they're certainly a lot better than instant. I figured that Lena would shower and dress too, so I made myself a cup and waited for her to appear before making hers.

I was sitting drinking mine when I heard a signal from my phone. Someone had sent me a text message. It was Carlos. He named a diner and proposed we meet for breakfast at 7.30.

We arrived perhaps a minute or two late. I confess I hadn't told Lena of our planned meeting. The diner was busy, but there was a spare booth beside the wall to the rear of the café. We took off our coats and sat side by side facing the door. I handed Lena the menu, a laminated typewritten sheet. We were deciding what to have when someone in a voluminous brown trench coat and a Dick Tracy style fedora mumbled his excuses and sat down opposite us. I was about to explain that we were holding the seat for a friend when I realized that this was Carlos! He put a cup of coffee on the table and, as he sat down, he whipped a dog-eared paperback out of his coat pocket and started, ostentatiously, to read it.

I wondered if the Hybrid had overdosed on American spy movies, what with his street evangelist antics the other day and now this risible charade!

Lena, who didn't even know we were meeting Carlos, was oblivious. As I watched with barely contained mirth, he raised his cup halfway to his mouth, his nose still buried in his book, and out of the corner of his mouth he rasped something that I didn't quite catch. I shook my head and roared with laughter.

Lena looked at me in amazement. Carlos, on the other hand, glared at me. I was helpless! I was rocking in my seat, tears beginning to roll down my cheeks. Carlos pushed open the corner of his mouth and hissed something else incomprehensible out of it. I had no idea what he said but it simply escalated my already out of control hilarity. I was aware that Lena was looking at me agape. I think I must have raised a hand and pointed to Carlos as the source of my mirth. The realization that Lena hadn't recognized him and simply thought I was being outrageously rude to a stranger only made me laugh all the harder. I thought, if I don't get this under control, they'll take me out in a strait jacket!

They say laughter is contagious and, by now, a couple of people nearby had noticed me laughing and were beginning to chuckle. This was ridiculous, I was almost hysterical!

Lena had laid her hand on my arm and, with her other

was stroking the back of my neck as I gasped for breath and rocked back and forth in my seat. Eventually I began to get myself under control, but even as it subsided, little aftershocks of mirth would continue to rock me. I cannot begin to imagine how long it had been since I had laughed like that; most of a lifetime I supposed.

As I regained control the bemused onlookers gradually lost interest and went back to their own conversations.

"My God, Jeff! What was that all about?" Lena asked, eyes wide.

"Oh dear," I said, still struggling a little, and then, lowering my voice conspiratorially, (which almost set me of again) 'this is Carlos."

Lena looked confused.

Carlos looked around furtively as if to see if I'd blown his cover.

I almost started laughing again.

I turned inward to face Lena and, with lowered voice, said to Carlos, "Listen sport, I cannot imagine why you think this whole cloak and dagger business is necessary but, given my little outburst there is nothing more natural than that you, as a stranger, should strike up a conversation with me."

He closed his book and stuffed it into his pocket as though it were something vaguely shameful.

"Lena," I said, in a voice that I judged would not be overheard in the general hubbub of the diner, "you saw Carlos as a hologram yesterday afternoon."

A look of comprehension dawned upon her face. Carlos

lifted the brim of his hat until it sat at a rakish angle on the back of his head. This nearly set me off again! Once Lena had nodded her recognition he pulled it back low, shadowing his face.

"We cannot be too careful." he said, barely audibly. "What on Earth were you doing laughing like that? Are you trying to draw attention to us?"

"I suspect you wouldn't understand," I said trying to suppress the laughter that I could feel stirring inside me again.

Lena glared at me which seemed to help a little.

"Alassay Harraan had arranged to meet with you today," Carlos said, evidently concluding he wasn't going to get a satisfactory explanation for my outlandish behaviour. "Well, she's not going to now."

"Oh," I said.

"No, she wants you to take Lena somewhere where we can pick her up and take her to our vessel."

"What, say, Central Park, Times Square?"

"Don't be facetious." Carlos frowned. "You already know that we will not put a scout down anywhere we could be intercepted."

"Well, I'm sorry," I replied, "but this is not the best time or place to organize such a rendezvous. To start with, I'm a stranger in New York, I have no means of independent transport, I wouldn't even know where to go if I did, and if there is any place on Earth where you are less likely to escape detection then I don't know where that is!"

Carlos appeared to take all of this in and ruminated upon it for a moment or two.

I cut in across his meditation. "Look, if you can persuade Alassay Harraan to wait a few days, we will be going back to Australia. It will be very much easier to arrange something there."

"Mm, I get the impression Alassay Harraan is impatient to move things along, but I get your point. I guess I can only try."

"Yeah, okay, send me a text when you've got her response."

"Oh, and by the way, he continued, "I'm sure I don't have to tell you that you must keep all of this highly confidential. I understand the Secretary General has required each of the delegates to commit to secrecy for fear of causing widespread panic."

"How would you keep something like this secret?" I asked.

"I think the plan is to let the world know that contact has been made but not to mention…."

I nodded.

Carlos made a show of finishing his coffee. He stood up and offered his hand and, in a voice too loud, said, "really nice to have met you folks." He shook our hands, turned up his collar and sidled out. It was all I could do not to burst out laughing again!

Chapter 30

I was given to understand that Alassay Harraan was irritated by my proposed delay, but she understood the logic. So, while she drummed her fingers with impatience, we flew back to Australia. I made that sound simple but of course it wasn't! The Secretary General had been present when Alassay Harraan had called a meeting with Lena and me for the following day and he wanted to be brought up to speed.

Baumann picked us up in a car that had been placed at his disposal. The driver dropped us at the main doors and took off. We were met inside the door by a woman in a business suit. She led us to a meeting room. Gustave Javier and Katherine de Villiers were waiting for us.

When I explained that Alassay Harraan had called off the meeting, I was pressed hard for an explanation. That put me in a quandary, but I chose, in the end, to tell them the truth.

"The simple fact is," I explained, "the Kareet have studied our planet and our people for decades now and have concluded that it is not safe to… to appear to the world, to

"

visit us if you like, because we cannot be trusted not to do something rash."

"Rash?" Javier enquired.

"Bring in the military, start lobbing bombs in their direction."

"Well, I suppose that's not unreasonable!" Baumann said. The Secretary General and the President looked at him askance. "Well, you've only to look at the world over the past… well, however long you care to look back," he offered a little bashfully.

"But I understood that the meeting was to take the same format as the one last evening—the alien… woman…'

"Alassay Harraan," I interposed

"Yes her, appearing as a hologram," he continued.

"I gather she only wanted to arrange for Lena to be picked up and transported to their vessel," I replied. I then thought it diplomatic to embellish the truth a little. "Alassay Harraan was unwilling to risk exposing a scout vessel to U.S. Military eyes. She wants us to return to Australia and arrange a rendezvous somewhere discreet."

"But now that we know about this we have merely to follow you to your discreet location," the President reasoned.

"Well, in the first place, I was not supposed to tell you any of this and, second, I am hoping you will see the futility of attempting any kind of interception. I am hoping you will allow us to return to Australia and arrange this transfer without interference." I hoped I hadn't pushed my luck too far.

There followed a short discussion between the leaders,

finally concluding that I was right, and any attempts at an interception could, at best, achieve nothing and, quite possibly, make matters worse, if that were possible.

However, what I should have foreseen, and stupidly didn't, was that they would latch onto the fact that Lena was to be going aboard their vessel. Surely this was an opportunity? Suddenly there seemed a chink in their armor, a glimmer of hope that there may be a way out of our predicament.

The President wanted to bring in the Chairman of the Joint Chiefs of Staff. Baumann was dreaming up substitution ploys while Lena and I were looking at one another in alarm, wondering just what I had unleashed.

"Madam President, if I may," I interjected haltingly.

Katherine de Villiers' eyes swung to me expectantly.

"Madam President, I am alarmed at what I am hearing! I really don't think we should be contemplating an aggressive act."

"But they are contemplating the ultimate aggressive act against us!"

"Yes, that's true, but they do hold all of the trump cards."

"Well, perhaps not any more. Perhaps we do have a card up our sleeve."

"I can only guess that you're thinking of a Trojan Horse." She nodded. "But if we fail…'

"What is the worst that can happen? We're already facing the greatest human catastrophe since mankind walked the Earth!"

"But you'd be putting Lena at unacceptable risk."

She looked at me as if I had taken leave of my senses.

"So, it's okay for…'

"No, no," I held my hands up in surrender, "I'm sorry, I get it. I really do."

"Can I make a suggestion?" Lena interposed. "Unless Jeff can tell us, we have no knowledge of their screening process for people coming aboard their vessel."

"Well I can't help you. I was taken aboard unconscious. When I woke I was naked. They had removed and quarantined my clothes. I have no idea whether they scanned me or probed me or… whatever."

"So, I suggest that before we make any decisions, if I am to go aboard, I should carry nothing with me. I can then ascertain what security measures they take. Then, if it is feasible to do so, I could carry something with me on a subsequent visit."

"What if there is no subsequent visit?" the President asked.

"I'm sure I can manufacture a reason to have to go back on board."

"How? You don't know what they are going to do with you on the first visit."

"Well, I'm sure they intend to ascertain my competence in micro-biology and will, no doubt give me instructions…'

"And the seed material for this vaccine, and send you back to Earth. So why would you need to go back again?"

Lena didn't have an answer for that. The question was left hanging.

"Well, we'll have to give it some serious thought. When do you plan to return to Australia?"

"As soon as possible. I gather Alassay Harraan is impatient to begin!"

We returned to our hotel. I was pensive and somewhat taciturn. We sat in the armchairs in my suite and I poured us each a glass of Baumann's Glenlivet. Lena seemed similarly preoccupied so we sat in companionable silence. What was bothering me was my apparent aversion to any notion of retaliation against the Kareet. I couldn't understand it. I am a pacifist by disposition, but I am sufficiently pragmatic to recognize that there are times, in the face of 'clear and present danger' when it is necessary to make a stand. Nobody could dispute that the Kareet represented 'clear and present danger', greater, no doubt, than any mankind had ever faced. I should be in favor of popping a thermonuclear device into them, and ridding ourselves of them and the threat they posed. Yet I wasn't.

I mulled it over. I rationalized that even if we did destroy the alien vessel, all that was likely to do was to enrage the powers-that-be back on Kareedias who would then, in all probability, send a punitive force. Not that this wasn't a punitive force but, I suppose what I was thinking, was any action we took now, if it were successful, would only delay the inevitable.

I think I realized that, although this was undoubtedly true, I had only now just thought of it, so it was unlikely to be the source of my reticence. I wondered if I felt some sense of attachment to Lauren and Carlos and the other Hybrids; Alassay Harraan even. I thought I probably did but, obviously, if it were a choice between them and eighty per cent of humanity there was simply no contest.

But then I wondered if perhaps I was actually sympathetic to the Kareeti cause. That was a dreadful thought! No, God no! No, I couldn't countenance the mass destruction of all of that human life, not in a million years. Yet, there was something that Lena had said that had triggered something in my brain. What if she were able to release a virus that would make human beings infertile? There would be no mass extinction event, no immediate loss of life. People would die in the natural course of events and they simply wouldn't be replaced.

"You seem deep in thought," Lena said.

"Er, yes, yes I am," I replied, shaking myself out of my reverie.

"What are you thinking about?"

"Well, I'm thinking hard about why I feel so reluctant to become involved in action against the Kareet. And I'm thinking a great deal about your infertility virus."

"Ah," she said. "Yes, and what were you thinking?"

"Well I suppose I was thinking it would be a very good thing if we could release that rather than the Kareeti virus."

"I've been thinking the same thing. I'm trying to think how I might persuade them to cooperate with us and help me develop the antigen."

Later that afternoon, Martin Baumann called me on the phone he had given me. We arranged to meet in the cocktail bar of our hotel. All very informal and incognito. He arrived in a heavy, dark green overcoat scarf and woolly hat. Snowflakes were still melting on his shoulders. A waitress helped him out of his coat and took it to a cloakroom. He joined us at a table beside a window looking out over a winter wonderland.

"A little different to Sydney!" he said as he sat down opposite us.

"Not too unlike Salzburg," Lena replied drolly.

We ordered drinks from the waitress and made small talk until they arrived.

"Well, it's all been decided," he said as he tinkled the ice around in his glass. "You can fly back tomorrow. I've had someone book you on a flight, and the details will be sent to your mobile phone. They've agreed not to attempt to smuggle anything aboard but, Lena, you are going to have to pay very close attention to their security systems so we can work out how we can get something aboard."

"You do realize, don't you," I interjected, "if we somehow manage to destroy the Kareeti vessel, it will be only a matter of time before they return with a fleet of ships ready to exact awful revenge."

Baumann made a thin line of his mouth and shrugged. "I think worrying about global security is a little above your pay grade, don't you?"

"I most certainly do!" I re-joined. "Especially since I don't even have a pay grade!"

"Ah well, now that's something I've been thinking about, and I think we can perfectly reasonably bill the United Nations for consultancy fees. But leave that with me, I don't think you'll be disappointed. As to the Kareet and our response to them, I fear that is out of our control. All we can do is counsel as we see fit and follow orders if our advice is declined."

I could have argued with that, but I thought it prudent to keep my own counsel!

Chapter 31

To Martin Baumann's eternal credit, he had booked Lena and me into first class. I had never had the privilege of travelling in such style before. The food was excellent and, of course, we had beds! What luxury! We were able to get a really good night's sleep. I had certainly never disembarked an airplane feeling more refreshed than I had before I'd boarded it, yet this was exactly how I felt when we arrived in Sydney. Consequently, the interconnect to Ballina was not nearly as arduous as I had anticipated.

Having said that, we were both of us exhausted by the time we pulled up at the house in Iluka. I took the bags upstairs. Lena peeled down to her underwear and plonked herself on a recliner on the deck. It was 85^0 and it was seven in the evening. It had been below freezing when we left New York. It took a bit of keeping up with, this inter-hemisphere travel! I handed Lena a glass of ice cold beer. She smiled her appreciation.

"I'll have to get used to this heat again," she said, sipping her beer, "but, God it's good to be back here away from all of that." She waved a hand as if to flick something unpleasant off her fingers. We sat and gazed out across the Clarence towards Yamba. The sun was still nearly an hour from setting.

"I've been thinking," I said, "I'm not going to let you go up there alone. I'm coming with you."

Lena looked at me wide eyed. "Will they let you?"

"I think so. I'll tell them that if they don't agree I won't cooperate with taking you to meet the scout."

"Is that a good idea?"

"I don't see why not. What are they going to do? They don't want to bring their scout down anywhere near civilization. You have to get there somehow. I don't have to agree to help them."

Lena thought for a while. She held up her empty glass and I ambled off to the fridge.

"Well I would certainly appreciate the company," she said with a soft laugh. I smiled too. She had made it sound like we were discussing a stroll to the shops!

I confess I didn't feel much like confronting Alassay Harraan with my ultimatum, so I dug out the syncom and attempted to call up Carlos. Let him be the messenger, I reasoned. I checked my notebook. My memory is not all it may once have been. I had assiduously written out all the gestures I needed for the syncom. I waved my hands about and said 'Abracadabra!"

Nothing much seemed to happen, so I tried again (without the Abracadabra!) Again— nothing. I was desperately checking my notes when suddenly the blue light flashed a couple of times. I looked up and Carlos shimmered into existence.

"Hello Jeff, where on Earth are you?"

"Welcome to Iluka, Carlos. What happened to the super sleuth? I thought you knew our every move."

Carlos managed to look confused, hurt and angry all at the same time which I thought was a pretty good effort!

"How's the weather in New York? Bit bloody cold I expect! Nice and warm here!"

Lena, who had wrapped a sarong around herself, raised a glass to him. "Cheers Carlos."

"I have a message for Alassay Harraan, old chum. I need you to tell her I will be coming along with Lena."

"You mean bringing her to meet the scout?"

"No, I mean coming aboard the scout and accompanying her onto your main vessel."

"Oh, I don't think that would be acceptable."

"Not negotiable, sport. I come with her or I don't take her to meet the scout."

"Why don't you try telling Alassay Harraan?" he asked, evidently peeved.

"You're the go-between, mate, your job. Oh, and that's non-negotiable too!"

We had no food in the house, so we wandered down to Sedgers again. We were very lucky to be served as they were shutting up the kitchen as we arrived. It was a choice between the greyhound racing in the bar or the mozzies outside. We had slapped on repellent before leaving the house, so chose the latter.

Our dinner plates were empty, and we were on the last of the wine when my mobile phone buzzed. It was a text from Carlos; grudging approval from Alassay Harraan. I was to nominate a time and location within twenty-four hours. I texted back acknowledgement and told him I would work out a rendezvous and let him know later that evening.

"Are you nervous?" I asked Lena as we lay in bed later that night.

"Yes, of course," she replied.

I squeezed her hand in what I hoped was a reassuring gesture.

"Have you given any more thought to how you'll persuade them to adopt your plan?"

"I've hardly thought of anything else. I suppose I hope she'll see reason. I mean surely she can see that this is a far more humane solution."

"I'm not entirely sure the Kareet do 'humane'."

"But you told me Alassay Harraan seemed intelligent, sensitive...'

"Yeah, but she's not *human*. To the Kareet, humans are a pest, a parasite that's killing its host—this world! They may well have no more concern for our wellbeing than we do for a tape worm."

Lena turned her head and stared at me, aghast. "Do you really mean that?"

"Well, I don't actually *know*. I suppose I'm trying to think of all this from their alien, perspective. Anyway, Alassay is our best hope; as I said she does seem to have some sensitivity. Let's hope, eh?" I finished lamely.

"Well, I've tried to think of other ways to persuade her, but I keep drawing a blank. One thing's for sure, I'm not going to try to covertly take anything aboard their vessel until I've been there and know a lot more about their screening processes."

"No, of course not, nor should you. Have you worked out how to wangle your way back on board a second time?"

"Mm, that bit doesn't bother me too much. It will be easy to make a compelling case that an assistant failed to follow correct procedures and contaminated the material."

"What, the material they give you to work on?"

She nodded.

"That could make them pretty angry. What if they then don't have sufficient… material, as you put it, to resupply you? They might go back to Plan A, i.e.: Guurtsaad Duurn's way of doing things!"

"I guess I'll have to get some sense of the available quantities when I'm with them. Otherwise I'll have to come up with something else."

"Like what?"

"Oh, I don't know!" I sensed her irritation, so I didn't pursue it.

~

The following afternoon we set off in the Land Rover for Jackadgery, a small rural town north west of Grafton. Beyond the township, about halfway to Cangai, the Jackadgery Bridge crosses the Mann River. A few miles on from there, just past the Cangai Creek, a small track crosses the Gwydir Highway; take the left-hand track and it takes you up a spur with open land on either side. I had reasoned that few, if any, people would be around at sunset. I had picked that time of day because the Kareet had insisted on twilight when they picked up Lauren.

The sun had set some time before I pulled off the track and trundled a short distance across the short grass. I was right, there was no one around. We hadn't seen any sign of life since we passed the Mann River Caravan Park—well, human life anyway. I tucked the car in under some trees, pretty much out of view from the track. Just in case, I left a note on the dashboard: 'Gone Hiking'.

"It feels strange taking nothing," Lena said as she pushed the door closed.

"Yeah, I hope you're not too attached to what you're wearing because it may be the last you'll see of it."

We walked out into the clearing. I scanned the sky but could detect no movement. I placed the syncom in the palm of my hand and gestured in the manner Carlos had described earlier that afternoon. The blue light flashed, nothing else. I shrugged and slipped it back in my trouser pocket. I put an arm around Lena. "How're you feeling?"

"I'm terrified!" I could feel the tension in her body.

"Fair enough," I replied, "it's not every day you go for a ride in a space ship." She dug her elbow into my ribs, but I could sense her relax just a little.

I thought I noticed a glint high in the now violet sky. I tried to track it, but it eluded me. Barely a moment later I heard Lena gasp and felt her clutch at my arm. Her eyes were wide and directed down the hill below the level at which we were standing. I followed her gaze. The scout came drifting up the hill towards us at a leisurely pace, barely three feet above the ground. It stopped perhaps twenty yards away from us. A line of light appeared in the lower section of what I suppose I'd call its hull, and then the telescoping walkway folded out towards us. We stood a moment or two, spellbound. Nothing further happened. I snapped out of my reverie. "They're waiting for us to go aboard," I said. I took Lena by the elbow and we made our way haltingly to the scout.

Part 5

Chapter 32

Lena and I were led into separate cubicles. White clad Kareeti medicos surrounded me. I was told to undress—by sign language, as these aliens did not speak English. My body was scanned by some device, a sample of my blood was taken, and my mouth was swabbed. That seemed to be all. I was left sitting on an examination table with a light blanket around my shoulders. Perhaps fifteen minutes elapsed, during which I sat alone with my thoughts, and then the door swooshed open. A medico walked in carrying one of the outfits they had made for me on my previous visit.

Once I was dressed, I was again left to wait. Eventually the door opened again, and I was summoned to follow the Kareet. As I emerged into the corridor Lena was ushered out of the adjacent cubicle. She too was dressed in the familiar Kareeti tunic and leggings and, like mine, hers was the same deep claret color. I thought she looked very appealing in her outfit. The expression on her face told me she was struggling to come to grips with all that was happening to her, and I could certainly understand that.

"Hello, Jeff."

I looked up, startled. Since we had climbed aboard the scout we had not encountered anyone who spoke English.

It was Miriam. Miriam the beautiful, Miriam who looked young enough to be my granddaughter but was, in fact, (if the Hybrids were to be believed) forty-eight years old!

"Hello Miriam, this is Lena."

Miriam smiled brightly and advanced with her hand extended. She welcomed Lena warmly. I was grateful for this small mercy because I could feel Lena let go some of her tension.

"Come on you two, I'll show you to your quarters."

We had only a few steps to make it to a lift. The lift ascended. We emerged into a corridor that looked exactly the same as any other corridor on the ship that I had ever been in. I wondered how the Kareet ever learned to find their way around their vessel. We walked perhaps twenty yards and came to one of those, by now familiar, hexagonal vestibules. Miriam stroked a panel and two adjacent doors slid open.

"Yours," she said with a smile, looking at me and indicating the door to the left. "Perhaps we can go into yours first, Lena," she said, indicating the other doorway, "and have a little chat."

I had Lena sit in the comfortable recliner while Miriam and I swung stools out from beneath the bench. Lena's eyes were still wide and staring, and I was very conscious of her inner turmoil.

"Miriam, any chance of a drop of araanschoz for Lena? I think this is all a bit overwhelming."

"Oh yes, of course, how remiss of me!" She reached into her tunic and produced a flask. "I had it with me but I just—' She poured some into a cup.

Lena looked to me for reassurance and, in response to my smile of encouragement, ventured a sip of the liquid. She evidently found it inoffensive for she quickly drank the rest of the cupful.

"So, how are you Miriam?" I asked in a fatuous attempt to make conversation. I didn't want Lena to have us focusing on her. Let the araanschoz work its wonders and then we can get down to the business Miriam was doubtless charged with addressing.

After we had chatted for a few minutes, talking of the work the Hybrids were doing on the vessel and who knows what else? (I wasn't exactly concentrating!) I looked across at Lena. I could see the Kareeti potion had worked its magic. She looked calm and alert.

"Well now, Miriam, I said, changing the subject, "what's the programmer for tonight?"

Miriam, too, glanced at Lena, as if to confirm to herself that she was up to it.

"Alassay Harraan is eager to talk to you, Lena. She will be eating now so I will order food for you then, when you've eaten, I will take you to her."

"That's both of us, you'll take both of us to her."

"Well, no, actually Alassay Harraan wanted to speak to Lena."

"But I insist on going with her. I didn't come aboard here to twiddle my thumbs."

"Twiddle your thumbs?"

"It's perhaps an idiom you haven't come across; it doesn't matter. What matters is that I get to accompany Lena."

Miriam looked uncomfortable.

"I will order you food and speak to Alassay Harraan," she said, then left us alone.

"Wait till you see the food!" I laughed

"Terrible?"

"No, not terrible, it's okay; but completely different to anything we are used to."

When the food did come it was the same as the first meal they gave me when I first came aboard.

"There's not much variety either, as far as I can tell."

"Mm, it's not bad, really," she mumbled with a vaguely puzzled look.

We were washing down our repast, such as it was, with a glass of water, when the door beeped, a blue light flashed and after a pause the door slid open.

Miriam stepped in. "I'm not disturbing you? Only you didn't respond to the entry request."

"I wasn't aware that there was such a thing as an 'entry request', and would have no idea how to respond to one even if I did."

Miriam took us to the panel adjacent to the door and explained a few of the workings.

"Ah well, that's enlightening," I muttered. "I don't think such niceties were afforded me on my last visit!"

Miriam chose to ignore this. "Alassay Harraan is ready to see you now and, yes Jeff, you can go too."

"Ah, good!" was all I said in reply.

The door to Alassay's suite slid open and we stepped inside. Miriam took her leave. Alassay was standing, as was her wont, it seemed, at the large porthole gazing out at the universe. The door closed, and she turned.

"Welcome aboard our vessel, Lena," she said walking towards us wearing the Kareeti version of a smile. "And you, *Mr. Ridsdale*," she said somewhat icily, "can be very difficult to get on with!"

I smiled. "You are not the first to observe that!" I replied.

She gestured towards the 'coffee table' as we would term it, although I had never seen the Kareet indulge in anything that at all resembled coffee.

"Perhaps a little hiftervess will make you a little more agreeable." She brought goblets and a bottle of the amber liquid. "Please, do sit."

We arranged ourselves comfortably around the low table. Alassay poured, we raised our goblets in an awkward, inappropriate salute, and then drank.

"So, what is behind this difficult behaviour of yours, Mr. Ridsdale?"

"Difficult behaviour, *Mr. Ridsdale*? Whatever became of 'may I call you Jeff'?"

"When I feel better disposed to people I am more likely to feel inclined to address them by their forename."

"Well, I'm perfectly happy for you to call me Mr. Ridsdale. Since I do not feel 'well disposed' to you I would not expect you to be so to me!"

"Mm, we are churlish today! Should I expect this to

continue or is it just a passing mood?"

"Listen, Alassay, I am not in a particularly bad mood. You are talking about killing most of the population of my world, so you can hardly expect to be on my list of favorite people. I have not been particularly 'churlish'. What I have been is utterly determined to stay beside Lena throughout all of this."

"Why? Is she not grown up enough to do this on her own?"

"Lena is very capable, but it is very stressful and confronting for any human being who, until a few days ago, did not believe in aliens or, if they did think there could in theory be extra-terrestrial intelligence, didn't believe that we would ever be visited by it. To now come face to face with the reality; especially when that extra-terrestrial is hell bent on wiping out civilization as we know it…well! So, I want to be here to lend her emotional support."

"Why?"

"Because I love her!"

I glanced at Lena, realizing as I said it, that I had never actually told her that I loved her.

She smiled at me warmly.

"Ah *love*! You humans and *love*! I'm convinced half of the problems you have on this world are because of *love*!"

"Maybe so," I said, bristling and ready for a fight, "but it is also because of love that we have such extraordinary achievements in art, literature, music and architecture."

"Do you not have love on your world?" Lena cut in.

"Well, we do; but it is not the irrational stupefying

affliction that it appears to be on Earth."

"But you have love and compassion for your fellow Kareet and you must love your children, surely?" Lena continued.

"The Kareet *care* for one another," Alassay replied, I thought a little guardedly. "We are inculcated with a sense of duty from birth."

"Not love? You must surely love your children?"

"Those of us that have children appear to 'love' them. You have to understand, Lena, that few Kareet ever have children."

"Few? Why is that?"

"Well, to start with, we either lacked in the first place, or had bred out of us, the compulsion to procreate. Not every Kareet wants to parent children. If they do, then they must first gain a permit."

"A permit?" Lena asked, startled.

"Yes. And I fail to understand why it isn't so on your world. Compared with humans, the Kareet are very much more disciplined, considered, thoroughly socialized and more highly educated. Even having said that, many of our people we consider unsuited to procreation. Therefore, if a couple wants to have children, they must first satisfy the authorities that they would make suitable parents."

"By what criteria are they judged?" Lena asked.

"They are genetically tested to eliminate, as far as possible, genetic defects, their level of education is taken into account, they are quizzed on their values and their attitudes, their income and income security is assessed, and an evaluation of their relationship is carried out to ensure, as much as one can, that their children will grow up in a nourishing, well balanced family setting."

"My God! It sounds awful—Orwellian," Lena said.

"Really? I observe your world where people are allowed to breed without constraint and what I see is utterly dystopian. I see millions in devastating poverty bringing babies into a world of pain, starvation and misery. I see people with gross genetic disorders bringing children into the world who will, in turn, suffer the same fate as their parents. I see terrible family violence and the abuse of children replicating itself from one generation to the next. I see parents who lack education, have no real moral compass, no appreciation of ethics, who don't even understand the basics of nutrition, having one baby after another who grow into obese, ignorant, uneducated, unemployable adults who will be a drain on the welfare system for the rest of their lives and, in all likelihood be perpetrators of crime. Is this your idea of Utopia?"

Lena fell silent.

"You must have a very small population," I ventured.

"We do have a small population, compared to that of Earth. We ensure that we have a population that does not consume resources in excess of the planet's ability to regenerate them."

"How then does your economy function?" Lena asked.

"Ah now, this is another great fallacy that afflicts humanity. Your economic models are predicated on annual growth."

Lena nodded as though it were axiomatic.

"If your economy can only function if it achieves growth then you must, of necessity, have an ever-increasing population and that ever-increasing population will consume an ever-greater quantity of resources. Your population is already consuming vastly more resources than the planet can replenish, and your population steadily grows!

"It should be immediately apparent to anyone with basic arithmetic skills that you cannot continue to grow your economy."

Lena looked at her questioningly.

"You are familiar with the effect of compound interest; little growth is experienced for a long time and then, if represented on a graph, the curve starts to rise much more rapidly until it becomes effectively vertical. Or, to put it another way; assume you start with an economy of a billion dollars and you require a growth rate of 3% per year to make your economic model work. After a hundred years, the economy will have grown to 19.2 billion, which seems reasonable and within the realms of your current experience of economies. After five hundred years though, the economy, if it has to continue to grow at 3%, will have grown to 2.62 quadrillion dollars!"

It didn't take a genius to see that that couldn't work!

"How do you know these figures?" I asked.

"I just worked them out." She saw the look of disbelief on my face and smiled. "I think I've already told you, Jeff, the Kareeti brain is wired very differently to the human brain.

"Ah, so it's Jeff now!" I said by way of a pathetic retort.

"Lena," she said, choosing to ignore my infantile taunt, "you are an intelligent woman, you can surely see the devastating effect that overpopulation is having on the Earth: the mass extinctions, the degradation of the soils, the air, fresh water, and what you're doing to the oceans is simply insanity."

"But the solution you are proposing—'

"Would not have been necessary had the world taken sensible steps even fifty years ago. The population was far too large then, at perhaps 4.2 billion, but had the world followed China's lead in 1979 and introduced the 'One Child' policy, global population would have declined significantly. With a smaller population you would use fewer resources, you would require less energy and you would require less of the Earth's surface for habitation and agriculture, which would mean you would need to destroy far less of the natural habitat and produce much less pollution."

"And you don't have any of these problems on your planet?" I interjected.

"No, as I have told you, we have a sustainable population. We do not degrade our world, we do not threaten the existence of other species and we do not have millions, if not billions of people starving and living in the most abject poverty."

I glanced at Lena, who looked as glum as I felt.

Alassay Harraan poured more hiftervess into our goblets.

"Alassay," Lena began, tentatively. "Believe it or not I

have considerable sympathy with the views you're expressing. I too hold very grave concerns for the future of Earth but I, as a microbiologist, have contemplated a different solution."

Alassay Harraan looked interested. "Go on," she said.

"I have actually developed a virus which directly attacks the human reproductive system. If this were to be broadcast in the manner in which I imagine you must be planning to seed the planet with your pathogen, then it would put an immediate hold on population growth. That way nobody need be forcibly killed and the same objective is attained, but I'd need your help to develop the antigen."

"Too late," Alassay replied peremptorily. "Had you released that fifty years ago it would have been the correct solution. Now it is too late. The devastation your species is wreaking on the planet with your current population is not sustainable. We cannot wait for natural attrition to address the problem. And did you say you have yet to develop the antigen? Even further delays and, frankly, I am having considerable difficulty persuading Guurtsaad Duurn to remain here while we go through this process with you."

"But what alternative does he have?" Lena asked, clearly puzzled.

"Ah ha! You do not know Guurtsaad Duurn! If he had had his way we would have arrived in your solar system, sent our scouts out to sow the virus and departed without you even suspecting our presence."

"But what about the antigen? How would any human life be preserved?" Lena asked, shocked.

"Please do not think, for one moment, that Guurtsaad Duurn could care less if your species were to become extinct. He has no more concern for you or your wellbeing than you have for an annoying house fly! He is a very ambitious Kareetur—we don't talk of men and women, male Kareet are Kareetur, female, Kareeten—and as far as he is concerned, opportunity is passing him by while he languishes in this desolate solar system so far from home."

"But won't you please at least consider my proposal?" Lena pleaded. "Our species may not be important to the Kareet, but it certainly is to us."

"No, it is out of the question. You will rest for what would be 'the night' in your frame of reference and 'tomorrow', we will introduce you to the Kareeten who runs our laboratories. She, at least, speaks your language."

And, with that, our interview concluded. Miriam was at the door to escort us back to our quarters.

Chapter 33

We remained, that night, in our own separate quarters; the bunks provided in those cabins were barely large enough to accommodate my frame, let alone the two of us. The following morning, or when I woke, (morning noon and night having no context on a vessel cruising the outer solar system!) the light in my quarters was bright. In the absence of sunshine, the Kareet manipulated the cabin lights to synchronize with our circadian rhythms.

When I emerged from the bathroom I noticed a tray on the bench near the door. I smiled. It was not so much different to a motel back home. The hatch opens, and your breakfast is shoved in for you.

I had just finished eating when the light flashed a couple of times. I had come to realize this was the equivalent of a knock on the door, I tried to recall what Miriam had taught me about the comms panel beside the door the night before. I pressed a button, the door whooshed open and Miriam stood at the threshold.

"You seem to have mastered the door controls," she smiled

"Well, now I know how, I can go and visit Lena."

"Well, no, actually you can't," she replied, "she's gone to the laboratories."

"Oh," I replied, a touch crestfallen.

"But I've come to invite you to the Hybrid Club," she said cheerfully. "There'll be some you already know there, and they're keen to meet you again."

Katrina and Stephan greeted me warmly as soon as I stepped inside the room, whereupon Lauren emerged from the kitchenette alcove. She seemed genuinely pleased to see me, which surprised me not a little! The last time I had seen her she had seemed quite cool and detached, apart from the sudden hug. Ah well, that's Hybrids for you, I thought wryly. I glanced around the room. There were others whom I had not yet met.

"Would you like a cup of tea, Jeff?" asked Lauren.

"I didn't know you had tea!"

"Well, it seemed so popular in Australia that I was given permission to bring a very small, quantity on board. We took it to the labs and they have synthesized it."

Clearly my face betrayed my thoughts, ('synthesized tea? You can't synthesize tea! That would be awful') because Lauren giggled.

"I think you will be pleasantly surprised," she said and disappeared into the kitchenette again.

"So, no Carlos?" I asked conversationally.

Katarina shrugged.

"I believe he's still in New York," Miriam said.

"Good luck to him." I grinned. "Bloody cold there at this time of the year!"

Stephan beckoned a couple of Hybrids over to come and meet me.

"Jeff this is Varsha."

She smiled, stepped forward and took my hand.

"And this is Bohai."

He also shook my hand.

"I gather your name reflects that of your human parent," I said, "so does that mean your mother came from India?" I asked Varsha.

"Well, actually in my case the donor was my father. I don't know if he was asked what name he would like me to have or whether the Kareet simply gave me an Indian name."

"Yes, well, my donor was a Chinese man and I believe his name was also Bohai," the other Hybrid offered before I could ask.

Stephan indicated some easy chairs and we all sat and chatted. Lauren appeared with a tray.

"Tea!" she said perkily, "white, no sugar, I believe," and placed a steaming mug before me.

"Milk? Synthesized I take it!"

She nodded. Lauren was right, I was pleasantly surprised. The tea seemed every bit as good as any I might make in the old teapot at home.

Varsha and Bohai both seemed very eager to chat about Earth. Their work did not require them to visit the planet, so they had never been. I answered innumerable questions until Varsha seemed suddenly to realize they were monopolizing my time. I, on the other hand, was keen to ask a few questions of my own. I had not even begun to think of strategies or angles, but I figured I should get to know as much as I possibly could about how the Kareeti vessel operated. Anything at all I could glean about their systems may, in the future, prove useful.

I was also very keen to get a feel for any hint of pro-Earth sympathies that I might, at some point, be able to exploit, though how I had no idea. I knew I had to be very, very discreet; it would not do to raise suspicions about my line of questioning. I had to appear to be motivated simply by the natural curiosity of a human newly confronted with extra-terrestrial technology. I must say I was feeling very much out of my depth. Nothing in my life had prepared me for this kind of subterfuge, Besides, I could hardly think of what I might try to uncover. I wished desperately that Lena was here; she at least had a scientific brain. I determined to try to engineer an invitation for her to the Hybrid Club.

Several hours later, Lena and I were, at last, alone in her cabin. Frankly, she looked drained.

Fortunately, I had had Miriam get us a large flask of araanschoz. I poured her a glass and she drank from it deeply and gratefully.

"Wonderful stuff, isn't it?" I asked after a few moments. I could see the color coming back into her cheeks and the tension begin to drain from her face. "So, how was your day?"

"Mm, sort of okay I suppose."

"You don't sound convinced."

"Well, working side by side with an extra-terrestrial bio-chemist, when only a couple of weeks ago I didn't even believe there were such things as extra-terrestrials, trying to get my head around scientific concepts that are way beyond anything we know about on Earth and knowing, all the while, that you are working together in a lethal plot to devastate the human race is not the sort of day you would normally put in the okay category!"

I saw tension reclaiming her and hurriedly passed her the glass of araanschoz.

"Anyway," she said, putting down the glass, "I have learned what the scans and tests we had to have when we came aboard are all about. It seems that the Kareet are familiar with just about all of our bugs. There's not much chance we can surprise them but, just to be absolutely sure, they scan all of our external body surface, swab our saliva and take blood and urine samples. If they had found anything they hadn't come across we would have been placed into quarantine and none of the crew from the quarantine station would have been allowed to enter the rest of the vessel until their scientists had analyzed it and, if necessary, destroyed it."

"Oh, okay, then nothing more invasive than that?"

She shook her head. Then she stood up and motioned me to follow her. We went behind the screen to her bathroom facilities. She turned on a tap and the 'shower'. To be perfectly honest the two combined made little sound, but I guess she convinced herself it was sufficient to mask her voice.

"Do you think they're listening in on us?" she whispered.

I shook my head. "I don't think so," I whispered back.

"But you don't really know?"

"No." I thought for a moment. "I don't believe Alassay Harraan would, but Guurtsaad Duurn… well he's another kettle of fish altogether!"

Lena nodded.

"I'll try to get one of the Hybrids to take us to the Observation Deck," I said, "I can't imagine they would have that bugged."

As it transpired, shortly after our conversation, we received a visit from Miriam. Apparently, she thought we might like to eat in company and we were cordially invited to the Hybrid Club. Well, I engineered that well!

Once we were comfortably ensconced in the Hybrid Club, introductions made and drinks in hand, Lena and I tried some delicate probing. I was taciturn and wore a decidedly glum expression. This led Katarina to enquire as to my gloomy disposition which, of course, provided an opening for me to start talking about the impending 'intervention'—now there's a euphemism for you!

It was an interesting, if not very helpful conversation. It became apparent that at least some of the Hybrids were highly conflicted. None, however, was prepared to support us openly, or to outright condemn the Kareeti plan. Lauren probably summed it up best.

"There are very few worlds in our galaxy that support sentient life. Kareedias, Earth, Albarus and Prandys. I haven't been to Prandys but, by all accounts it's no holiday destination! Albarus is quite pleasant but the climate has very severe extremes and there is very little bio-diversity. Kareedias too has a difficult climate, it has greater bio-diversity than Albarus but, compared to Earth…! Earth is a jewel; utterly unique. The climate is incredibly benign, the number and variety of life forms are truly staggering. If the Kareet were all of the same mind as Guurtsaad Duurn they would simply wipe out humanity and colonize the planet themselves. Fortunately, the Kareet are a peace-loving people."

"Peace-loving?" I grumbled. "I don't call the destruction of over six billion people peace-loving!"

"And, from your point of view I can certainly understand that. You have to understand that we… er, the Kareet, take no pleasure from this action. It is something that has been discussed for a very long time, ever since we first started to observe your world. It is not a decision come to lightly. But you know full well the devastation humanity is leaving in its wake. It is difficult now but in a hundred years, when the Earth is beginning to recover and nature to return to balance, those humans living on your world then will be thankful."

When Lauren stopped talking a silence descended upon our group as we digested what she had said. From a coldly intellectual perspective she was probably right but humanity is all about emotions, sentiment, morals, ethics; few humans are capable of such detached, dissociative thinking.

"Tell us about Kareedias," Lena ventured.

"What would you like to know?"

We learned that the Kareet spent much of their time in large underground cities. Because of a highly elliptical orbit around its sun, the winters on Kareedias were similar to our

Antarctic winters. The summers were impossibly hot. Their 'year', as measured by their orbit around their star, was equivalent to a little over three of our years. During each orbit Kareedias experienced, effectively, eight seasons.

"Beginning with the planet at its point of closest proximity to the sun, the temperature is very warm," Katarina explained. "Daytime temperatures frequently exceed 120^0—not that we use the same temperature scale as you do—but that's what it equates to. Then the temperature begins to moderate, and we move into a period of very pleasant temperatures. Gradually it becomes cooler and cooler until we enter into one of our two winters. As Lauren said, these would be similar to the winters you have in Antarctica. Then we begin to move into another… spring I suppose you could call it, before we move into the second hot season. Then of course the whole thing begins again."

"So, in one orbit you have two winters, two springs, two summers… each, what, about five of our months?" I asked.

"Yes, that's about right." Katrina said

"That must make life very difficult for plants and animals," Lena said.

"Oh, yes," Varsha agreed, "but life is so adaptive and resilient. Our plants have a very short time in which to germinate, grow and reproduce. Many produce ballistospores. On Earth, I understand, few of your plants—ferns some fungus and mosses—reproduce in this way. On Kareedias the majority of our plants produce these spores."

"Spores are, of course, an ideal means of dispersal and survival, in highly unfavorable conditions," Lena acknowledged.

"We have few animals, compared to Earth, but those we have are very hardy and have found ways to adapt to the difficult conditions," Lauren added.

"Do you have seas?" I asked.

"No, not as you would know them," Katrina replied. "Those we do have are close to the poles and lie beneath permanent ice caps."

We learned that the Kareet had, for millennia, excavated their homes and cities out of the bedrock of their planet. They had formed massive transparent domes to let in the light from the surface. Their micro-climate was controlled, and they had large open vegetated spaces. They had plant forms similar to our grasses and some similar to our trees. Because most of their plants reproduced by sporogenesis, they had almost no fruit or cereals or grain, as we would know them. They could, however, extract good, nutritive substances from many of their plants from which they make their food. The various Kareeti dishes that I had eaten on their vessel were examples.

Having mastered nuclear fusion many centuries ago, all of their energy needs were readily satisfied without damage to the environment.

"So, I presume you use deuterium to deuterium reaction and not tritium?" Lena asked.

"Oh, you know something about nuclear fusion?" Stephan asked with some surprise.

I was surprised too! I had heard of the new wonder technology that was going to provide unlimited clean energy that had, for about forty years always been about forty years away from becoming a reality, but I knew almost nothing about the science behind it.

"Well, I certainly don't know *much* about it," Lena replied. "I know that at extremely high temperatures isotopes of hydrogen can be made to fuse together giving off considerable energy. I believe that current research on Earth is focused on a deuterium—tritium reaction. But I understand there are risks associated with tritium because it is radioactive and can be difficult to contain. I have been told that a deuterium—deuterium reaction would not have the same radioactive risks associated with it but that the reaction is only possible at far higher temperatures. I gather we are having enough trouble managing temperatures adequate for the D-T reaction!"

The conversation rambled on until I found an opportunity to mention the observation deck. I waxed lyrical about the view, telling Lena all about the fabulous encounter I had had with Saturn. Lena seemed impressed and, as there was still some time before the Hybrids were planning to eat, Stephan very kindly volunteered to take us to the deck.

We were not in proximity to any planet, so Lena didn't get the sensational view I had, but Stephan showed us how to rotate the vessel to capture whichever view took our interest. He also showed us how to call up an interactive map of the galaxy on the large touchscreen table display. It was like a super high-tech version of the displays one sees at scenic lookouts on Earth. The problem was, it was all in Kareeti, so it wasn't much help to us!

Stephan chuckled. He pointed to a bright dot a little

above our eye line. Then he adjusted the console and we could see that the table mirrored the view we could see through the porthole. He touched the table display and a line shot out from the edge of the screen to the image of the bright orange dot and a word appeared beside it.

"Jupiter," Stephan translated. He tapped the screen again and a dialogue box popped up beside the Kareeti word for Jupiter. "This tells you that Jupiter is a gas giant, comprising mostly hydrogen, roughly 90%, and helium, roughly 10%. It has a diameter of… oh, let me see," he pulled out his syncom and fluttered his fingers in some arcane gesticulation, "just converting into units you will be familiar with; 89,000 miles. It has an average distance from your star of…' some more finger fluttering, "483.4 million miles and it has sixty-nine moons. That's just a brief description. If you want to know more there is a link in the side bar to vast amounts of data." Stephan seemed rather proud of the display.

"That's great Stephan," I said. "But it's of little use to us if it's in Kareeti!"

"True enough," he said, nodding. "If there's anything," and here he gestured to the magnificence of the universe, "that is of particular interest…" At that point his syncom lit up and he spoke briefly with it. "I'm sorry, I have to go," he said. "Some technical issue requiring my attention. Will you be all right here for a while?"

"Oh yes, I'm sure we can amuse ourselves here well enough," I responded. "We may not know what we're looking at, but it's all pretty spectacular and we could certainly never see it like this from Earth."

"I shouldn't be too long," he said, turning and making for the door.

When the door closed, I looked at Lena.

"That was a stroke of luck!"

She nodded.

"What do you think?"

"What do you mean?"

"Well, have you had any thoughts about any… I don't know, weaknesses, chinks in their armor? I mean, what do you think of the nuclear fusion thing?"

"What do you mean, 'what do I think of the nuclear fusion thing'?"

"Well," I said feeling a little exasperated, "could that be exploited? I mean could we somehow sabotage that? I don't know much about nuclear fusion, but I know it produces huge amounts of energy. If we could sabotage it, could we blow this vessel into another universe?"

Lena rolled her eyes. "Jeff, I think you've seen too many James Bond movies!"

I looked at her askance.

"One, I cannot imagine how we could possibly persuade any of the crew to take us to the reactor. Two, if we did, we wouldn't have the first idea what we would be looking at. Even if I saw a reactor on Earth it would just be a block of machinery with wires and tubes connecting to it. I wouldn't have the faintest idea what any of them did. The Kareeti reactor is likely to be so much more sophisticated than anything we might have produced on Earth and I'm damned sure it would be absolutely fail-safe and idiot-proof! Three, even if we could sabotage the thing we'd blow ourselves into sub-atomic particles along with the ship and all aboard!"

"Well, we'd have to consider doing that for the greater good," I replied lamely, perhaps a little unwilling to concede she may be right.

Lena turned to the window again and gazed out. I stood beside her, wishing I could simply enjoy this extraordinary privilege of seeing the universe from somewhere far out in the solar system.

"Smallpox," she said, almost under her breath.

I looked at her questioningly.

"Smallpox," she said again, nodding. "I was talking to Zherch—she's the Kareeten scientist I have been working with today. I asked her how long the Kareet have been studying and collecting Earth's micro-organisms. Since about 1980, it seems."

"So?"

"So, the last known case of smallpox was in late 1977. No case of the disease has been reported since, and the global eradication of smallpox was declared in December 1979. In other words, the Kareet have no knowledge of the disease and, therefore, no protection against it."

"Wow!" I said. "But, hang on, you just said it has been eradicated."

"There are still small stocks of the virus in two secure laboratories; one in the United States and one in the Russian Federation. I happen to know the head of Russia's State Research Centre of Virology and Biotechnology; they call it the VECTOR Institute."

We continued to talk in hushed tones for a few minutes, trying to formulate some sort of plan. Then the door whooshed open and Stephan returned.

~

The sound of my breakfast sliding in through the hatch roused me from a troubled, dream-filled sleep. It was perhaps not too surprising that spectral wraiths should haunt my slumbers, given the circumstances. In any case I woke with a foul taste in my mouth and reached for water.

This whole Kareeti experience, being aboard the alien vessel, eating their strange food, sleeping in the too short, narrow bunk and using their strange ablutions was becoming all too familiar, and yet, how long did it actually amount to, this time I had spent on board? I had lost track, but it could only be a few days. The food was very familiar, and it occurred to me that the Kareet enjoyed little culinary variety. Still it seemed to hit the right spot!

I dressed and went to call on Lena. The moment I stepped out of my door and into the small vestibule I became aware of an armed Kareeti eyeing me warily from perhaps ten yards away. I guessed he had been tasked with keeping an eye on me. It occurred to me to wave to him, but I thought better of it choosing instead to go directly to Lena's door and 'ring the bell' so to speak. There was no response. Damn! I bet she was in the lab again.

I didn't suppose I could simply go for a wander; presumably that was what the little man in blue was there for. I didn't know how to summon any of the Hybrids on the syncom, so I had little choice but to return to my room and cool my heels. I wouldn't have minded a book to read; there was nothing to do. There wasn't even a porthole for me to sit at and gaze out. I tried to set my mind the task of working out a strategy, some means to maybe get Lena's smallpox thing to work. My brain let me down. I couldn't concentrate. Too many extraneous thoughts kept whirling through my mind and, when I did focus and start thinking, I kept hitting up against things I simply didn't know.

I used to be a good strategist, back in my corporate days. But this was like trying to build a rescue plan for a failing business client without having a list of creditors or knowing his level of debt, or even what his product or service was! I gave up. What could I do? Lena was probably in a much better position to work out a plan.

I was sitting with my head in my hand feeling glum when the door flashed and buzzed. It was Lena.

"Well, we're off," she said.

"Off?"

"Home."

"Home?"

"Are you simply going to repeat everything I say to you?"

"Sorry, I'm a bit lost and confused. You say we're going back to Earth? What about your… have you finished?"

"Yes. I spent about an hour with Zherch, and we went over everything I learned yesterday. She's satisfied that I know what I'm doing. They've prepared a case of breed stock and they're loading it onto the… scout?"

"Yes, well, that's what I call it."

"Then I was summoned to see Alassay Harraan."

"Alassay?"

"There you go again!"

"What did she want?" I asked

"I think you would call it a 'pep talk'," she replied.

Chapter 34

"There *has* to be a way to stop them!" Cliff Glasson said, with a note of desperation in his voice. The National Security Advisor and Admiral Joe Morrell the Chairman of the Joint Chiefs of Staff had flown to Canberra to meet with Lena and me at the earliest possible time after our return from the Kareeti vessel.

"Could you see no way at all to penetrate their defenses?" the Admiral chipped in.

Lena shrugged and looked at me.

"Admiral, we are not military people. We are not trained to analyses an enemy's strengths and weaknesses. If this were a Russian ship I would have no idea what to look for, let alone a piece of alien technology who knows how many years in advance of our own!"

The Admiral nodded resignedly.

"Even if I had found some chink in their armor, how on Earth would you exploit it? Have you even tracked their vessel yet?"

"No," he admitted. "But could you smuggle something

aboard, I don't know, an explosive device? I'm sure our people can come up with something."

"Admiral, we don't have an invitation to return aboard and, even if we did, the Kareet put you through a thorough scanning process. There's no way you could slip a bomb past them."

"But we can't just stand back and let this happen," Glasson said in anguish.

No one replied. What could one say?

Lena and I had discussed her idea of using the smallpox virus and had decided not to mention it to the Americans, or any other nation's security people for that matter. It just seemed to us that they would find some way to screw it up! Either they would find it impossible to agree with the plan to curb fertility, and we certainly didn't have time for long, drawn out discussions, or they'd want to deploy the virus to simply kill all of the Kareet, not accepting that while this was going on the Kareet would simply release their virus and there would be no time to grow the antigen to save at least some of the world's population.

"Anyway," the Admiral said, "you can be sure we have all possible resources deployed trying to locate their vessel."

I had no doubt that was true but just what good it would do, even if they found it, was a mystery to me.

~

For Lena to begin work on the Kareeti antigen it was necessary for her to return to her laboratories in Geneva. This would leave a gulf in my life but there was nothing we could do about that. I think Martin Baumann had worked out there was something going on between us, but we never openly broached the subject. Before she left she confided in me that she would be getting in touch with Victor Orlov who was the head of VECTOR.

"Victor from VECTOR!" I noted with a chuckle.

Having been caught up in a whirlwind of activity and emotions for the past few weeks I found myself utterly becalmed once Lena had left. News and current affairs was filled with vacuous nonsense about the 'alien contact', with spokespeople from every imaginable specialist field speculating upon the potential benefits and bounties that were soon to be bestowed upon us. One or two took a contrarian and somewhat pessimistic view of what an alien civilization might think of humanity, but they were very much in the minority and were marginalized and treated dismissively by the media.

There was nothing for me to do and no one for me to be with, so I did what I knew best. I went sailing.

Each night I checked my emails. Usually I would find Lena had sent me something. To her credit (at least in my eyes) she didn't indulge in schmalzy lovey-dovey language, although she would normally end on a note of endearment.

The days passed. I took advantage of a predicted sou' westerly to do an overnight sail to Brisbane. It was an opportunity to catch up with Midge and take her for a sail on Moreton Bay. She didn't mind wafting around in the sheltered waters of the bay, but she suffered badly from sea sickness as soon as there was a swell, so she wouldn't go to sea.

It was in the early evening, back in the marina at Manly, as we sat in the cockpit with a glass of wine, when my phone pinged. I glanced at it. It was an email from Lena:

"SP just arrived. Looking forward to introducing him to our friends. Bad news from the lab—I was confident I had this new technique under control, but I have somehow managed to contaminate the breed stock I've been working on. I'm going to have to find a fresh supply. Hope all is well with you. Love, Lena."

We had discussed, only in general terms, how we were going to engineer a situation that would get Lena back on the Kareeti vessel. This then, if I were to join the dots correctly, was how we would do it.

"You got yourself a girlfriend, Dad?"

"What? Why would you think that?" I asked, a little unnerved by her penetration.

She chuckled. "Female intuition," she said.

"Mm. Well, yes," I mumbled, a little embarrassed. "I have met someone, but it's early days yet."

"Tell all."

"No, not now. I will, in due course, I promise, but not now, please; bear with me, okay?"

She could tell I really didn't want to talk about it, so she kindly let me off the hook.

'How about you, how's Asif?"

"Oh, Asif and I are no more."

"Oh dear," I said with what I hoped was the appropriate degree of concern.

"Oh, don't worry. I dropped him. He was just too much hard work."

"Hard work?"

"Yeah, like I told you at Christmas, he likes to think he's very progressive, he says he no longer subscribes to the Moslem faith, but his whole… I don't know, attitude… the way he treats women, me, his views on morality, relationships… all just patriarchal, chauvinist bullshit. So, anyway, he's gone."

"Have you got anyone else lined up?"

"I thought of screwing my supervisor—see if I can get a distinction—but he's married!"

"Some of Asif's morals must have rubbed off on you!" I jested.

"Fuck off, Dad! I had a set of moral values long before I met bloody Asif!"

Nevertheless, she did have plans for the evening, so I walked her out of the marina back to her car and, when she was gone, I sauntered off down the street to a restaurant for my evening meal.

Back on the boat, I poured myself a scotch, not the Glenlivet—that was long gone—and rummaged in my pack for the syncom. I carefully rehearsed the gestures that should summon Carlos, and also the story I would tell him. I drained the glass and poured another.

"Alakazam!" I muttered wryly. Nothing much seemed to happen, and I was just wondering whether I had stuffed it up when Carlos shimmered into existence.

"Ah, Carlos," I said with some relief, "how are you?"

"Yes, I'm well thank you, Jeff."

"Okay, good, look, the reason for my call is I've just heard from Lena."

"Good. Is she progressing well?"

"Well, no, actually, and this is the reason for my call. It seems she has got something wrong with the technique and has somehow contaminated the 'breed stock'—if that means anything to you. I'm afraid I'm no scientist."

Carlos sat in reflective silence for a moment or two and, as he did so, his countenance became increasingly somber.

"This is not good, Jeff, not good at all."

"I suppose not."

"Alassay Harraan will be furious. This will set back the program and she's already under considerable pressure from Guurtsaad Duurn. Are you sure all of the sample is contaminated?"

"Well, I'm not there with her; I'm only going by what she told me in her email. She said she would need new breed stock, so I assume she has nothing usable left. She also seemed to suggest that she has failed to get the technique quite right so, I don't know, maybe she needs to go through it with your scientists again?"

Carlos let loose a string of Kareeti which I thought I could probably translate into English pretty accurately!

"Leave it with me, Jeff, I'll get back to you." He shimmered back out of existence.

"Whew!" I said and drained the second glass.

I awoke startled and not a little confused shortly after three in the morning. A blue light was flashing accompanied by an angry buzzing sound. It took me a couple of seconds to gather my wits about me and realize that it was the syncom. I passed my hand over it and Carlos appeared again.

"As I suggested," he said without preamble, "Alassay Harraan is furious! Can you contact Lena?"

"Yes."

"She is in Geneva, yes?"

"Yes."

"Good, tell her to wait on the corner of Quai Bezanson Hugues and Pont des Bergues at three o'clock tomorrow afternoon."

"Oh, whoa, okay, let me get a pen and paper. You'll have to spell that out for me; I've never been to Geneva."

Part 6

Chapter 35

Carlos appeared to particularly relish telling me that, on this occasion, I would not be accompanying Lena. "And *that* is not negotiable!" So, for what happened after that I have had to rely on Lena's recollections and by reference to a journal she periodically updated.

Lena

It was freezing! A northerly wind swept across the lake bringing blinding flurries of snow. How I wished I was back in Iluka with Jeff! I stamped my feet to restore circulation and peered bleakly through the whirling snow for any sign of this Carlos. I tried to remember what he looked like but all I could recall was Jeff's hysterical laughter and some character looking like a detective from a black and white 1950s American movie! I glanced at my watch; it was 3:03. Three minutes late, in this weather! I supposed I couldn't be too critical. At that moment a car pulled up alongside me. The driver's side door opened, and a man got out, put out his hand, and touched my upper arm.

"Lena, I hope you haven't been waiting too long. The weather is horrible. You may remember me, Carlos? We met briefly in New York."

"Oh yes, yes I remember."

"Please, get in the car. I have the heater on." It took at least five minutes before I began to thaw out. By that time, we were heading north west along the Route de Meyrin.

"Where are we going?" I enquired.

"Up into the mountains. We will be met there by one of our small craft."

"In this weather?" I asked incredulously. "If it's this bad down here what will it be like in the mountains?"

"I believe this is passing quite quickly and there is better weather behind it."

"I hope you're right."

Of course, he was! The Kareet seemed to have a much better idea of what was happening in our global systems than our own meteorologists did. The forecast had been for increasing snowfall. As we began to climb through the foothills the clouds began to clear and soon we were driving in sunshine.

We parked alongside an Alpine meadow. There was no one around. The sun may have come out, but now it was setting, and, under a clear sky, it was bitterly cold.

"Here it is," Carlos said.

I could see nothing but, following his lead, got out of the car. I closed the car door and turned around and, apparently out of nowhere, the scout was there, barely five yards away.

I had no idea how it could move so rapidly and so silently. The ramp extended from the bottom of the body of the vessel. Carlos took my arm and steadied me as we waded the few steps through the deep snow and clambered up the steps. He helped get me seated then, with a small wave, left and returned to his car.

Once aboard the main vessel, I was subjected to the same routine scans and checks I had undergone on my previous visit. They were thorough, without being overly intrusive. When they had finished their examination, I was ushered into an anteroom. A Kareeti nurse remained with me for the fifteen or so minutes it took before I was given the all-clear. At this point I was given the outfit I had worn when I was here before.

As I was dressing I heard someone say, "Excuse me."

I turned, and there in the doorway was Varsha, one of the Hybrids I had met on my last visit.

"Oh, hi, you're…"

"Varsha."

I had remembered; she obviously thought that I would not!

"Yes, of course, Varsha; how are you?"

She smiled, by way of reply.

"I understand you are here to see Oortcyl Zherch; I am here to take you to her."

"Oh, good, thank you. But, er, before we go, can I… can I use the toilet?"

"Oh, yes, yes, of course." She led me out of the quarantine rooms and a short way along a corridor before she stopped outside a door which she opened for me. "I'll be right here outside."

I must say I was very relieved. I had gambled that, given the apparent complacency with which the Kareet had scanned us when we came aboard last time, they would not take any particular notice of the fact I was wearing a tampon. I now had to get that tampon out for, hidden within it, were two small, but distinctively different-looking glass vials, one containing the smallpox virus the other, my sterility virus. Once I had removed them from their secret hideaway, I placed them carefully in separate pockets of my tunic, washed my hands and rejoined Varsha waiting in the corridor.

"Right, I'll take you to the laboratories."

"Oh dear, Dr. Sandmeier, what have you done?" Oortcyl Zherch looked grave. "Alassay Harraan has made it very clear that she is most disappointed at this delay!"

"Yes, I'm sure she is," I replied as humbly as I could contrive. "However, this is new technology to me, and I had not only to remember how to work with it myself, I had also to teach my assistant. Something went wrong. I'm sorry; what can I say?"

"Well, I'm sure we can soon set you back on the right track. I have already started to produce new material for you. Let's—' The door flew open and an angry looking Kareetur stormed in. He appeared, to my relatively untrained eye, to be an officer. He was accompanied by two armed foot soldiers (well, I assumed that's what they were). The officer began barking orders in Kareeti. I, of course, could understand not a word, and simply stood staring in utter incomprehension. Oortcyl Zherch was arguing angrily back at the officer. The foot soldiers looked angry and brandished their odd-looking weapons.

Zherch whipped out her syncom. The officer snatched it from her. There were more heated exchanges. The officer seemed menacing. Zherch appeared to move reluctantly towards a bank of cupboards along the wall. As they turned with her towards the cupboards, I was vaguely aware of movement behind me and Varsha saying something very quietly. I glance behind me in time to see her return her syncom to her tunic.

I was very apprehensive. I had absolutely no idea what was happening, but I knew it could not be good. Zherch put her hand to the panel beside a door in the wall. This resulted in a red light flashing and further remonstrations between the protagonists.

"What's going on?" I whispered to Varsha.

"This is very bad!" she whispered back. "They are ordering Zherch to release the virus ready for loading onto the dispersal vessel."

"What virus? We don't have any vaccine…!"

"Zherch cannot open the door on her own; she must have secondary authority."

At that moment, the officer rounded on us and snarled something in Kareeti. I looked to Varsha for an explanation. She merely raised her finger and placed it across her lips.

Zherch and the officer were arguing. The officer handed her back her syncom. She spoke into it briefly then placed it back in the waiting hand of the officer. A pregnant hush fell upon the room, during which one of the armed soldiers appeared to regard me suspiciously.

The main entry door slid open. A Kareetur in an olive-green tunic came in. I vaguely thought I may have seen him before when I was last in the labs but, I confess, the Kareet all looked so similar to my eyes. The Kareeti officer growled something at the newcomer. He appeared alarmed and looked to Zherch, who said something to him. To the extent that I could read Kareeti body language, it appeared he walked resignedly to the door where Zherch stood. They both touched their hands to the panel. The door opened to reveal three shelves packed with canisters. The two scientists stood back. The officer snapped something, and the soldiers gestured with their weapons. Again, with evident reluctance, Zherch and her assistant began to unload the canisters from the shelf.

It was as they were doing this that the door slid open again and in stormed Alassay Harraan. She was diminutive in form, but her authority was towering. The officer and two soldiers withered before her. The officer, however, clearly had orders of his own and, to his credit, he squared his shoulders and responded to Alassay's harangue in what sounded a reasonable tone. The senior diplomat's tone in response did not match that of the officer! He dropped his gaze in deference, but then looked up and, producing his syncom, spoke again. Alassay Harraan nodded curtly and dismissively. He gestured with the communicator and, after a brief pause, began to speak into it.

Alassay Harraan turned her attention to us.

"Thank you Varsha," she said. Evidently, as I had deduced, Varsha had used her syncom, surreptitiously, to call Alassay.

"Dr. Sandmeier," she said turning her eyes to me. "This must be very distressing for you."

"I barely know what is going on," I replied, although, in truth I knew perfectly well.

"It appears Guurtsaad Duurn has decided, unilaterally, that no further delay can be brooked. He has ordered the release of the virus."

"But we have no vaccine!"

"No, you haven't; but that, I gather, is your fault."

There's diplomacy for you!

"I do believe we will very soon be graced by the presence of our Captain who will, no doubt, explain his decision with his accustomed sensitivity!"

And, indeed we were. Within minutes Guurtsaad Duurn stormed into the room with a retinue of fellow officers, including his interpreter, and four armed guards. There ensued a blazing row. Varsha endeavored to give me the gist of it. None of it was good. After several exchanges, none of which, I gather, was couched in terms of endearment, Alassay attempted to assert her authority as Commander of the Mission. Guurtsaad Duurn, however, was unfazed by this. Instead he had his interpreter tell us in English, that he no longer accepted the authority of Alassay Harraan. She, and her senior team, were to be arrested and held in detention. The virus was to be loaded onto the dispersal vessel and seeding would commence as soon as the equipment was primed.

With that Duurn gestured to his guards. They grasped Alassay Harraan by her arms and frog-marched her out of the lab. Duurn growled something and pointed at Varsha. Two guards took up position on either side of her, ready to escort her to wherever they were planning to hold her.

"And what about me?" I asked, terrified.

"You? You, are of no interest to us. You will be disposed of."

Chapter 36

Lena

The moment was at hand, as terrified as I was, I could delay no further.

'Wait," I said, "I think I may be of considerably more interest to the Kareet than you think."

The interpreter looked at me as though awaiting further explanation.

"I have here," I said, holding aloft the glass vial, "a quantity of smallpox virus. I have merely to squeeze the glass between my finger and thumb and the glass will break spreading the virus through your ship."

The interpreter translated this for Guurtsaad Duurn. The latter snarled something which somehow sounded derisive.

"We are not concerned by your silly threats. We have studied Earth's micro-organisms for many of your decades and we can protect ourselves from all of them."

"Not smallpox. We had eradicated smallpox before the

Kareet ever started to investigate our microbes. You have no cure for this and if I release it you will never be able to return to Kareedias without wiping out your entire species." My God, I was getting carried away with the rhetoric—it must have been nerves!

"Well now you've got them worried!" Varsha muttered as the Commander and his interpreter traded several terse exchanges.

"They are going to check with the chief science officer," Varsha offered.

"Silence you!" The interpreter pointed an angry finger at Varsha. As she fell silent he pulled out his syncom, there was a moment's delay and then he began to speak urgently into the device. He put it back into his tunic pocket. My nerves were taut as violin strings and I wished I had taken the opportunity to urinate when I was in the toilet.

A few moments passed. I stood quaking, wishing I could at least sit down. Guurtsaad Duurn glowered at me and the interpreter waited nervously, I assumed, for the chief science officer to get back to him. I glanced at Varsha who looked bewildered and, I thought, frightened.

The interpreter whipped out his syncom. There was a brief exchange. He spoke to his Commander.

"You're right, they haven't got anything on smallpox." Varsha said. Duurn glared at her.

I took a deep breath.

"I demand that you immediately release Alassay Harraan and deliver me to her keeping. If you fail to do this or attempt in any way to trick or deceive me I will break this vial," I said, holding it aloft again.

"But then you will die yourself!" spat the interpreter.

"Not necessarily, I was vaccinated against smallpox as a child. Even were I to contract it and die, do you suppose I would hesitate to release it when the future of my species is at stake?"

He had no response to that.

~

"Well, you seem to be a very resourceful woman!" Alassay Harraan said with some asperity. She did not seem particularly grateful to me for her deliverance. "What do you propose to do now?"

"Now?"

"Well, you clearly brought that virus aboard with some strategy in mind. It was not to set me free because you couldn't know I would be detained by Guurtsaad Duurn."

We were in her quarters and she had not invited me to sit down. She stood beside her desk, tapping her foot in apparent irritation. I was exhausted from nervous tension and could have done with a hug, at least. Even though I had been planning to threaten her with the smallpox virus in order to get her to agree to my demands, some part of me had been expecting… what, gratitude, a sense that it was us against Guurtsaad Duurn? I don't know. It was silly really. I took a breath and steeled myself.

"I asked you to reconsider your approach to this intervention and to consider assisting me to develop an antigen to the virus I had made which would cause sterility in my species. I thought it a comparatively humane and reasonable alternative, but you would not even consider the proposal. Well, now you will."

She fixed me with an unblinking stare and I could feel the anger behind her eyes.

"Don't you see it's too late?" she hissed.

"No, I don't. I grant you that before declining to the levels you have in mind, humans will continue to do terrible damage to our ecosystem, but it is a very resilient planet and, when the population does decline, it will soon begin to recover."

She made a derisive sound. "Well, it seems I have no choice in the matter."

"You don't, but at least this way you will get to achieve your ultimate goal, one which I wholeheartedly share with you."

"Guurtsaad Duurn is seething!"

"I'm sure he is," I replied, "but let him be warned that this vial," and I held it up for her to see, "will not leave my hand until I am back on Earth. Any attempt to stop me or to interfere with me and I will snap it open."

As I said that I realized there was a flaw to my plan that I had not foreseen and had made no contingency for. I knew I had to keep that realization from appearing in my eyes.

"Very well." Alassay Harraan sighed heavily. "I will summon Oortcyl Zherch."

Once we were safely ensconced in Zherch's lab again, and she was busy examining my virus, I spotted some medical adhesive tape lying on a bench and used some to tape the smallpox vial to the inside of my wrist. I put the remainder of the roll in my pocket. I then addressed my mind to solving this latest problem I had identified. As I had been talking to Alassay it had belatedly occurred to me that, even if I got my antigen, as soon as I returned to Earth there was nothing to stop Guurtsaad Duurn re-arresting Alassay Harraan and seeding the original virus!

"I think we can synthesize a molecule for this reasonably easily," Zherch said, after a few minutes of examining the virus. "I will have my assistants start work on it immediately."

"Ah good," I said, "is it really that easy?"

She smiled. "Your science is coming along very well but it is still a long way behind ours.

"You must be tired," she added, and no doubt my appearance would have suggested that. "You should rest and have food."

"Yes, that would be good," I admitted.

Zherch passed a hand over her syncom and, after a pause, muttered something in Kareeti into it. Shortly after that the door opened and Varsha appeared.

"If you would please follow me, I'll show you back to your quarters and order you some food," she said.

I followed her gratefully.

There was a wearying degree of uniformity on the Kareeti vessel which made it almost impossible to know where you were. When we arrived at the door of 'my quarters', it appeared no different to any other vestibule and doorway leading off any other corridor, except for the somewhat more generous dimensions afforded senior Kareet such as Alassay Harraan. Varsha put her hand to the panel and the door slid open. It may or may not have been the room I had been assigned on my previous spell on board, but it certainly looked no different.

"Will you come in?" I asked, as I entered.

Varsha appeared to hesitate a beat before accepting my invitation, but then, with the merest hint of a bow, she entered. She went directly to the communication panel beside the door. I assumed she was ordering my food; I would hesitate to call it dinner, based on prior experience!

"You might appreciate this is a very stressful experience for me," I said to her. "Last time I was here, Jeff was able to give me a drink. I don't remember what it was called but it certainly had a calming effect."

"Ah yes, that would be araanschoz. I'll order some for you."

"Will you sit down?" I asked, as she turned from the coms panel. Again, I felt I could detect a reluctance on her part but, nevertheless, she swung out a stool and perched upon it. I watched her eyes drift to the vial taped to my wrist. Instinctively I crossed my hands in front of me and took the wrist in my other hand. Her eyes darted away guiltily almost as though I had caught her looking at me inappropriately.

"Does the fact that you are a Hybrid make this difficult for you? I mean, do you find yourself with conflicted loyalties?"

"No," she said after a moment's thought. "Intellectually, I can comprehend your distress and sympathize with your predicament, but I am Kareet. The fact that my father originated on Earth is of only passing interest; I never met him. I was raised, nurtured and educated as a Kareeten. I have a very satisfying medical career mapped out for me. There is no congruence between human interests and my own."

"Mm, that seems pretty cold and dispassionate."

"Perhaps, but it is true, and I cannot pretend otherwise."

"Well, anyway, I am going to need your help."

"Help, how?" she asked, surprised.

"Just how much do you know about my current status here on this vessel?"

"Well, that you have somehow messed up the materials you were given to work with and you need retraining and more material."

I told her all about my proposed alternative to the Kareeti intervention and Alassay Harraan's rejection of the idea. I explained that the smallpox was a rather desperate but, I thought, effective strategy to prevent the cold-blooded murder of vast numbers of my species.

"You will understand," I continued, "that I am a scientist, not a spy or a secret agent. I am not trained to plan an operation such as this. Consequently, I only became aware of a flaw in my plan after I had arrived aboard."

Her eyes lit up with interest. Any hopes my words may have raised in her, however, were soon dashed as I explained that I would not leave the vessel until I was one hundred per cent sure that my sterilization plan had been fully implemented.

"But how can you do that?" she asked in a tone that

suggested that she too had identified a problem. "You cannot be in two places at the same time."

"No, I realize that, and that, of course, was the flaw in my plan. But I have a solution and I will require your assistance."

"Why would I help you?"

"Because, if you don't, I will snap this vial and infect your ship with deadly smallpox," I answered simply.

There was a silence while Varsha processed this. I could see she was desperately seeking an alternative solution. She shook her head. I took this to mean she had not found an alternative.

"I have an assistant in Geneva who has been working with me since I first returned to the laboratories with the Kareeti breed stock. He is very capable and I am sure he can be relied upon to produce the vaccine without my assistance. So, when Zherch has prepared the breed stock for my vaccine, I will need you to deliver it to him."

"I don't have Earth clearance."

"You need only deliver it to Carlos. He is still in Geneva. He could meet the scout and receive the vaccine from you."

Varsha nodded, pensively.

"To help me to coordinate this on Earth, I am going to need the help of Jeff Ridsdale. I need you to get me a syncom and teach me how I can contact Jeff on it. I don't need it to do all kinds of fancy tricks, I just need it to work like a cell phone."

"I think, under normal circumstances, we may have some trouble getting you a syncom, but I suppose these are hardly normal circumstances!" She smiled wryly. "So, do you intend to stay here, on board, until this is all over?"

"I don't see that I have any choice," I replied.

"It's going to be a very hard and lonely time for you."

"Yes, I suppose it is."

"You will not be able to move freely around the ship with that vial."

"No, I suppose not." I stood up and wandered over to the door. "I suppose that, even if I were able to lock this door, the lock could be overridden?"

Varsha nodded. My mind was racing. As she had said, I would be a long time on board. I had to sleep. Guurtsaad Duurn would try anything to get his hands on the vial. He might think me vulnerable when asleep, and attempt to capture the vial then. He couldn't risk waking me, so he could have my food or drink tampered with. Hell, this was getting complicated! If I had planned all of this properly on Earth I could have thought up contingency plans.

As this was all tumbling through my head, the blue door light flashed, and a tray was slid through the hatch. Damn! How was I going to handle this? I eyed the tray speculatively. I was on my own and could not expect help or support from anyone on board. I had to get this right.

"So, Varsha," I began; a strategy beginning to form in my mind, "what do you think? Will it be the food or the drink that will have the poison in it?"

Her eyebrows shot up as though on springs.

"Poison?" She had clearly not considered this possibility.

"If you were Guurtsaad Duurn, how would you go about

getting your hands on the vial and ridding yourself of me?"

She looked completely at a loss for a moment or two. Then she nodded slowly.

"You see," I continued, "if I began to suspect I had been given something in my food or drink, and I must get some physical warning—nothing can act instantaneously—I would snap the vial."

"I don't think they would have tampered with this… I mean they may plan something, I really don't know, but this is too soon. They couldn't have planned it and put the plan into effect this quickly."

I was inclined to agree with her.

"Nevertheless," I replied, "I cannot afford to take the risk. I suggest you find out whether or not they have tampered with it, because I am going to have you eat and drink some of everything before I go anywhere near it."

"What if I won't cooperate?"

"Then I won't eat or drink any of it."

"You'll soon get very hungry and dehydrated."

"And if that happens…' I held aloft my wrist with the vial attached.

Quite honestly this whole thing was becoming utterly bizarre; nothing in my background or experience came anywhere close to preparing me for this… this… well it was the sort of thing you read in cheap novels on trains or planes! My stomach was churning, my stress levels were through the roof and I had no idea what I would do next, or how this madcap scheme could possibly end in anything other than disaster!

I picked up the flask, which I assumed contained the araanschoz.

"Just drink some of this," I demanded.

If there were glasses available, I didn't know where I might find them. She looked for a second as though she might ask for a glass but then, with the slightest of shrugs, she put the flask to her lips and drank. As if anticipating my suspicions, she held her mouth open, so I could see the liquid pooled under her tongue, then she closed her mouth and swallowed. I waited for half a minute then took the flask from her hand and drank deeply.

It took a moment or two but gradually I began to feel my heart rate calm and the churning in my gut abate. As the minutes passed my inner state became almost serene. It was quite amazing, the effect of this stuff. But, although my anxiety was eased, I was not released from my predicament. Perhaps a calmer mental state would provoke clearer thought.

I stopped my pacing, which was ridiculous in so confined a space anyway, and sat in the recliner. An idea was forming in my mind. If I were to have Varsha take me to the Hybrid Club, if we were all to eat together, I could swap plates randomly…

Varsha whipped out her syncom. She spoke briefly in Kareeti, looking at me as she did so. She nodded.

"Lena, Alassay Harraan would like to see you again."

"What, so that she can berate me some more?"

"No, it seems she has had a change of heart."

Chapter 37

Lena

"Quite frankly, I'm struggling with this; why should I trust you?"

"Doctor Sandmeier." I had noticed that I could tell much about her mood by whether she addressed me formally, or called me Lena, so I reacted appropriately.

"Yes?"

"Whatever you may think of my mission here, I can assure you I am neither duplicitous, nor do I bear you any personal animosity."

"You seemed anything but friendly at our last meeting," I replied tersely.

"I was, I admit, angry. I was annoyed at your having challenged and, indeed, thwarted my purpose. I was also extremely angry with Commander Duurn."

I said nothing but continued to regard her speculatively.

"I have had a chance to reflect and have simply concluded that, although I am not at all happy with your solution, it will doubtless achieve our ultimate goal, albeit at the cost of the extinction of innumerable species that may have otherwise been saved. As you seem to have us over a barrel, we may as well cooperate as best we can with one another."

"So, this means…?"

"Well, as long as you are on your own and feeling threatened, and you have that vial in your hands, the whole ship is in imminent danger. I fear Guurtsaad Duurn will make every effort to regain control by whatever means he may and I consider that a very high-risk strategy.

"I suggest you move in here with me; we can watch one another's backs, so to speak."

Well, that was the gist of it. As a member of a different species, I have not the in-bred skills to read the body language of a Kareet. Could I believe her? What could I do? I seriously doubted my ability to keep this ludicrous situation going on my own, although I certainly didn't give any hint of this to Alassay Harraan.

"Why don't you sit down?" she asked in a kindly voice.

I did so, suddenly very tired and grateful to take the weight off my feet. She produced a flask and poured us each a goblet of hiftervess. She raised her glass to her lips and, when I saw she had indeed swallowed some, I too took a sip.

It took me a while to really come to terms with Alassay Harraan's intentions. Yes, she was annoyed that I had subverted her plans, but she was very much angrier with Guurtsaad Duurn and apprehensive as to what he might do next.

"Guurtsaad Duurn is a very ambitious Kareetur. There

has come the news of the death of a senior commander and the retirement of another. There will be much maneuvering in the senior ranks for promotion. Duurn is extremely anxious to return to Kareedias. He opposed the inclusion of me and my diplomatic contingent from the very start but was overruled. He has barely tolerated me all along. Your intervention was what I believe they call in English, the last straw.

"Standing between Guurtsaad Duurn and his ambition, is a very dangerous space to occupy."

It became apparent, upon reflection, that Alassay Harraan had come to the conclusion I could be of considerably more value to her as an ally than as an additional existential threat.

Whether it was the hiftervess (we'd had a couple of glasses) or fatigue, or just my desperate need to have someone on my side, I gradually found myself beginning to trust her. Not entirely so but, shall we say, on the balance of probabilities.

Alassay Harraan showed me her sleeping quarters and then arranged a bed for me in a corner of the main room, adjacent to where we had sat. She offered me the use of her bathroom and, while I was in there, it occurred to me to relocate the smallpox vial so that, should I sleep heavily, she wouldn't know where it was, and it would not be easily accessed. I taped it to my groin. Surely no one could get at it there without me knowing!

I returned to the stateroom but didn't lie down until Alassay had gone to her bedroom and closed the door behind her. Even then I was hesitant to lay myself down to sleep.

I woke up with a start.

It was that feeling you had slept too long; that you would be late for work. I sat up and gazed about me uncomprehendingly. It took a moment for me to recollect my circumstances.

"Oh, you're awake at last!"

I looked in the direction of the voice.

"You must have been tired!" Alassay sat at her desk, apparently working at a console of some sort.

I blinked rapidly several times, trying to clear my thoughts. "How long have I slept?"

"That's a difficult question to answer. You see, we don't denominate time the same as you do but, as a quick calculation I'd say it would be about nine of your hours."

"Nine hours! Are you sure?"

"Near enough; and you slept very soundly too. I called your name several times quite loudly, but there was no rousing you!" This was alarming news. I glanced fearfully at my wrist. The vial was gone! Then I remembered I had moved it somewhere safer. I looked back at Alassay, a little guiltily. She merely smiled although I am sure she had followed my thought process.

"I have food for you, but I expect you would like to use the bathroom first."

While I was freshening up, I thought long and hard about my position. I was ridiculously vulnerable. It was preposterous to think I could continue to get away with this! If I didn't have the vial actually in my hand, someone could grab me by the wrists and I would be helpless. With my wrists bound I could be searched; game over! The only chance I had was to ensure that I was only ever in the company of one other—probably Alassay Harraan—at any time. If the situation arose where I could not avoid others being near, then the vial must be in my hand, and visibly so, to deter anyone from thinking they could overpower me. I thought about how long I may need to keep this up and shuddered at the prospect.

The day passed quite uneventfully. Alassay Harraan worked at her desk for some of the time, while I looked out at the universe through her large window (should that be 'port hole', Jeff?)

At one point, Alassay looked up from her work to say, "I believe we will be in proximity to your planet Neptune tomorrow. You may enjoy the view from that window a little more then."

We were delivered food at what I will choose to call lunch time (in that two or three hours had passed since I had woken). Alassay broke from her work and we ate together. I found it both difficult and embarrassing to ask her to eat some of my food before I would touch it, but I felt I really did have to take every precaution. Alassay was quite relaxed about it.

"I'm not sure if I'm a very good choice of food taster for you; I think Guurtsaad Duurn would be very happy to poison the pair of us!"

I glanced at her in alarm, but she chuckled in that strange Kareeti way and said, "I don't think he will attempt to put anything in our food. He is intelligent enough to know that nothing he could put into our food would have such an instantaneous effect that you wouldn't have time to snap open that vial."

"What do you think he will try to do?" I asked in the hope that this new-found, apparent ally might give me at least some insight. After all, I was at my wit's end.

"I don't really know," she replied thoughtfully. "I am quite sure he is seething. The problem with Duurn is his ambition far exceeds his ability."

I looked at her quizzically.

"He was so desperately anxious to return to Kareedias to be in consideration when the new senior appointments are to be made, that he took precipitous action against me. He obviously hadn't thought through the consequences of his actions. How does he imagine he will explain his behaviour when we return? This is not the sound, strategic thinking we expect of someone in high office. If it were only me, he might have arranged for me to mysteriously die, and explained it away as a natural death or perhaps an illness, but I have a delegation with me, and staff. He can't get rid of all of us."

"Yes, I see, he certainly does have a problem!"

"I suspect he is in his cabin berating himself for the fool that he is and coming, grudgingly, to the conclusion that there is almost nothing he can do."

"So, what about me? What do you think he will do to me?"

"I don't really think there is anything he can do. He's put himself in a very difficult position. He cannot afford to take any action that could risk the release of the smallpox virus. I think he has to just let things take their course and hope he still has a job when we return home to Kareedias—any job!"

I meditated upon what Alassay had said. I couldn't fault her logic, but it occurred to me, it was not her, but Guurtsaad Duurn's logic we were dealing with and, as Alassay had already pointed out, his decision-making was not always necessarily rational. Nevertheless, I felt a little less stressed in my situation.

As our talk became less and less to do with our circumstances, I began to appreciate Alassay Harraan as a conversationalist. Her knowledge on so many different and diverse topics was truly impressive, and her ideas and attitudes were underpinned by a deep understanding of Kareeti philosophy.

I learned that their philosophy is not so different to our own. All of their people, however, learn philosophy, from early childhood going forward throughout their years of education. As with we humans, the Kareet have their fair share of esoteric, academic philosophers who get bound up in the arcane and all but incomprehensible facets of philosophy, but the general population pays little heed to them. Their focus is ontology and, as a result, for the most part, theirs is a peaceful and caring society; they have very little crime, murder is virtually unheard of, and they don't even have prisons.

Alassay Harraan told me how horrified she was watching our world and its people. She could not believe we could have wars and weapons of mass destruction, terrorism, torture, genocide. She was appalled that we could allow millions to be born into abject poverty, to leave them to starve to death in times of drought. She was clearly outraged that an individual could own billions of dollars and vast portfolios of real estate and other property while their fellow man starved to death. None of that could ever happen on Kareedias.

Our discussions were interrupted by Alassay's syncom. It was Zherch. She had completed the formulation of the anti-viral molecule.

"Well, what's your plan now Doctor Sandmeier?"

I glanced at her nervously, given my earlier observation that the form of address she adopted was indicative of her mood. I needn't have worried. She had a twinkle in her eye.

"I have been giving this some thought, Alassay," I replied. "I believe I need to remain on this vessel with you until the vaccine has been produced in adequate quantities and dispersed among the population. I have a highly qualified assistant who I am confident can produce the vaccine."

"Oh, and how do you propose to get the molecule to him, may I ask?"

"I thought Varsha, or one of the other Hybrids, could deliver it to Carlos who, I believe, is still in Geneva. I wondered, Alassay, whether I might be provided with a syncom so I can contact Jeff Ridsdale. I don't need to be able to do anything more than just hold a two-way conversation with him—in private—we do have an emotional attachment. If I can speak with Jeff I can give him all the details he will need to coordinate this."

~

I had always thought myself reasonably well coordinated, that is, until Alassay placed a syncom in my hand! It took me simply ages to get the thing to respond in any way to my gestures and strokes. It was so frustrating. Alassay was very patient with me, thank goodness, and, little by little I began to get the hang of it.

Watching the Hybrids and the Kareet with their syncoms, you would think it's all perfectly simple and straightforward; the merest of gesture, the tiniest movement of a finger.

"You have to remember, Lena, we have been partnered with these things from early childhood. You mustn't expect to master it in one day. Here, your middle finger down the side, yes, like that, and just a small backward stroke." And so it went on.

"There's a lot to be said for our smart phones on Earth," I grumbled.

"There's a lot might be said about their limitations too," she replied, pulling my focus back to the task at hand.

Chapter 38

Jeff

I was back home in Iluka. It was early evening, warm and humid. I was sitting on my deck, feet up, drinking a beer. I heard a buzzing from the bedroom and got up to investigate. It was the syncom. Oh, God, now what was it? I made the gestures I had been taught and, fully expecting to see the bold Carlos, was more than a little surprised to see Lena come shimmering into view.

"Now here's a vision splendid! How are you, how's everything going? So, they've given you a syncom too."

"Yes, well I barely know what to do with the thing. I told Alassay I only needed the functionality of a cell phone, but she knows we are… anyway she insisted on showing me how to do this hologram thing. She's been very kind."

"Kind? I find that amazing. Given your plans with the smallpox and all that, I thought you would be her mortal enemy!"

Lena brought me up to date with events as they had

unfolded for her. I must confess I was in awe of all she had accomplished. I duly took down all the contact details for Daiki Shimizu, her assistant, and I undertook to contact Carlos.

"Do I need to coordinate all of this?" I asked.

"No, as long as Carlos has Daiki's contact details, Alassay will contact him when we have everything ready here."

"Okay; and you're all right? You're handling all this?"

"Well, of course, I'm finding it all very stressful but now that Alassay appears to be on-side, and as long as I get regular infusions of araanschoz, I seem to be coping.

"Oh, and Alassay has also taught me how to use the syncom as a recording device so I'll try to record my recollections of this whole thing," she said, then, almost as an afterthought: 'how's everything going back on Earth? God, I can't believe I just said that!"

"Well, not very well," I replied. "Some idiot who was present at the UN when Alassay spoke, notwithstanding all of the delegates undertaking to maintain complete secrecy about the Kareet's intentions, has let the cat out of the bag."

"Oh, my God! What's happening?"

"A little as you might imagine; some, probably most, are scoffing at the story but there are plenty that believe and, I suppose understandably, are panicking. Across the world there are outbreaks of lawlessness; people desperately trying to get their bit of the good life before it all comes to an end. Religions are booming. There is nothing, but nothing in the media, on the radio, on television, except 'the aliens'! Oh, other than, to its credit, ABC FM which keeps on doggedly, or perhaps stoically, playing classical music and refraining from comment."

"How is all this affecting you?"

"Well, I'm trying my best to ignore it all; impossible of course, the press won't let me be. I'm back in Iluka which, as you know, is normally pretty sleepy and laid back, but is currently swarming with news reporters all trying to get hold of me. I've beefed up the security on the house, I keep the phone turned off most of the time, and I'm staying out of sight as much as possible. I hope they'll give up soon. I had been doing a bit of sailing, locally; yacht deliveries have dropped right off—go figure! And I've shut out all media except my own music collection. And, I'm missing you."

Once Lena's image had flickered out, like phosphorescence in the wake of the boat, I poured myself another beer and checked the time. By my calculations it was mid-morning in Europe, as good a time as any to call Carlos (a pity it wasn't three in the morning! Still…)

It was not long after I had spoken to Carlos that the PM's 'hot phone' rang. It seems almost unbelievable, looking back on it, that we had engineered this whole smallpox thing without telling anyone about it. And, yet, that is what we did. You may well imagine the reaction I got from Martin Baumann!

"You have done *what*? Are you totally mad?"

"Martin, we didn't think we had any other option."

"No other option! What, like discussing it with me, with the President. That wasn't an option that occurred to you?"

"We needed to act decisively and without delay. Can you

imagine the furor, the wildly different opinions, the endless arguments that would have ensued? The Americans had nothing. They couldn't even find the Kareeti vessel. Even if they had, what could they have done? The best they had to offer was for one of us to smuggle a bomb on board!"

"So, let me get this straight, the Kareet are going to seed this planet with a virus that will wipe out our ability to reproduce, is that it?"

"Yes, except we will have a vaccine that we can administer to… however many people."

"So, you and Doctor Sandmeier have taken the unilateral decision to take away the reproductive rights of most of humanity?"

"What was the alternative? If the Kareet had had their way, and frankly we had absolutely no way of stopping them, they would have wiped out most of the human race, and left those remaining to cope with the corpses. At least this way life will go on as usual except that, as people die, as people do, they won't be replaced. Seems eminently the better of two alternatives."

There was a protracted silence from the PM. "Well, you two have taken on one hell of a responsibility, and with no authority whatsoever to do so," he finally grumbled.

"That's as may be," I replied, "but, under the circumstances, I consider that Lena Sandmeier should be recognized as an absolute hero."

"Well, you may think that, but let me tell you; you had better be prepared to defend your actions before the United Nations because people are going to want explanations!"

I confess that the prospect of addressing the UN had me quaking in my boots but, if that's what had to be done, then that's what had to be done!

A week or more slipped by. I was almost a prisoner in my own home, under siege by the press. To while away the time, I began to write up my recollections of this whole bizarre adventure. Throughout that time, I heard nothing further from the Prime Minister or Carlos or Alassay or even Lena. I assiduously avoided the news channels and kept working away at my memoir.

After a few days, I did poke my head out to check the enemy's positions and was somewhat relieved to find their numbers significantly reduced. Later that day, in need of supplies, I brazened my way out through the front of the house and hopped into my Zodiac. Luckily, the motor started on the second or third pull and I was able to drown out their clamoring and surge away from the jetty leaving them squawking questions and frantically gesticulating behind me.

I nipped over to Yamba and, with my hat down low over my sun glasses, I headed to the local supermarket. No one, apparently, recognized me, which was a relief, and I made it back to the boat without being accosted. It was inevitable, of course, that I would have to run the gauntlet when I returned, and so it was. As I came alongside the jetty, a stream of reporters emerged from the shade of the trees and blocked my path.

"Mr. Ridsdale, Mr. Ridsdale!" One reporter appeared to have the tacit approval of the pack to ask the first question.

"Mr. Ridsdale, you have met these aliens, what do you say to the story getting about that they are going to wipe out most of the human race?"

"Ladies and gentlemen," I replied with a hint of exasperation in my voice, "I can assure you that the Kareet are not going to be killing any of us."

"But then, what are they planning?" another reporter asked.

"I cannot tell you that."

"Cannot, or will not?" someone else called out.

"Both," I retorted tersely. "First of all, I have been bound to secrecy by the Secretary General of the United Nations, and by the President of the United States and by our own Prime Minister. Second, through a bizarre set of circumstances, I became the conduit between the Kareet and the world leaders. Having made that initial connection, a communications protocol has been established and I am no longer in the loop, so to speak." That wasn't entirely true, but desperate times call for desperate measures!

"How did *you* get to become the 'conduit' as you put it?"

I thought about this for a moment. How much could I tell them without telling them everything, how much would Baumann accept seeing in the papers before he considered I'd gone feral?

"I happened to be in the wrong place at the wrong time. I was in the middle of the Tasman Sea on a yacht, in a storm, when I had an accident that knocked me unconscious. When I woke I was aboard the Kareeti vessel. It was explained to me that I would have a device inserted into my neck that would allow the Kareet to use my sight, hearing and voice centers to receive sight and sound through me, and to use my voice to talk. I was then returned to Earth. I ended up at the UN being, as I say, the conduit for the Kareet. That function having been completed I am now no longer involved. Lines of communication have been opened and I am not required, nor am I party to the conversation. Now, if you please, I have ice cream in here that I need to get into the freezer."

It is amazing the respect Australians have for ice cream; the crowd parted like the Red Sea did for Moses! Random questions pursued me all the way to the house, but I had said all I was going to say, and I closed the door behind me.

Chapter 39

Lena

It was fantastic to have been able to speak to Jeff. I understand he was able see me as a hologram. I couldn't see him, of course—we're neither of us that skilled in the use of these things. He is a wonderful man; I can hardly believe some woman hadn't already snapped him up. I'm really looking forward to this terrible business being over so I can go back and be with him. Although I do wonder at how things will work out. He is so happy living the quiet life, away from all of the hustle and bustle. I really cannot imagine him wanting to live in Geneva, and I certainly can't do my work in Iluka.

After the chat with Jeff, things went back to the boring, repetitive routine of life aboard the Kareeti vessel. The fly-by of Neptune truly was the most spectacular thing I have seen in my life, or am ever likely to see. The planet filled the entire sky. I had seen the pictures NASA published from the *Voyager* mission, but nothing I had seen was even remotely on the scale of what I saw during the fly-by. The large dark spot and 'the Scooter' took up the entire porthole in Alassay's room. I could very clearly see the methane clouds; it was astounding.

But, as Neptune shrank into the distance, it was back to the confines of the stateroom. Alassay had work to do; she couldn't spend all her time entertaining me, but we did have opportunities for conversation and I found these sessions endlessly fascinating. The more she told me of life on Kareedias the more insane our human existence seemed to me to be.

I think I may have mentioned that the passage of time on the spacecraft was difficult to ascertain, there being no day and night as we know it on Earth but, as well as I could estimate it, about three days passed by before Oortcyl Zherch paid us a visit.

She reported that the antigen had been synthesized, in the appropriate quantity, and was ready now for shipment to Earth.

"And what about Lena's molecule?" Alassay enquired.

"We have concentrated upon the antigen because we know it will take them time on Earth to manufacture it in volume. While they are doing that, we can make up the virus ready for dispersal."

"Good."

"I would like to come to the lab and inspect the molecule before it is loaded for dispersal," I said, trying to keep the quaver from my voice.

"Ever suspicious!" Alassay chided.

"There's far too much riding on it. I owe it to my *species* to check every single aspect of this."

She nodded in acceptance.

After our meal, Alassay put aside her work and we sat across the table from each other in the easy chairs. She poured us a glass of hiftervess.

"Tell me more about Kareedias," I urged her.

"What would you like to know?"

"I don't know, everything really."

She chuckled.

"What are your houses like?"

"Well, houses are houses wherever you are. They perform the same function on Kareedias as they do on Earth and on Kareedias, perhaps to a greater extent than on Earth, form follows function."

"I didn't think you had been on Earth," I interjected.

"I don't need to; your internet has all the necessary information for me to research almost anything I want to know about your planet, housing included."

Alassay went on to explain that, because the Kareet lived in temperature-controlled environments beneath vast glass domes, protected from the harsh effects of the environment on the surface, the building materials did not have to be as durable as those used on Earth.

We talked for some time about houses, and then I asked about their society, how it functioned, what sort of government they had, how their economy operated.

"You seem inordinately interested in our world," she said with just a hint of weariness.

"Inordinate? I wouldn't have thought it inordinate," I replied. "I would have thought that anyone encountering a hitherto unknown alien civilization would be endlessly fascinated by every aspect of their world."

She didn't reply immediately; she seemed lost in thought. She topped up our glasses.

"Why don't you come to Kareedias and learn all about us first hand?"

It was fortunate that I didn't have the glass to my lips, or I might have choked at that moment!

"Go to Kareedias?" I must have been the very picture of bewilderment for she chuckled, and took a drink of her hiftervess.

"Why not?"

"You can't be serious!"

"Again, why not? What an opportunity; for you to study and learn about us and for our people to meet a citizen of another world."

"But... but... how would I get back? I mean it's not as if I could pay you a visit for a few weeks and jump on the next spaceship home!"

"Ah yes, there is that, of course. You may, conceivably, have an opportunity to return at some point in the future, but that certainly can't be guaranteed. Still, you may be happy there."

"What would I do?"

"Well, I dare say you would be perfectly capable of studying and, eventually, acquiring the knowledge to bridge the gulf between your present level of comprehension of micro-biology and ours, but it is probably fair to say you will never again be at the cutting edge of your area of specialization.

"I'm sure you could earn a very decent living giving talks and presentations to our people about Earth, your civilization, the history of your development, your arts."

"But probably never again be with my people, with the people I know and love."

"Oh well, Lena, it was just a passing notion, not something I had given any prior thought to. Perhaps it is not a particularly good idea. I imagine I would have to wade through a considerable amount of bureaucracy to get the necessary permissions."

"So, you weren't serious?" I asked, not knowing whether I was relieved or disappointed.

"Oh, I think I was serious when I made the offer, if a little impromptu, spontaneous. You can think about it if you like, if you decide you'd like to, I'm sure I can arrange it, but don't feel under any pressure."

I was completely flabbergasted! I didn't know what to think. I slept poorly that night, turning it over and over in my mind. I bounced back and forth between the excitement, the thrill of visiting another world, another, wholly new civilization and being the first human being ever to have done so, and the despair of never again seeing family, friends, loved ones, Jeff, my familiar world, leaving my career behind; no, it was out of the question!

Chapter 40

Jeff

The days went by slowly, so slowly. As far as I could ascertain, the reporters had decided there was little more they could get from me and had decamped. I went for a sail one day, to pass the time, but my heart wasn't in it. I had an overwhelming sense of futility; I was in the center of an immense situation over which I wielded not one whit of control. I wanted desperately to speak to Lena. No, I wanted desperately to have Lena here, by my side, sharing a glass of wine. I wanted this whole Kareet business to be some bizarre dream from which I would just wake up, and it would all be over. I wanted all of these things and could have none. Here I was a man who had done pretty much whatever he wanted for the past however many years and now, now I just felt helpless!

I couldn't call Lena; my facility with the syncom was almost non-existent. The damn thing sat there on the coffee table contumaciously silent. I stared at it balefully, willing it to come to life. And then, one afternoon, suddenly, without any warning its little blue light sparkled brightly, and it started purring. I was so startled I fumbled clumsily with it, almost dropping the thing on the floor. Finally, I arranged my fingers in the prescribed fashion and suddenly I heard Lena's voice:

"Jeff, Jeff, can you hear me?"

"Oh my God, Lena, yes, I'm here. Where have you been?" Completely dumb question; I knew exactly where she'd been. "I've really missed you." Oh, how true that was! For years I had been perfectly content living mostly in my own company but, now that I had met Lena…! We spoke for a while saying the sorts of mushy stuff that couples say that I don't particularly want to record here, and then she said, "Well, the work is done here." Apparently, Varsha had carried the vaccine to Earth, and handed it to Carlos. Carlos had taken Daiki Shimizu with him to meet the scout. As soon as he had received it from Varsha, Carlos handed the material over to Daiki and climbed aboard the scout with Varsha and returned to the main vessel.

"Great, so when do you come back?"

"Well, not for a while, I'm afraid."

"Pour quoi?"

"Jeff, I'm committed to seeing this thing through…'

"But haven't you done everything you set out to do?"

"Yes and no; I have forced their hand, and now they have manufactured the antigen for my virus but, if I came back now, how could I be sure they wouldn't simply revert to Plan 'A'?"

"I thought you had convinced Alassay Harraan, I thought she was on your side."

"I have *forced* her, Jeff, not convinced her. Her current acquiescence is pure pragmatism. Given her own way, she would certainly carry on with her original plan."

"But why? Why is she so pigheaded? Surely she can see the sense in your proposal?"

"No, she doesn't. Well, she does see the sense from our, human perspective, but she is not much concerned with our perspective. She is looking at it holistically, from a global perspective. I think a good metaphor might be that of the oncologist. If you go to the doctor with cancer, he will want to cut it out, or hit it with chemotherapy, straight away. If the cancer could talk and say, "but hang on, that chemotherapy stuff doesn't really work for us," the doctor is hardly likely to sit down with the tumor and work out a solution that is more to the cancer's liking!"

"So, that's all we are, a cancer?"

"Well, look at it from the Kareeti perspective."

"So, then, how long?"

"I don't know, Jeff. How long will it take Daiki to manufacture the vaccine? How long will it take the UN to distribute it and how long for the nations to administer it?"

These were all questions I had asked myself, to some degree, over the past few days. Not that I'd come up with any answers.

"I imagine Guurtsaad Duurn must be getting edgy," I said eventually, having no answer to Lena's questions.

"I haven't seen him once since his aborted attempt to detain Alassay Harraan."

"What do you think he will do?"

"I quizzed Alassay on that. She seems to think he made a serious error in judgement and has now realized that he screwed up. She doesn't think there is anything really that he can do."

"I think the whole process around selecting who will and who will not receive the vaccine will be incredibly difficult and I'm sure the UN is going to ask for more time," I said, looping back to Lena's earlier questions.

"Yes, well, you'd better warn them that we really do not have any extra time. The Kareet are very impatient, even without the Guurtsaad Duurn factor. If the world is seen to be prevaricating or playing for time, all bets are off."

"But you still have the smallpox."

"Jeff, do you have *any* idea just how tenuous a hold I have? I am just one woman, on her own. I have to sleep. I am sure that Alassay Harraan could contrive to separate me from that vial if she chose to do so and, frankly, I wonder that she hasn't already."

"Yeah, okay, yes, I get it, I do; I do understand. I think you are incredibly brave, I really do. You just be very careful, okay?"

"Just you make it very clear to the UN that they have to make this happen quickly or… God knows!"

After I ended the call with Lena I used the 'hot line' to call Baumann. Parliament wasn't sitting, so I reached him straight away. We exchanged brief pleasantries and then I brought him up to speed with all that Lena and I had discussed—well, insofar as it related to the Kareet!

"Martin, I cannot over-emphasize how important it is to get all of this done as quickly as humanly possible."

"Yes, of course, I understand but you have to understand…'

"No! Martin, no! No, *you* have to understand, you *have* to understand, if we delay, in any way, if we are seen to be deliberately holding up the process or even, for that matter, just blundering around in a blind bureaucratic delirium, there is a very real chance that the Kareet will find a way to overcome Lena and revert to their original plan only, this time, there will be no vaccine, no guarantee that any of the human race will survive. We could face total extinction! Tell me you do, actually, comprehend that."

Baumann stuttered and stammered for a while but then he gathered himself and I really think he had grasped the full gravity of the situation.

"Martin, I can't do anything more. It is up to you. *You* have to take this message to the UN and you *have* to drive it home. You do understand that, don't you? This is no time for political shilly-shallying."

"No, yes I do, I do fully understand. You're a good man, Ridsdale, a damned good man."

Chapter 41

Lena

I began to settle into a routine. I won't say I was relaxed, but Alassay Harraan continued to show me nothing other than good will, and my strategy of remaining alone with her and not venturing out of the stateroom was making the management of the smallpox vial easier than it might otherwise have been.

Alassay continued to captivate me with tales of Kareedias, their society, the planet itself, its biosphere, the flora and fauna. She spoke of their strange biology which led to her suggesting I might like to spend some time in the lab with Oortcyl Zherch; it would be a chance to talk to her about micro-biology. I was in two minds. On the one hand, I would absolutely have loved to be able to talk to Zherch, to pick her brains, to learn even a fraction of what they must know that we have yet to discover. I must have had a million questions I wanted to ask her ('Lena,' my father would say in a mock stern voice, 'I have told you a *million* times not to exaggerate!'), On the other hand, Zherch was a Kareeten. She had only ever been polite and, I thought, kindly disposed to me, but I certainly couldn't consider her an ally. She and Alassay could plan to beguile me with their science and, having me off-guard, attempt to trick me or overpower me.

"I would love to spend some time with Oortcyl Zherch," I said after a moment's consideration, "but not in the lab; it would have to be here."

"Oh, why is that?"

"You put me in a difficult position, Alassay. You have treated me kindly and appear to have accepted my alternative solution, but the stakes are too high. I feel I have a modicum of control of my situation while I am here with just the two of us but, in the lab, or on the way to the lab, with others around, I would be vulnerable."

"Yes, I understand, you have a predicament. And it's because I understand, that I am not angry with you for implying that I might be duplicitous! You can be assured that, although a determined Kareeten who will work assiduously to attain her ends, I am not deceitful, double-dealing or treacherous."

I hung my head like an admonished school girl.

"However, as I said, I do understand and will not take umbrage. I will see if Oortcyl Zherch can spare you some time."

"Thank you," I said, simply.

And she did spare me some time. She was most gracious, and it was incredibly exciting. It's funny, when you know a lot about a subject, when you are working at the cutting edge, it feels as if you are always working at the limit of your intellect but, when something is uncovered for you, when you are shown the next step, it all seems incredibly obvious; simple even.

Zherch was an excellent teacher; she would reveal something new to me and then leave me with a set of problems to solve. I was having a wonderful time.

Chapter 42

Jeff

Perhaps I am reclusive by nature. I'm sure I wasn't when I was younger. Then again, perhaps I was. I don't suppose I was ever what you would call an extrovert. Well, anyway, whatever I may have been in the past, I was certainly feeling and being reclusive now. I didn't want to have anything to do with this whole Kareeti business. I didn't want to talk about it, be interviewed, express an opinion or, even, think about it. How was the world going to manage the vaccine business? How would they select who would receive it and who would not? Frankly, I didn't care! It was above my pay scale. A far as I could see the world had managed to make a total mess of everything thus far; I'm sure they would be perfectly capable of making a total balls-up of this without any help from me!

Time went by, and once in a while I'd get a call from Lena. It was great that I could see her hologram, but I'd much rather have seen her in person. She seemed to be doing really well. Apparently one of the Kareeti scientists was coaching her in micro-biology and she was loving it. I was immensely relieved to learn she was no longer feeling the same level of stress.

One evening when Lena called, we had an almost farcical situation as she attempted to coach me in how to use the syncom to listen to her journal. Apparently, she had recorded her recollections of her experiences since she went aboard the Kareeti vessel and Alassay had shown her how to send the file to my syncom. All we had to do now was to get 'Old Dexter Dan's' fingers to do the walking!

On one of her calls, Lena seemed very tense again.

"How is the vaccine program going, Jeff? Alassay Harraan is getting a hell of a lot of pressure from Guurtsaad Duurn and she wants some answers!"

"Hello Martin, what's happening?"

"Happening? What do you mean?"

"I mean how is the vaccine program going? Lena has been on to me. Apparently the Kareet are becoming very impatient."

"Christ's sake, Jeff, do they have any idea how incredibly complex this whole exercise is?"

"I think they can probably work it out, but I don't think they care; they just want to get their job done and go home."

"Jesus, Ridsdale, can you hear yourself? 'they just want to get their job done and go home'! Their getting their job done is about to have the most monumental impact on the human population since life began!"

"I'm sorry, Martin, don't shoot me, I'm just the

messenger! But they're looking for answers so…'

"I'll have to get back to you on it. Can you give me a couple of days?"

"I can give you as long as you want, but I can't speak for our little men from outer-space! Get back to me as soon as you possibly can, and you are going to have to really hammer it home to your mates at the UN that we don't have time to play with!"

It occurred to me, sometime after we had ended our call, that Baumann was wrong; this would not be the most monumental impact on the human population since life began. According to my reckoning, (and with a little help from the internet) the world population had grown from 1.6 billion in 1900 to 8.5 billion in 2029; that's an increase of 6.9 billion without any extra-terrestrial help at all! My back-of-the-envelope calculations suggested that if only 10% of the current population of child bearing age are administered the vaccine then, in a hundred and thirty years, there will still be more people than there were in 1900. There's your bloody catastrophe!

The more I thought about it the more I found myself coming around to the Kareeti viewpoint. With Lena's modification, I mean; I certainly couldn't come at the wholesale death and destruction they had had on their playlist!

~

It was well into March, around about the time of the equinox, when I received he bombshell. Lena and I had been talking, on and off. I had to wait for her to call me because

I hadn't learned how to call her. Alassay Harraan had called me. I had talked to Baumann again. The PM assured me the vaccine deployment was well and truly underway and that my family would be provided for. Then, one evening, when I was at home, Lena called me.

"They are going to start seeding the atmosphere with the virus in a few days." I felt my heart begin to hammer. I reminded myself no harm was going to be experienced by anyone, still…

"So, you'll be back… when?" There was a long pause. I looked at her, well, her hologram. She appeared uncomfortable; she was biting one side of her bottom lip in a way I had become familiar with. "Well?" I pushed.

"Jeff, Jeff… this isn't easy for me… I'm not coming back."

"What, what do you mean you're not coming back?" I asked, aghast.

"Alassay Harraan has invited me to return with her to Kareedias."

"To Kareedias! What do you mean? You can't go to Kareedias!"

"I'm sorry, Jeff, I've thought very long and hard about this. You are very special to me too and it's very difficult, but I just can't let this opportunity pass."

"But…' I spluttered for a while, trying to get a coherent thought past my tongue, "how long will you be gone?" I asked eventually, lamely.

"I don't think I'll ever be back. I think it's a lifetime commitment."

What could I say? I was devastated. I hadn't really considered my future with another person, until I met Lena. Now I couldn't imagine it without her. Well, I could, but I didn't want to. I desperately wanted to talk her out of it, change her mind, have her come back to me but I knew that would be unfair. She had already told me she'd thought long and hard on it, and it must have been a difficult decision. The offer to go to another planet, to see another, alien civilization, truly was a unique experience. I almost asked if I could go with her, but I didn't. I don't know that my life was so altogether special here on Earth, but I rather liked it, and I had my family to think of as well.

Lena asked me to send a letter to her family and friends. She said she would compose it and then send it, along with names and addresses and contact details of her people, appended to the next instalment of her journal.

I agreed to do so, of course, but I was feeling truly forlorn and wanted desperately, at that moment, to do nothing other than curl up on my bed and, probably, cry.

Epilogue

All of that was, of course, a very long time ago now. Thanks to the genetic augmentation I received at the hands of the Kareet, I have enjoyed extraordinary longevity. My time is coming to an end, I know that. I'm not unhappy about it; I've had a good enough innings. Good Lord, I was sixty-eight when this all happened. Realistically, at the time, I probably thought, optimistically, I might have had another ten years of sailing in me. I finally gave up the boats almost five years ago, when I turned 170!

It has been a very strange life. I've watched my son and daughter and even my granddaughter, Millie, grow old and die of old age or age-related illnesses. My great-grandson Hammond is eighty-six. He's living in a nursing home with dementia. Even Rafe, my great-great-grandson, is sixty-seven and has retired; he and his wife Elspeth came and stayed the weekend only recently, and yet I live on. Not much longer I suspect.

To think, these journals have sat on a solid-state drive, and not seen the light of day in over a hundred years! They may well never again have come to light had not the most extraordinary thing happened.

About three weeks back I was pottering around the house. I've moved now, to Ashby, just up the river. The old house was going under water because of rising sea levels. This one stands proud on a hill high above the flood level, and has magnificent river views; but I digress. The phone rang, I answered it.

"Hello, is that Jeff?" A woman's voice, somewhat aged I thought.

"Yes, this is he."

"Well, well, well, Jeff Ridsdale! Who'd have thought? This is Lena."

"Lena? Lena who?" I asked, puzzled.

"Lena Sandmeier, of course!"

Well, you could have knocked me down with a feather, as the old saying goes!

It transpired that the Kareet had decided to come back and see how planet Earth was faring after their dramatic intervention. When Lena learned of the mission, she hitched a ride.

Well, of course we arranged to meet. She was staying in a Hotel in Brisbane. My neighbor, Gus, was happy to take me to Byron Bay in his air car and from there I was able to pick up a Strato-Cab straight to the roof of the hotel.

I made my way to reception and asked for Lena, then took a seat in the lobby to wait for her. It was odd, sitting there and trying to think back over all those years. I had been in love with Lena—like a love-struck teenager! Of course, I didn't feel anything like that now; it takes a lot of oxygen to keep a flame burning for more than a century!

After a few minutes, I saw an elderly lady step out of the lift and peer about the lobby. Was that her? Could I even remember what she looked like? I remember she had been reasonably tall, slim and very upright in her stance; would she still be? This lady certainly fitted the description. I stood up and the movement caught her eye. She squinted at me and then her face lit up.

They were serving morning tea in a lounge adjacent to the lobby, so we settled into a pair of voluptuous armchairs with a cup of tea (coffee in Lena's case) and a plate full of patisserie delights that would have turned the weight-conscious young green with envy.

Of course, we both started talking at once, both eager to hear the other's tale. If you have met up with a friend who has been overseas for a couple of years you will know how much there is to talk about. Lena had been to another planet for over a hundred years and had been instrumental in changing life on Earth in ways she could not even begin to imagine!

I suppose, because Lena had anticipated our meeting for longer, she had had time to consider how we might handle this information overload so I acceded to her plan of attack and found myself telling her all about the past hundred years or so here on Earth.

"How did they decide who to give the vaccine to?" she asked.

"I don't really know. Here in Australia and, I think the

US, the UK, they administered it to young couples of child-bearing age between the ages of twenty and thirty who met various suitability criteria the government thought appropriate."

"But the virus affected only females, and the child-bearing window is far more than ten years."

"Yes, but, it's not like we were short of candidates, and I think the strategy was to try to get the best possible outcome so… I guess the twenty to thirty age group was seen as having the best prospects for healthy, successful pregnancies. The couple requirement probably came about to best assure a secure family environment for the offspring.

"As for what happened in other countries… well, I can only guess. I confess I didn't take a great deal of interest."

"Really, why ever not?"

"I seem to recall, at the time, being overtaken by an overwhelming sense of lassitude. After all we had been through, had been central to and had agency in, suddenly there was nothing more for me to do and, frankly, I was enormously glad of it."

The vaccination program must have been the most outstanding example of human cooperation in the history of the world. I cannot imagine how it was all managed. I know the whole operation was a public information nightmare. The fact that we had been visited by extra-terrestrials was, by then, generally known. What could not be made public, under any circumstance, was the true nature of the Kareeti mission; not even with Lena's hard-won amelioration. There would have been utter chaos.

World governments put out information bulletins that nobody believed. The commentariat all had wildly differing opinions and social media was abuzz with speculation and 'facts backed by irrefutable evidence'. Yet, somehow, despite it all, life managed to carry on and, as it did so, surreptitiously and under who knows what pretext, millions of women around the world received an injection.

It was only months later, when the seeding of the virus was complete and the Kareet had left our solar system, that it became gradually apparent that there was a sudden, inexplicable drop in pregnancies globally. It was not until that fact became front page news and the dominant subject of television news and current affairs programs that the Secretary General of the United Nations announced that he would make a public broadcast.

"You can well imagine the furor that erupted when that bombshell was dropped! To his eternal credit, Gustave Javier repeatedly hammered home the fact that, had it not been for the intervention of Lena Sandmeier (who must justly be regarded as one of the world's greatest heroes and who gave her life in the process) the aliens would have exterminated ninety per cent of the world's population."

I looked at Lena. Her eyes were like saucers, one hand atop the other over her heart.

"Well, it was true enough. The very few who knew the truth about where you'd gone were not going to say anything. As far as they were concerned you might just as well have been dead; they were never going to see you again."

Lena looked forlorn. I chose the moment to catch a

waiter's eye and ordered her more coffee, this time with a glass of cognac. She looked as though she could use the fortification.

As time went by, the white-hot indignation that lit up the media began to cool. Instead, the headlines began to focus on the financial repercussions that were beginning to surface as the uncertainty of the world's economic future came into question. Where would growth come from in a world of rapidly dwindling population? The entire global economy was based upon consumerism.

"Yes, that's interesting, how did all that play out?" Lena asked as the waiter placed her coffee before her.

"Well it took a while, I can't remember how long—it all begins to blur—but the years after the intervention became increasingly difficult, chaotic really."

And they really had! There was, as you might well imagine, a hell of a furor about the aliens, the intervention, the people's right to procreate, outrage from the majority who missed out on the vaccine… where does one end? In democratic countries, governments were turfed out of office by a bellicose electorate and were replaced by radical, populist governments. The global economy went into a tail spin; fear and uncertainty being anathema to the markets. As more and more of Greenland and the Arctic melted, low lying lands were inundated. Vast areas of countries like Bangladesh and many Pacific islands went under. Millions of people were displaced and came knocking on the doors of the first world nations whom they, not unjustifiably, asserted had caused the problem in the first place.

The first world countries were not without their own problems. Trillions of dollars' worth of canal and seafront real estate was being rendered worthless as lawns began to disappear beneath high tides. In many countries, certainly in Australia, there was already a housing shortage so adding hundreds of thousands of people, suddenly disenchanted with waterfront living, to the 'open for inspection' queues, was the perfect recipe for chaos. Little surprise, perhaps, then, that climate change refugees received short shrift!

The United Nations, historically never much good in a crisis, was entirely useless. I think delegates continued to go to the Assemblies to squabble, but nobody, not even the media, took the least bit of notice. Several wars broke out. Fortunately, no one resorted to nuclear weapons so cataclysmic environmental harm was avoided.

Eventually, after thirty or forty years, things started to change for the better. The rapidly declining population was acting like a pressure release valve. The same problems continued to exist but there were fewer people experiencing them and at least greenhouse gas emissions and pollution in general were trending strongly in the right direction. People were dying without offspring who, ordinarily, would inherit their estates. Their accumulated wealth went into government coffers and, little by little, it became apparent that there was enormous wealth on tap. That was when things began to change most dramatically.

They called them 'the First Generation' which, of course, after the Intervention, they were. Amidst all the chaos of the time these children were nurtured and educated like no generation in the history of the world. They were such a small cohort. Schools that had been accustomed to burgeoning classroom sizes now found themselves with resources to spare. Teachers who may have dreamed of making a difference in the lives of their young pupils suddenly found they could.

Admittedly I can only speak for Australia and, to a limited extent the U.S. and Europe (Charlie travelled quite extensively on business) but generally, it seems the authorities, when selecting candidates for the vaccine, had chosen young women with a good academic track record. It was widely recognized that, with the growth in artificial intelligence and robotics, there would be fewer and fewer opportunities for those with limited education. Consequently, the teachers were encountering kids who carried with them an expectation of achievement. Class sizes were dramatically smaller, and the disruptive element was all but absent.

As the First Generation grew up, entered the work force and, eventually, began to assume leadership roles, radical new ideas about how to organize societies and economies began to emerge. By the time the kids of the 'Second Generation' started leaving the universities and making their way in the world, we were beginning to see extraordinary new levels of international peace and cooperation.

By then we had long had a Universal Wage. With the vast wealth of deceased estates flowing into government coffers it was eminently affordable and, in any case, made enormous sense. Poverty has long been recognized as the principal factor behind crime, prostitution, mental and physical illness, poor nutrition and drug and alcohol abuse. All these have an enormous societal and economic cost. Better to ensure everyone has access to adequate resources to fund a meaningful existence, and to contribute to society in their own way.

"Something that always worried me was how you, I mean the world, would cope with the virus after the initial vaccination project." Lena broke into my narrative.

"Ah, yes, well that was something your assistant—what was his name…?" I could tell from her expression that Lena couldn't remember either. "Ah well," I said, "it was over a hundred years ago. Japanese bloke, anyway. He explained the virus might well hang around and infect the new generation, so he was invited to head up a project to make the vaccine available in adequate quantities."

"Well, of course, he would have first had to work out how to make it. The Kareet only gave us enough to create adequate quantities of vaccine for the number of people we were to be allowed to vaccinate to achieve the population levels they considered appropriate. Ah well, Daiki Shimizu… there, I've remembered! Daiki Shimizu really was an excellent micro-biologist, a very smart man. I'm sure he would have been able to reverse engineer the technology without too much trouble."

"In any case, he was obviously successful because all female children now receive the vaccine at birth," I replied.

We talked for ages. I realized I was hungry and checked my watch. It was after 1:30! I proposed we had lunch. The hotel has an al-fresco dining area on a deck overlooking the Brisbane River and, as neither of us was as nimble as we once were, that suited us fine.

"You haven't been to Brisbane before have you?" I asked, as we sipped at a chilled Chenin Blanc.

She shook her head.

"Ah well, she's not the sparkling, bustling city she was in the old days." I gestured in the direction of several large, derelict and partially demolished riverside apartment blocks. "Everywhere you look these days, I'm afraid."

"No one to live in them? What ever happened to… to houses… to… well, I mean the whole real estate market once the population started to fall?"

"Ah well, now, that's a whole story in itself!" I took another sip of wine and tried to compose my thoughts. We had been through so much turmoil it was hard to know where to begin. At first, nothing much changed, other than the general sense of outrage from those denied their reproductive rights. The rate of population growth plateaued of course, but that did nothing to ease the housing shortage because rising sea levels were creating vast numbers of climate refugees. For some time, there had been a spike in housing values because of the huge demand but, little by little, people died, their children moved into their parents' houses and then, eventually, died without having children of their own. Gradually, at first, the demand for housing fell. As time went by the rate of demand fell below supply levels and continued to decline at an accelerating rate.

Real estate prices plummeted in lock step with

population. The governments, as beneficiaries of thousands of deceased estates, found themselves in control of vast real estate portfolios. However, houses were worth next to nothing. The property market ceased to exist. Real estate ceased to be an asset of any real value. One of the prime underpinnings of the economy was gone. It was time for a new paradigm.

Together with the 'living wage', the government leased houses to people at peppercorn rents. Folk who, hitherto, could barely afford a dilapidated cottage in the outer suburbs, found themselves living in multi-million-dollar properties in absolute prime locations, well, not waterside perhaps! As for the outer suburbs, well they became ghost towns.

Production and consumption—key drivers of the economy—were gone too. The idea that you constantly produce materials to make products to satisfy an endless human demand was suddenly no longer true. People began to realize that there was more 'stuff' in the world than we could ever use, or need for that matter. Extractive industries ground to a halt. We didn't need to cut down trees for timber or dig up more iron ore for steel. The previously insatiable demand for electrical power seemed finally sated. Of course, we still needed electricity, but manufacturing had ground to a halt and there were fewer and fewer people. Energy from renewable sources could easily cope with demand, so no more coal was needed.

Many of the companies who had been engaged in the extractive industries turned their hands to mining resources through recycling: timber, bricks, steel, tiles and furniture were stockpiled, as deserted suburbs were carefully demolished. Huge city office and apartment blocks yielded glass and air conditioning units, cable and computer systems. Millions of cars sat idle on roadsides and in people's garages. Thousands upon thousands of airplanes sat idle in hangars. There were more resources on hand than the population could use over the course of several generations.

Lena listened attentively as she removed the snapper flesh from its bones with surgical precision. Neither the passage of time nor her extended stay on Kareedias appeared to have dampened her enthusiasm for wine, so I ordered another bottle.

"I've never understood velootskur… oh sorry, that's Kareeti, isn't it? I mean economics, I've never studied it, or thought very much about it. But, I suppose one absorbs quite a lot just from living with it. It must be very different from when I was here."

"I expect you can speak Kareeti now, can you?"

"Oh yes, fluently. I think in Kareeti! I have to translate my thoughts from Kareeti to English to talk to you. Isn't that amazing? I even have to do the same thing with German, my native tongue!"

I shook my head and looked suitably impressed—and I was, don't misunderstand me.

"Yes, the whole economic model collapsed many years ago now." I tried to put together in my own mind the sequence of events but, frankly, economics wasn't my pet subject either, and it had also been a while since I had consumed this much wine in one sitting. I drained the last of my glass and topped us both up, there, that should help!

"I suppose, when you think about it, capitalism could never have survived this scenario. I mean, even before all of this, I think it was staggering around like a punch drunk heavyweight boxer in the twelfth round, his knees refusing to finally buckle and drop him to the canvas. The Intervention was the final round, and they carried him out on a stretcher never to re-enter the ring again. The whole capitalist system was based on there being an ever-expanding market, i.e. population, and a two-tiered socio-economic system. Those with the money, the capitalists, identified opportunities within the market and established responses to those opportunities. Those without money provided the labor.

"The Intervention put an end to the continuously growing market. Instead it was in rapid decline. The opportunity to make lots of money simply evaporated. Over time, as the governments became increasingly the fount of all wealth, they began to re-distribute that wealth in ways I've already mentioned: a universal living wage, low rental housing and by pouring vast sums into health, education, aged care and scientific research.

"No doubt the selection process used by the world when it had to decide who would get the vaccine would have skewed the demographics markedly but, in any case, crime all but disappeared. I guess people no longer needed stuff the way they had. As money and housing and health and education all became universally available, the pressure was taken off people. Drug abuse, often a response to abject need, is all but unheard of.

"The arts are flourishing. Those who do work are well paid and are keen to support the arts. Those who don't have regular employment can manage comfortably on the 'living wage' and that frees them up to release their creative side."

"Science?" Lena enquired.

"Also flourishing; I'm sure we're still a long way behind the Kareet, but I think we've come a long way. I suppose a lot of the brain power that was devoted to the development of weaponry is now better deployed. We seem to be curing all sorts of diseases that we never could before. They've made good progress in longevity. It's not at all uncommon to hear of one-hundred-and-twenty-year-olds, nowadays."

"Space?"

"Yes, we're still doing that. Back then we were talking about colonizing other planets because, the way we were going, this one would be buggered in a few generations. Now we have a colony on Mars and a permanent staging station on the moon but, it's more about scientific research than any real need to live anywhere else."

"So, how is the world going?"

"Pretty good, I think. We still have enormous problems getting rid of all the junk seven billion people left behind, but nature is reclaiming vast tracts of land everywhere. Future generations will hack their way into a jungle and find overgrown suburbs in pathetic imitation of Angkor Wat! The new growth, the trees, are sucking up carbon dioxide and we aren't producing the stuff anymore. There is evidence that the carbon in the atmosphere has peaked and may be declining. Of course, with nowhere near the number of mouths to feed, we have cut back the livestock herds, which has dramatically reduced methane production… but they've still got me of course!"

She looked at me quizzically.

"There's not much you do better as you get older but one of them is farting and I'm very old!"

Lena laughed and smacked my hand as it lay on the table. "You've still got the same sense of humor!" she scolded.

"I'm surprised you remember, it's been a long, long time. But, hey, that's enough about me, I've talked for hours. Tell me all about you, about Kareedias… everything."

"Jeff, I've kept a journal over all these years and I've sent it all to you on your syncom. I'm guessing you haven't seen it, but I think you'd better, because we don't have time for me to tell you everything here."

"My syncom? I haven't seen it for… God knows how long! I don't even know if I still have it. Even if I do, surely the battery will have gone flat decades ago."

"Oh Jeff, I cannot believe for one moment that you don't still have it. Are you telling me you looked at it one day and said, 'won't need that anymore', and threw it in the rubbish? Of course you still have it! As for the batteries, as you put it, they won't run out. Your syncom runs on radioactive decay energy. And, no, there are no health implications," she said in response to the question she doubtless saw on my face.

I was in two minds about all of this. Of course, I wanted to hear all about Kareedias and her experiences, but I also recognized that the shadows were already lengthening, and I think we both were feeling tired. So, I didn't pursue it.

"But what will you do now?" I asked her.

"I don't really know, to be honest," she replied, a little forlornly I thought. "You are, obviously I suppose, the only person on this entire planet that I know."

"Family back in Austria, Switzerland?"

"Everyone who ever knew anything about me is long dead."

"Oh, I don't know, I bet you're a legend. I bet your story has been handed down through the generations."

"So, what, I should go and see them, turn up on their doorsteps like an ancestral portrait come to life? I don't think so!"

"Would you return to Kareedias?"

"No, I don't think I could survive the trip. Coming back almost killed me. Besides, I think I'd like to end my days on Earth; it's where I came from."

I was suddenly overtaken by a maelstrom of conflicting emotion. Here I sat, an ancient, old man, surely soon to die, opposite this kindly, dear, very elderly lady whom I had once loved. I no longer loved her; too many long years had passed. Here she was, possibly the most influential person in the history of the world and yet not known to a single living soul, save myself.

Was I duty-bound to invite her to come and stay with me—not conjugally, of course—and be her friend and companion for as long as I may have left to me to offer such comfort? Did I want to? My first reaction was: no! I have been living on my own for a very long time. I'm happy. I have my own little systems and routines with which I'm quite comfortable. It's a bit damned late to be bringing someone home now!

On the other hand, she's right, she will be completely alone, and I probably should make the effort.

Then again, she did choose, all by herself, to leave Earth and all her relatives, friends and contacts (and me) and make a new life for herself on an alien planet.

I'll have to sleep on it.

Biography

Patrick is married and lives a life of semi-retirement in Northern New South Wales. Once an incurable optimist, he has been drawn, inexorably, into a state of deep pessimism as to the future of the planet. He says: "We have made a terrible mess of our world, and any hope that we could clean it up and take strong positive action to reverse the terrible effects of our grossly mistaken policies are fanciful as long as the Barbarians remain in control."

His natural optimism in all other matters remains firmly in place, however, as is manifest in his belief that someone out there will buy and enjoy this book!

Visit The Intervention Facebook Page.